The Bringing
of Wonder

Recent Titles in
Contributions in Comparative Colonial Studies

The Bringing of Wonder

Trade and the Indians of the Southeast, 1700–1783

Michael P. Morris

Contributions in Comparative Colonial Studies, Number 36

GREENWOOD PRESS
Westport, Connecticut • London

Library of Congress Cataloging-in-Publication Data

Morris, Michael P., 1959– .
    The bringing of wonder : trade and the Indians of the Southeast,
1700–1783 / Michael P. Morris.
        p.   cm.—(Contributions in comparative colonial studies,
    ISSN 0163-3813 ; no. 36)
    Includes bibliographical references and index.
    ISBN 0-313-30843-8 (alk. paper)
    1. Indians of North America—Commerce—Southern States.
    2. Indians of North America—Southern States—Economic conditions.
    3. Indian women—Southern States.   4. Southern States—Commerce—
    History—18th century.   I. Title.   II. Series.
    E78.S65M67   1999
    381′.0975′09033—dc21   98–28290

British Library Cataloguing in Publication Data is available.

Library of Congress Catalog Card Number: 98–28290
ISBN: 0-313-30843-8
ISSN: 0163-3813

First published in 1999

Greenwood Press, 88 Post Road West, Westport, CT 06881
An imprint of Greenwood Publishing Group, Inc.
www.greenwood.com

Printed in the United States of America

The paper used in this book complies with the
Permanent Paper Standard issued by the National
Information Standards Organization (Z39.48–1984).

10 9 8 7 6 5 4 3 2 1

The work is dedicated to those history Ph.D.s who did not graduate from Ivy League schools and who received little information about the job market prior to graduation. It is written for those who had to work as adjunct faculty for years while watching others sail into tenure-track jobs. It is published in honor of those who had to shuffle into the industry through the back door of the academic plantation.

Contents

The author gratefully acknowledges the aid of the Computer Services Department of the University of South Carolina at Aiken in the preparation of this manuscript.

1

The Language of Trade

The practices of trade and exchange existed in human history long before the specialization of labor and the Industrial Revolution. In modern life, many aspects of trade and exchange are routine, even mundane, with little or no meaning attached to these transactions. Yet, trade and gift-giving enjoyed much deeper meanings in the egalitarian societies of pre-Columbian North America. When such practices take place between two cultures of disparate technologies, trade and gift-giving especially take on a deeper meaning, which may be lost on the more technologically sophisticated culture. Such was the case of trade and gift-giving between the natives of North America and the Europeans who colonized and eventually assumed control of the continent. Through the use of trade, both Native Americans and Euroamericans tried to control each other. In order to understand this process, it is necessary to review traditional native concepts of exchange and trade in order to illustrate the major impact of European goods on native cultures.

Karl Marx noted that all societies, when stripped of their veneers, represent a certain economic organization. The political, business and religious values of any culture will reflect its economic foundation. Similarly, one author has described exchange as the cement which holds society together. In simpler, tribal societies it consists of a system of reciprocal services and obligations which bind society together; in industrial democracies it takes the form of services guided by a very specific set of prices subject to market fluctuation.[1]

A parallel practice, gift-giving, also appears in human society. Gift-giving involves a return obligation which may be repaid immediately or at a later date and introduces an emotional aspect to a relationship.[2] Since it involves the notion of eventual reciprocation, gift-giving forces the recipient to make decisions of status--determining his own and that of the giver. The status, age and financial condition of the giver and recipient color the choices in each case.[3]

At least one colonial observer in the eighteenth century challenged the notion of reciprocal obligation in Native American culture. In April 1773, an anonymous writer penned a tract stating that he observed no bonds of obligation among the tribes in which he traveled in North America. The traveler stated that North American Indians gave gifts out of a sense of affection, not obligation. While always pleased at receiving gifts, the writer believed, Indians felt no future obligation towards the giver.[4] Available evidence indicates that Indians across North America did view such matters as reciprocal; this writer's opinion may best illustrate the lack of understanding Europeans had about such matters.

Simple economies in less stratified cultures are organized around notions of reciprocity and redistribution. Reciprocity entails gift-giving with the mutual understanding that an obligation is being created. Redistribution involves wealth accumulation for dispersal among others at some future time. It is the distribution of wealth which indicates the status of the donor, not the accumulation. Such gift dispersals are often tied to special events.[5] Thus, clearly the definition and purpose of wealth in the more egalitarian societies of North America differed significantly from the wealth concepts of colonizing Europeans which linked wealth to amassed fortune.

In fact, the "wealthy man" in the less industrialized societies of North America was the man who could redistribute the best resources most widely. Since gift-giving at this level incurs a debt of repayment in kind at a future date, the donor has, from the native perspective, contributed to an indigenous form of social security that, barring disaster, will contribute to his own welfare one day. Further, the simple knowledge that he had the wealth to redistribute is what made him a powerful man in his own society, not the steady accumulation of wealth, as in the long history of Western society.[6]

The very notion of quantifying wealth also differed greatly between the economies of early Western Europe and the basic economies of North America before contact. Money in Western Europe was and is all-purpose money with widely understood value. Few transactions take place without money in one form or another: coin, currency, check or in colonial America, the bill of exchange.

In the egalitarian societies of North America money was not general purpose. Here items of exchange were limited in what they could purchase, though this knowledge was understood by all. Transactions were linked and inseparable from social obligation, unlike the impersonal exchanges in stratified society.[7]

In societies organized at the tribal level, like those in precontact North America, social interaction takes place on a highly personal level and there is little specialization of labor. Thus, one man's repertoire of work skills was much like that of any other man. The same may be said for women as well. Daily life revolved around food procurement and processing and, when necessary, defense. Such basic economies remain static unless changed by two forces. First, technological innovation could cause a change in a basic economy. Egalitarian societies that were isolated from one another were, in a sense, less likely to experience innovation. Endowed with a limited set of ideas and bound by survival needs to respect the tried and true methods of living, egalitarian societies were not prone to technological innovation. The second alternative to such a static economy was craft specialization, the option followed by the Native Americans of North America after European contact. This option allowed basic societies to capitalize upon an existing skill while allowing certain other skills to fall away. This labor specialization was dependent upon the ability of the egalitarian society to compensate, in some manner, for the skills which were allowed to languish.[8] Native Americans maximized their relationship with intruding Europeans through the fur trade, though it created a cultural dependency upon manufactured goods which forever changed the patterns and rhythms of native lives.

The Indian role in the fur trade business was an example of a specialized existing skill. Tribes of the Southeast hunted the white-tailed deer in greater numbers after the arrival of Europeans and exchanged the hides for a host of European trade items. The nation states of fifteenth century Europe participated in this international fur trade, in which they competed with each other for control of the peripheral area of North America, a region lacking a nation-state government.[9]

As a response to European intervention in their own economies, Native Americans became craft specialists in order to obtain the manufactured wares of Europe. In the process, Native Americans adapted their economic strategies, known as scheduling. Scheduling in the precontact period involved organizing food gathering so that results were maximized. Indians planted crops in the spring and harvested them by late summer. They gathered nuts when they fell in the fall and hunted deer when rutting behavior brought the animals to peak visibility in the late fall and winter. After European contact, native peoples altered their schedule to hunt more so that they might procure European goods. Though Native Americans learned to exercise their own controls over this new economy, their involvement never stimulated them toward true nation-state development. Rather, European economic strategies were adapted so that they fit within traditional roles whenever possible.[10]

In southeastern North America, contact with representatives of European nation-states stimulated the static, subsistence economies of the Native Americans to focus on deerskin procurement as an economic craft specialization, much as the Indians of what is now Canada focused on beaver pelt procurement. Since the more advanced economies of Western Europe were able to offer items the Indians wanted badly, such as metal tools, cotton cloth, guns, ammunition and liquor, native economies reoriented themselves to focus more and more on the items needed to trade with these advanced economies. Competing economic tasks that were necessary in the precontact period, but now diverted time and energy from deer hunting, tended to languish. Tasks such as food and clothing production were abandoned if trade with the advanced economy could provide substitutes, further making native peoples of North America more dependent upon Europe.[11]

One of the reasons that Europeans needed American furs so badly was that their own supply was practically gone. The European type of beaver was nearly extinct by the 1500s, found only in short supply in Russia and Scandinavia. Thus American furs were valuable to Europeans because their own supplies were nearly nonexistent. The furs were lightweight and easily transportable in high bulk, making the trade quite profitable. At one point, French fur traders sold the Indians a manufactured item worth 1 livre for a beaver robe worth 200 livres in France. Native Americans performed most of the work; pelts were primed for European processing by both planned native processing methods and the simple act of wearing them.[12] While the market for skins would seem limited only to upper classes, their distribution in Europe was much wider. Unlike North American craftsmen, European clothiers did not create full-length fur coats from the pelts. They were used to make muffs and trim work on silk and velvet worn by the upper classes. Members of Europe's royal houses wore ermine and sable; lesser nobility contented themselves with marten, lynx, fox and otter. Native American craftsmen provided Europe's lower classes with leather, also in short supply in Europe, for use in work pants, aprons, shoes, saddles, saddlebags, bookbindings, covered seats and luggage.[13] Europe provided a ready market for American furs and skins.

Historians speculate that the European practice of trading for pelts began as a secondary occupation of European fishermen who had been dispatched to North America. By the beginning of the sixteenth century, both Britain and France sent fishing fleets to the coast of Canada every spring for cod. Merchants from Bristol may have been sent to the New World as early as the 1480s.[14] This new staple, called "poor john," helped feed Europe's masses, including armies, navies, urban lower classes and peasants. European Catholics also welcomed the import of cod, since it gave them a meat alternative for the 165 days each year when meat consumption was forbidden.[15]

The fishermen dried the cod before returning home; they most likely came into contact with the Indians ashore as they preserved their catch. At first, the trade was merely a means for the Europeans to augment the monetary reward of their fishing expeditions. The initial trade between Native Americans and Europeans was also a way for the latter to replenish their supplies. After ships trekked across the Atlantic, they needed new supplies of firewood, food and fresh water. The natives usually gave the wood and water for nothing, but the Europeans had to trade for their food. Early on, European sailors learned the lessons of reciprocity; when they gave their hosts tokens they ensured hospitable treatment in the future.[16]

Trade items in the beginning were those commonly on hand--not specifically designed for trade with the Indians as in later years. The archaeological record reveals a host of metal implements found in the ship's rigging but not essential to its operation, such as metal rings. Indians also traded for the earrings that sailors wore to ward off bad eyesight and for the blue beads that sailors wore as protection against the evil eye. Indians trading for brass kettles and steel axes reworked them to make knives, ornaments, chisels and adzes. The earliest artifacts date this trade at about 1550 A.D.[17]

The reason these exchanges took place at all was that people of cultures on both sides of the Atlantic understood the concept of trade, at least to a certain point. Native Americans had not reached a point where they understood notions like accumulated debt or used currency in the exchange process. That Europeans understood these things needs little or no explanation. Native Americans participated in a series of complex trading networks linking distant peoples long before European contact. Indians living in the future state of Michigan mined and traded copper as far away as Jamestown, Virginia. Natives in the area of Minnesota mined catlinite stone, used in ceremonial peace pipes, and traded it across North America. Obsidian, volcanic glass, was traded to Indians of the east coast from several hundred miles away. One group was known as the "Tobacco Indians" because they produced that crop in such quantities for trade.[18]

After contact, the new business partners approached each other with caution. Indians often hid when European ships entered their harbors, and the practice of abducting natives for transport and display back in Europe surely encouraged this precaution. Europeans found they had to leave trade goods in open places to lure Native Americans from their hiding. Once a mutual trust was established, trading sessions often became quite festive as British traders discovered music improved sales. Europeans were used to dealing with representatives of nation-states; in tribal societies they learned to discern leaders by their special dress and the deference others showed them. The French adopted reciprocity and learned to give gifts to the women and children of a tribe when leaders agreed to permit trade.[19]

Of course, as Indians became dependent on gifts and other trade items, they shifted from subsistence hunting to commercial hunting. That transition forced Native Americans to abandon their traditional conception of animals. In the precontact period, most Native Americans viewed animals as gifts of the Supreme Being who "surrendered" themselves to the hunter because of his need and because he had followed a specific ritual preparation. While Western Europeans regarded game as merely meat to be taken, Indians perceived animals to be intelligent, coresidents of the universe who, like them, held specific roles to play. Essentially, through a set of rituals, the hunter "overpowered" the spirit of his prey, who then surrendered. The animals surrendered if the hunters had shown their species "respect" during past hunting expeditions, by using every part of the carcass, allowing nothing to be wasted. For a time after the kill, the carcass was treated as a sacred object.[20]

In the Southeast, the Cherokees prayed to the wind to cover their scent to facilitate good hunting. They delivered prayer to the hunted species asking forgiveness for what they were about to take. After the kill, they offered the first carcass to the four winds, in hopes of preventing foul weather. Natives also did not eat the first kill, out of respect for that species, fearing that if angered, it might not allow itself to be captured again.[21]

Indians hunted from midautumn to early spring. Animal pelts were in prime condition during this time, having thickened for colder weather. Ritual preparation, hunting, killing and transportation of the animals home were men's tasks. Indian women assumed a vital role in the process at that point. The contributions of both sexes have been lost as a result of the stereotype of the lazy Indian. Since hunting was a leisure activity for many Europeans, they failed to acknowledge it as a legitimate contribution of men. Despite such prejudice, Euroamericans did not tackle the difficult job of hunting and processing skins until the late 1700s.

As noted, hunting involved complex preparation for the actual event. Next came the hunt itself, the killing and the transport of the animal carcass back to the village. In the South, hunters retrieved deer skins, which women processed in an elaborate manner. They soaked and scraped the skins and treated them in a heated solution of the animal's brains. Afterwards, they scoured the skins again, twisting and untwisting them, then vigorously rubbed to dry them.[22] Since this was standard preparation of pelts for their own clothes, the first serious European fur traders bartered for the skins that Native Americans were wearing at the time; the Indians were thrilled to exchange their "old clothes" for new manufactured items and believed they were getting the best of their trade partners.[23]

In fact, the Indians believed they were selling their own trifles for the exotic wonder brought by these seagoing strangers. In addition to being exotic, these trade items were highly prized because they were often more durable than native counterparts.[24] Trade goods generally fell into two categories: those used for the same purpose by both cultures and those which the Indians used differently than the Europeans. In the first group, Indians readily recognized the planned utility of fishhooks, knives, spears, hoes, axes, and needles and bartered for them. These metal tools were much sturdier than Indian versions wrought in bone or stone. Native Americans also bartered for metal objects, which they put to uses other than those of the Europeans. Indians used objects made of shiny metal as body adornment, despite their original purpose; thus, buttons became decorations for the hair. The Spanish noted that native peoples loved to wear the tiny bells used to train hawks and falcons. Indians reworked brass and copper kettles to make traditional jewelry.[25]

Native Americans also adopted European clothes. In the Southeast, they especially liked European shirts because of their lightweight construction as compared to buckskin and because the foreign clothes were colorful.[26] By the eighteenth century, the British trade lists carried calico clothes as staple items.

As Europeans advanced farther into North America, trading practices fundamentally altered traditional Indian life. As demands for furs exceeded supplies, Native Americans shifted to commercial hunting, which quickly depleted their hunting grounds. When they were unable to supply their European business partners, many Indian groups found themselves abandoned. Despite their lack of "organic currency," most tribes at that point were addicted to the trade and sought new avenues through which to continue it. Some tribes opted to act as middlemen when their own game supplies were gone.[27]

The ever-increasing demands for furs forced many Native Americans to make a choice in the scheduling of various economic pursuits. Their choice to abandon some skills illustrates the value they placed on European goods. Those goods were not the worthless trinkets remembered in folk culture; values are relative to all cultures. In their own culture, processed furs, though hard to produce, were common. European trade goods, in comparison, were most uncommon. Further, Indians became quite adept at determining when they received shoddy merchandise. Inferior trade goods did not last long, and some, like guns, advertised their poor quality by exploding. Thus the Indians quickly established standards by which they judged the quality of European goods. They too were not above pawning off inferior furs on occasion as well. In addition to causing friction between Native American and European cultures, advanced trade prompted an increase in intertribal violence, arising from the competition for game. A certain degree of conflict existed prior to European contact as Native Americans became sedentary farmers. The new life-style prompted intertribal conflict among various groups over arable land.

The Cherokees are typical of a tribe with a long history as agriculturists. They tended to settle in riverine environments which both attracted game and were conducive to farming. Rivers often flooded, bringing the rich alluvial soils that revitalized their farm plots. By the time of European contact, they had mastered production of high protein crops. Grown in the field together, these nitrogen fixing and nitrogen absorbing plants prevented total soil depletion, thus lengthening the productive life of their farmlands.[28]

After European contact, groups like the Cherokees assimilated new fruits and vegetables into their production repertoire. The watermelon, originally from Africa, became a Cherokee favorite. They also planted peaches and figs, originally brought by the Spanish.[29] Among the new vegetables, the Cherokees began to cultivate cabbages, olives, okra, peanuts and onions. The Indians did not assimilate every new type of plant or agricultural technique, however. The Cherokees would not use the plow in their farming and this limited their ability to try such crops as wheat, barley and rye.[30] Prosletyzing agents of Euroamerican culture tried to convert the Indians like the Cherokees into completely sedentary agriculturists in order to "civilize" them.[31]

As agriculturists, groups like the Cherokees appreciated the value of productive, defensible territory. They came into conflict with other agriculturists over choice land, as well as with remaining nomadic tribes. This potential conflict was exacerbated with the shift to commercial hunting. Once Native Americans had made the transition, they either had to do the hunting themselves or have access to those who did. The introduction of European arms was critical in this struggle; Indians with guns were more likely to prosper in hunting and fighting than those without them. As Europeans moved farther inland from the coast, some Indians relocated to be near trading posts.[32]

Internally, the fur trade altered the social structure of most tribes in North America. Its introduction disastrously affected native religious beliefs and ultimately the special relationship Indians enjoyed with their prey. Native

Americans slowly lost faith in their own clerics, the shamans, when these native specialists could do nothing about the virulent diseases that came with the foreign trade. When the shamans failed, Indians lost belief in their own spirits and the sense of environmental balance their own religion had engendered. In fact, they often interpreted these new illnesses as punishment from the animals they hunted. Since most tribes believed that animals could retaliate in some way if improperly treated by humans, the seemingly unprovoked epidemic disease may have prompted Native Americans to turn on their game with a vengeance.[33] The Cherokees believed that man once lived in harmony with the animals, but his invention of bows, knives and other weapons gave him an unfair advantage over them. In retaliation, the animals invented new diseases to plague man; their plans were, in turn, thwarted by the plants who furnished man with herbal remedies to combat the new diseases.[34]

As pronounced as the effect of advanced trade was on native economies, it had an equally astounding effect on European ones. The demands of Native Americans on Europe's manufacturing capacity affected both imperial policy and industrial development. Britain in particular enjoyed a favorable balance of trade. Native American demands for manufactured items supported British industry; skins received in exchange for the manufactures far outweighed them in value and also enhanced the economy. The Indian commerce stimulated British markets until colonial populations grew enough to supply such a demand.[35]

In fact, certain industries survived because of the Indian trade. British wool producers had steady demands for their product from America when they were encountering difficulties shipping to the continent in the sixteenth century. One region, the Stroudwater Valley of Gloucestershire, owed its livelihood to the Indian trade. The area produced a scarlet and blue cloth which was shipped out of Bristol instead of London. Because strouds were cheaper than similar cloth in London, Indian merchants in the American colonies patronized Bristol dealers for the cloth from 1690 until 1760, precisely the period of Bristol's greatest trade prosperity.[36]

While the trade helped Europe achieve cultural and political dominance over North America, it reduced Native Americans to mere appendages of an invading culture. Demands for European goods stimulated industry at home; in America they prompted Indians to hunt for animal skins in such quantities that they exhausted their supplies and became habitual debtors to their European creditors. Worse yet, differing economic systems prompted the Europeans to look upon their business partners with disdain. Europeans and Euroamericans measured success in wealth accumulation; Indians measured success in wealth distribution. Those Indians who participated in the trade never got rich. Once game supplies were exhausted they sometimes sold their lands to pay for debts incurred in the trade, thereby removing their only remaining means of payment. Since their culture prevented capital accumulation, Indians received few long-term benefits from the trade. Their eventual impoverishment inspired scorn from the Euroamericans who only respected such life-styles among religious orders.[37]

Economically, North America actually served to stimulate otherwise depressed markets of seventeenth century Europe. The North American market acted to buttress fledgling economies in Europe by feeding them a steady supply of furs valuable in Europe while demanding manufactured items that were equally valuable in North America.[38] While both cultures understood the rudiments of trade enough to interact, trade and exchange folkways common to egalitarian societies prevented the wealth accumulation which strengthened Western Europe. Trade with Europe undermined traditional, conservationist values of native people and turned them into high volume consumers. Cultural taboos against wealth accumulation limited native abilities to regenerate their own purchasing ability; this, combined with their low level of technological development, prompted the now familiar outcome in this collision of cultures.

This study explores the impact of Euroamerican trade on the Indians of the southern colonial backcountry, in both familiar and unfamiliar ways. The fur trade brought European men into direct contact with Indian women and together they forged a relationship built on mutual needs. European men needed acceptance into the matrilineal societies of the various tribes. Further, the women served as cultural instructors, teaching their mates the rules of behavior in Native American society. The women likewise profited, though only in the short term, as fur traders gave them greater access to both luxury goods and necessities. In addition, many Indian groups attached greater prestige to women with Euroamerican husbands and mixed-blood offspring.

The Europeans who came to the backcountry as fur traders were mostly from Ireland and Scotland. They entered the profession in search of that ever elusive short path to riches, though most never found it. While desk-bound colonial officials formulated diplomatic policy to govern the relationship between the two cultures, it was the fur trader and later the Indian agent who wound up being the day-to-day representative of Euroamerican culture and policy. Because of the trade power they wielded, fur traders could be quite effective agents when they were of honorable character. When they were scoundrels, they could easily inflame relations between the two cultures. Since colonial governments never found an effective way to monitor and control their behavior, dishonest traders cost the British government no small expense in maintaining peaceful relations with the southern tribes.

With most tribes in North America, trade issues quickly became synonymous with diplomatic ones. Both colonials and Indians tried to manipulate each other through the Indian trade. Occasionally, minor misunderstandings over trade rapidly escalated into scenes of backcountry violence. More times than not, a greedy trader was at the heart of the matter. Intercolonial and international rivalries in North America empowered various tribes to make their own trade demands on colonial government. These governments often acquiesced to Indian demands from fear of losing their Indian allies and trade to rival colonies or nations. While the Indians became strongly attached to Euroamerican trade, the southern colonies and the British government felt nearly as compelled to supply that trade, often at great expense.

NOTES

1. Cyril Belshaw, *Traditional Exchange and Modern Markets,* Wilbert E. Moore and Neel J. Smelser eds., (Englewood Cliffs, N.J.: Prentice Hall, Inc., 1965), 6.

2. Ibid., 46-47.

3. Ibid., 49.

4. Anonymous, 12 April 1773, *Lloyd's Evening Post.*

5. George Dalton, "Economic Theory and Primitive Society," *American Anthropologist,* 63 (1961): 9.

6. Belshaw, *Traditional Exchange,* 48-49.

7. Dalton, "Economic Theory," 12-13.

8. Belshaw, *Traditional Exchange,* 51-52.

9. Nick Kardulias, "Fur Production as a Specialized Activity in a World System: Indians in the North American Fur Trade," *American Indian Culture and Research Journal,* 14: 1 (1990): 25-26. A nation-state may be characterized as having a strong central government, capable of defending the borders it claims. Its people share a common cultural and linguistic heritage.

10. Ibid., 28-29.

11. Ibid., 36.

12. Ibid., 36.

13. James Axtell, *After Columbus: Essays in the Ethnohistory of Colonial North America* (New York: Oxford University Press, 1988), 162-164.

14. Calvin Martin, *Keepers of the Game: Indian-Animal Relationships and the Fur Trade* (Berkeley: University of California Press, 1978), 40.

15. Axtell, *After Columbus,* 145.

16. Ibid., 153.

17. Martin, *Keepers of the Game,* 42.

18. Francis Jennings, *The Invasion of America: Indians, Colonialism, and the Cant of Conquest* (New York: W.W. Norton and Company, 1976), 85-86.

19. Axtell, *After Columbus,* 156-158.

20. Martin, *Keepers of the Game,* 42.

21. Timothy Silver, *A New Face on the Countryside: Indians, Colonists, and Slaves in South Atlantic Forests, 1500-1800* (Cambridge: Cambridge University Press, 1990), 41.

22. Jennings, *The Invasion,* 92.

23. Kardulias, "Fur Production," 38-39.

24. Axtell, *After Columbus,* 160-161.

25. Ibid., 167-169.

26. Ibid., 171-172.

27. Kardulias, "Fur Production," 41-42.

28. Gary C. Goodwin, *Cherokees in Transition: A Study of Changing Culture and Environment Prior to 1775* (Chicago: The University of Chicago, 1977), 55.

29. Ibid., 127.

30. Ibid., 128-129.

31. Ibid., 141.

32. Kardulias, "Fur Production," 46-48.

33. Ibid.

34. Silver, *A New Face,* 40.

35. Jennings, *The Invasion*, 98-99.
36. Ibid., 99.
37. Ibid., 102.
38. Kardulias. "Fur Production," 53-54.

2

Walkers Between Two Worlds: Native American Women and Trade

The introduction of manufactured trade items into the southern backcountry altered every aspect of Native American life. In particular, the trade drastically changed the lives of native women, but such change is difficult to document because of the lack of written records. In *Many Tender Ties,* Sylvia Van Kirk was able to document a process of cultural adaption by women in the Northeast in response to the presence of trade and Euroamerican men. These women, through liaisons with frontier men, transmitted the cultural information vital to the success of the Indian traders and later Indian agents. While they taught tribal language and customs, women absorbed elements of Euroamerican culture such as private ownership, literacy, materialism and pastoral farming. Native women adopted these new ideas at a pace related to the success they brought in everyday living and dealing with foreign encroachment. Thus, metal utensils and weapons were easier to absorb than concepts of Western government and religion.

Van Kirk was quite fortunate in her research to draw upon the records of proselytizing religious orders operating in the Northeast as well as records of large trading companies like the Hudson Bay Company and the North West Company. Similar documentation in the Southeast is much scarcer. No large scale company operated within the backcountry; instead a small, nearly invisible army of private traders worked the area, supplied by both public and private trading firms. Further, no religious orders invested heavily in the region. While Spain and France sent missionaries to their respective enclaves in North America, Britain from the beginning of its colonization efforts did not. In fact, Britain's political turmoil in the 1600s allowed its American colonies to expand the parameters of colonial governments. While the Church of England was the established church in several of the southern colonies, no proselytizing arm of it existed until the advent of the always half-hearted efforts by the Society for the Propagation of the Gospel in Foreign Parts in the early eighteenth century. Thus, the great bulk of Euroamerican contact with Native Americans in the Southeast took place without benefit of the rich ethnographic sources of the Northeast.

These complications in writing about Native American women are further exacerbated by cultural precepts of Euroamericans about the proper role of women. Women in the egalitarian societies of Native America possessed more integral roles than did their Euroamerican counterparts. Native American culture ascribed a certain importance to women for their part in childbearing and child rearing, as well as their contributions in agriculture. Women who performed especially outstanding services for the village in the Southeast might be elevated to the status of Beloved Woman and allowed to make civil and military decisions for the village. Euroamericans, by contrast, had segregated their women out of the public sphere. They believed that spinning thread and weaving cloth were the proper contributions of a woman to her home and society. Euroamericans often succeeded in getting native women to adopt such economic pursuits out of a perceived obligation to educate savages about the proper role of women.[1] Native women often adopted foreign economic strategies when advantageous, though they adapted them to fit within the bounds of traditional life when possible.

The Enlightenment reformed some notions that Europeans held about their women, although it ultimately reinforced the idea of separating women from power. François Marie Arouet, otherwise known as Voltaire; Montesquieu; Charles Louis de Secondat and John Locke probed and questioned the folkways of tradition. For example, Locke's notion of a tabula rasa had strong implications for a society acculturated to ideas of an ordained hierarchical world.[2] Taken further, this concept meant that beyond the physical differences between men and women, nothing should affect the opportunities available to each. Many authors called for the need to educate women better, though the Enlightenment was not a call for complete equality between European men and women. Reformers like John Locke wanted women to be educated better, not equally with men. Their roles as mothers and teachers of children required that they be better educated in order to produce a society of superior men.[3]

Yet, in this new and better society proclaimed as attainable by the philosophes, women did have a unique role. Men like Montesquieu ascribed a privileged, yet passive role for women. Truly civilized societies, according to Montesquieu, required that women be treated with a high degree of mannerliness, courtesy and consideration. The degree to which a culture offered this position to women in turn marked its level of sophistication. This need to "elevate" women was yet another way to distance them from the centers of power. Requiring them to be passive objects of social deference negated the prospect of having politically active women in a "civilized" society.[4] Most travelers who came to the southern, colonial backcountry in the eighteenth century were not the cultural elites who would have shared Enlightenment views. Still the Europeans encountered in America a world where women's roles were too closely associated with their own ideas of the proper role for men. The Europeans visited Indian villages during the summer when women's work, gardening, gathering nuts and fishing, was at its peak. Men's work, hunting and trapping, had peaked during the winter. To the Europeans, hunting was a sport, not a job, and so they created the myth of the squaw as drudge. Existing evidence challenges the European estimation. Mary Jemison, European by birth, lived as a Seneca woman and found the work load a reasonable one-- ameliorated by communal effort, the presence of children and a leisurely work pace.[5]

While a combination of low literacy rates, lack of a dominant institution with record keeping facilities and a negative attitude about the proper role of women in society minimizes the availability of references to native women, it may by safely said that few backcountry traders and Indian agents achieved success without the aid of an Indian consort. A relationship with native women gave Euroamerican men the linguistic and cultural instruction they needed, as well as the social acceptance required in a matrilineally ordered society. The intermarriage of native women and Euroamerican men created an invisible web in the backcountry, and few players in that drama were untouched by its social strands. Native women involved in the web ultimately lost political power as a result of Euroamerican society's efforts to reform native societies, especially women's roles. In order to document the loss, it is necessary to compare traditional roles with those created as a result of fusion with Euroamerican culture.

Creation stories in Native American mythology hint at the cultural clashes that were to come between Indians and Euroamericans. The mythology speaks of an orderly universe that always existed, as opposed to one created out of nothingness. Such explanations tell of men and women being created equally and concurrently, each endowed with their own nature with neither having ascendancy over the other, but rather separate spheres of equal importance.[6] Intrinsic beliefs about women's status differed from the European model.

Native American women in general were guided by strong spiritual concepts which influenced every facet of their lives. The religions practiced throughout North America were based on imitative and sympathetic magic aimed at meeting the needs of life.[7] They also strove to maintain the delicate balance of opposites in the world, a concept tied to Native American belief systems. The cosmology of the southeastern Indians generally held that the world was a great island suspended from the sky by four cords which prevented it from sinking into the sea. This island was round but divided by four lines, each representing points east, west, north and south, with a space at the center, which most tribes believed they occupied.[8] Southeastern tribes generally acknowledged the existence of a Supreme Being known by various names but often called the Master of Breath, who dwelled beyond the clouds. His realm offered plentiful game and crops and cheap trade goods. Conversely, those who violated tribal norms were consigned to a miserable, briar-ridden swamp within the bowels of the earth, where constant hunger awaited them.[9]

Earthly representations of these spirits existed as well. Southeastern Indians considered fire the symbol of the Great Spirit and revered it for its purity. Conversely, they considered water symbolic of the lower world. The southeastern Indians believed it was their task to maintain order on earth by ensuring the separation of disparate elements.[10] Thus women's roles in Native American society required their full participation in life, not segregation from it.

Indian women saw themselves as a natural part of the universe, coequal with men and possessing tasks as important as those of men. The social structure of tribal life reinforced that concept, beginning at birth. Among the Chickasaws, female children were placed on deer or bison skins while male children were placed on panther skins in hopes that both sexes would receive the positive attributes of those animals. Children of both sexes were breast-fed for a relatively long time.[11]

Children of the southeastern Indians were welcome additions to village life. William Bartram, a noted British naturalist, observed among the Creeks that the men were "courteous and polite to the women, and gentle, tender and fondling, even to an appearance of effeminacy, to their offspring."[12] Southeastern Indians handled childhood discipline differently than their European counterparts as well. Indian parents approached child discipline cautiously, fearing that excessive punishment might prompt the child to commit suicide. In Chickasaw society, parents did not punish male children directly. The oldest uncle in a clan performed that task.[13] Caleb Swann, a Euroamerican residing at Little Talassie (near present-day Montgomery, Alabama) in the 1790s, observed that Creek women often scratched the leg or thigh of a recalcitrant child until the wounds bled; in addition to punishing the youngster, southeastern Indian women were teaching their young that injury and the sight of blood were a part of the struggle of life and not to be feared.[14] Older Creek children of both sexes were admonished for their misdeeds through public scorn and gossip--punishment dreaded by all members of the tribe.[15]

Among the Creeks both female and male children went about naked until puberty, partially to condition their bodies to extremes of heat and cold.[16] Powhatan women in Virginia washed their children in rivers on the coldest mornings of the year to toughen their constitution.[17] Education and acculturation continued the notion of separate but equal spheres for men and women. Few facets of southeastern Indian life both fascinated and repelled Euroamerican visitors as did the sexual practices of groups like the southeastern Indians. Jean Bernard Bossu, a French traveler among the Creeks in the 1750s, noted that when an Indian male passed through a village, he was free to engage a young woman for sexual favors without stigma either to him or the woman.[18] Bernard Romans, a Dutch-born American traveler among the Choctaws in the 1770s wrote, "Fornication is among them thought to be a natural accident, therefore a girl is not the worse looked on for ten or a dozen slips."[19]

Indeed, both young women and men were free to pursue other singles as they liked without fear or rebuke. Among the Creeks, a young woman who had been considered popular within the village was all the more desirable to other males when she chose to settle down with a permanent mate.[20] Tribes like the Creeks perceived lasting relationships as evolving over time. The first step, courtship, began only after a young man had achieved success in battle. This achievement brought him adult status, which was necessary before he could approach the woman's maternal aunt to state his intentions, and she, in turn, discussed them with the family. While approval of the family was required, it in no way bound the woman to accept the man, unlike in some European cultures. Among the Chickasaws, a potential suitor sent a bundle of clothing to the parents of his intended mate. The parents were free to accept or reject the present; if they accepted it, they handed it to the woman. If she accepted the bundle, she indicated her interest in the man.[21] Afterwards, most southeastern Indian couples were free then to begin a sexual relationship. The relative ease in establishing such a relationship with Indian women coupled with the traditional desire for good gifts allowed Euroamerican traders to move quickly into village life.

Relationships were not considered finalized until the birth of a child. Even then, the ultimate sanction of the union took place at an annual event known as the Bus ke tau, the Busk or simply the Green Corn Ceremony. This yearly event honored the Supreme Creator for a successful year in hunting and harvesting. It was scheduled after the last harvest of corn in late August or early September, hence its British name. Indian cultures generally acknowledged the fragility of human nature. All relationships, including marriage, were adjusted during the time of the Busk. Young couples who had their first child were formally recognized as bonded. Either member of a mismatched union could request its dissolution, and divorce carried no stigma.

Euroamericans labeled Native Americans as promiscuous because young singles were given much freedom. Some tribes, however, enacted an equally swift and violent punishment for adultery from either member of a settled couple. For example, the Creeks perceived it as a threat to the earthly balance between elements of the upper and lower worlds. If a man suspected his mate, he would take both a member of her lineage and one of his own to a potential rendezvous spot. If successful in obtaining proof, the injured male presented his case to the village chief, who then scheduled a dance where all members of the village would be present. At the height of the festivities, the adulterous woman was thrown to the ground and mercilessly beaten, as was her lover.[22] William Bartram, traveling in the backcountry in the 1770s, met an Indian man in pursuit of an errant wife and her lover, bent on removing the ears of both.[23] Only the cuckolded husband could stop public punishment; once he did, he remanded her, beaten, dirty and perhaps mutilated, to her lover, who was in similar disarray. The woman was free to settle with her lover, but both had to leave the village.[24] Unlike the Creeks, the Cherokees did not require women to practice serial monogamy. Cherokee women, single or not, were free to have sex with whomever they chose, just like men.[25]

Women frequently became widows in an aggressive society motivated by retributive justice. Widows found their lives carefully regulated by their late husband's family, specifically his female relatives. It was they who formed a special guardianship over the widow that began with her husband's burial. At that time, they divested the woman of all colorful apparel and ornamentation to signify a period of ritual mourning, which lasted up to four years. She could do nothing in that time to enhance her appearance, nor could she remarry.[26] Many circumstances could alter this ritual seclusion, however. If the woman were especially dear to her former "in-laws," the guardian women could take pity on her and bring her out of her mourning period prematurely. They would proceed to her home, return her more festive items, bathe her and arrange her hair in an attractive manner. In so doing, they signified her social rebirth and her availability as a potential mate. A second alternative again revolved around the maternal side of the deceased husband's family. If any of his brothers or cousins from his mother's side wished, he could prematurely end the widow's seclusion by taking her as a second wife. Normally, a first wife had to give her consent in order for her husband to take a second wife, yet southeastern Indian men had an obligation to support their brothers' families which superseded a first wife's power to object.[27]

If a widow chose to break her time of seclusion, she risked provoking the wrath of the entire village. If she had a lover, they could try eloping. If they managed to elude vengeful members of the husband's clan until the time of the next Busk, they were free to return to the village as a couple without fear of reprisal.

Pregnancy and childbirth were natural parts of most relationships among southeastern Indians, although these stages were marked by periods of ritual seclusion from the group. Small group dynamics in tribal societies dictate a high degree of cooperation among members to ensure group survival. The possibility of alienating or offending certain members directly threatens the security of all. Therefore, many cultures weave a complex tapestry of cultural rules concerning ritual seclusion for members at special times in their lives so that they may avoid conflict within the group.[28] For example, warriors preparing for and returning from battle segregated themselves for short periods. Menstruating women likewise segregated themselves for the duration of their condition. Southeastern Indians took great pains to maintain the separateness of men and women; menstruating women were considered to have very powerful female natures which might contaminate unwary males if such women bathed or even stood upstream from them.[29]

Likewise, pregnant women due to give birth removed themselves from the village. In December 1790, Caleb Swann noted that four women came from Little Talassie (modern Alabama) one day to sell horse ropes. The weather was cold, rain mixed with snow, and the women decided not to return home that evening. During the course of the night, a pregnant woman went into labor. Though the woman's own mother was along, the pregnant woman went unattended into a nearby swamp at midnight to deliver. She returned the next day at 10:00 a.m. with her child and the entire group walked home barefoot in a snowstorm.[30] While seemingly harsh, these self-imposed seclusions served a deeper purpose. In societies bound by group interdependence, physical changes like menstruation produce mood swings that might provoke conflict within the group.[31] As both sexes practiced seclusion, it does not indicate women's subservience.

Finally, southeastern Native American women possessed a high degree of control over their own reproductive rights. Abortifacients existed and native women used them in their culture. Further, the right to terminate the life of a child was not confined to its inutero development. Euroamericans, like the Methodist minister John Wesley, noted that Creek women practiced infanticide.[32] In fact, new mothers had a one month period after the birth of a child during which they could end its life. Choosing to terminate a newborn's life might reflect an inability to support it or a desire to punish a wayward mate.[33]

Ultimately, the structure of Native American society in the Southeast reinforced the high status of women. At some point after hunter-gatherer societies were forced to adapt to widespread climactic changes around 6000 B.C., women were accorded a higher status because of their preeminent role in the cultivation of plants as replacement food sources for the dying megafauna which had heretofore been a major part of their diet. Many tribes in North America converted to matrilineal organization, which recognizes the relative ease in identifying one's true mother but the difficulty in ascertaining one's true father, given the fragility of human nature. Groups of matrilineally related people were organized into clans. A child then belonged to his mother's clan and the role of instruction and guardianship filled by the father in Euroamerican society was filled by the maternal uncle.

Clans were associated with some type of animal or natural phenomenon, such as the Fox or the Wind Clan, from which the group hoped to derive anticipated benefits. Clan membership was a vehicle through which one accessed rights and privileges; aliens had no rights within the village. The inclusive nature of Indian culture often prompted the adoption of members of other tribes or Euroamericans. Such adoption brought status equivalent to birth membership with its attendant rights and obligations.[34] Southeastern groups, such as the Creeks, practiced exogamous relationships. Two members of a clan could not form a permanent union as it would be considered incestuous and disruptive of the balance between upper and lower world elements. Indians put transgressors of this taboo to death, but one particular incident reveals the organizational fluidity of Indian communities. When two members of the Toad Clan among the Creeks fell in love, their community was faced with a dilemma. As both man and woman were highly respected, the town council created a new group, the Mole Clan, around the woman, thus removing the threat of incest or the loss of valued people.[35]

The benefits enjoyed by Native American women included property rights: the right of personal ownership and the right to give or will possessions to sons and daughters.[36] To the dismay of many Euroamericans, the boundaries between property and political rights for southeastern Indian women were uncomfortably close. The male and female children of a woman were part of the mother's clan. Groups like the Muskhogees called such a group an *owachira*. The land held by an owachira belonged exclusively to its female members. Married women of childbearing age in an owachira had the right to hold a council to choose candidates for chief and subchief of the greater clan. The head of an owachira was often its eldest female member. If the chief or subchief of a clan proved unsatisfactory, it was the women's council of the owachira which started the removal process. If a vacancy in the post of village chief arose, a prominent woman with exceptional wisdom and leadership often would be appointed to fill the vacancy temporarily.[37] Ultimately, a woman who performed an outstanding service to the village would be granted the status of Beloved Woman enabling her to participate in the village's political life. Euroamericans first encountering such high-ranking women mistakenly labeled them queens and princesses.

Christian Penicaut, a French traveler among the Mississippi tribes around 1700, observed that women did all the work in Indian society.[38] In truth, their sphere was the home, where they tended the elderly and the sick; fashioned pottery, clothes, robes and sleeping mats and also processed animal skins. Since women were honored for horticulture, the garden was an important part of their world. Men assisted them in the garden, clearing the ground and breaking it up for planting. Come harvest, men assisted in the actual transport of produce to storage facilities.[39] In the day to day process of gardening, women were not the drudges described by European men. As in most areas of life, they shared in the daily obligations and rewards of society with men. They also owned slaves, who assisted them with their work.[40] The routine of women's lives was interrupted by various sporting events, where they were both participants and spectators. They attended activities analogous to the quilting bee and attended ceremonial events forbidden to men.[41]

Southeastern Indian women, like their European counterparts, were socialized to identify with a wide variety of cosmetics and ornaments. They were especially fond of using body paint--a concoction of pigment, animal tallow and saliva. Since Indian clothing seldom had pockets, women always needed small bags and pouches in which to carry needles, thread, medicine and tobacco. They used animal and vegetable tallow as a hair dressing and scented herbs, fish and whale oil to make perfumes.[42] Women smoked tobacco in pipes, as did men, though European men seldom reported this fact. Both sexes smoked to enhance spirituality, however, not merely for pleasure.[43] Both sexes liked jewelry; Leclerc Milfort noted a Creek woman in the 1770s who wore silver pins, silver bracelets, earrings and colored ribbons in her hair.[44]

Women's hairstyles did not vary as widely within the tribe as did ornamentation. William Bartram described Cherokee women with plaited hair bound atop their head by broaches. John Lawson noted that Carolina women wore their hair long, adorned by beads, leather and strings.[45]

Southeastern women also used facial makeup although its use was more individualistic than hairstyles. Women painted empty or filled circles on the cheeks and around their eyes. They frequently drew two vertical lines between the forehead and the chin. In addition, they often pierced their ears and wore earrings.[46] Thus, southeastern Indians associated the use of cosmetics, perfumery and jewelry with the status of womanhood. Since Euroamerican traders could provide these women with a steady supply of such goods and other more practical items, the traders enjoyed an enhanced status in the eyes of the women. This led, no doubt, to the great proclivity for relationships between Indian women and Euroamerican traders.

Finally, with respect to personal appearance it should be noted that aside from hair on the head and eyebrows, Indian men and women in the Southeast depilated their skin using clam shells or wooden tweezers. In addition to removing body hair, the women and men often wore tattoos. Southeastern women, especially, were prone to have tattoos on their thighs, legs, trunks and arms.[47]

One ethnohistorian has observed that when two peoples of disparate origins meet, they first fight and later intermarry. The initial response of Native American women to the presence of Euroamerican traders in the eighteenth century surely must have been similar to the response of Native Americans to their initial contact with European explorers. Sadly, a lack of written records of those contacts leaves only educated speculation as a guide. An early Ojibwa account from central Canada of such a meeting described the Europeans as possessing odd skin that was the color of snow. The Ojibwa also noted that the Europeans did not remove body hair, but instead let it grow long, especially on the face.[48] During Arthur Barlowe's initial exploration of Roanoke Island he noted that the Indians "wondred mervelously [sic] when we were amongest them, at the whiteness of our skinnes, ever coveting to touch our breastes, and to view the same."[49] The Mongoloid stock from which Native Americans descended was relatively hairless. Since the people of many tribes depilated their bodies even further, the sight of comparatively hirsute Europeans must have been fascinating in a morbid way. Indeed, the Potawatomis and Menominees of the Lake Michigan region thought the French to be another species altogether because their bodies were covered with hair.[50]

Aside from curiosity over physical differences, many Indians initially thought the Europeans were their spiritual and technological betters. Spiritual power, they believed, allowed the Europeans to cure the sick if they so chose; it also allowed these intruders to kill the healthy. When Euroamerican settlers in North Carolina inadvertently infected the surrounding native peoples with European diseases, the Indians of Roanoke honored the colonists of Roanoke for their ability to kill over long distances without physical effort.[51]

Native Americans also were amazed at the Europeans' crafted tools. Indians often honored such items as guns as though they were deities. Yet, they were fascinated by cleverly designed objects of any purpose, such as clocks as well as cloth goods and wooden articles. To Native Americans, such items were nothing short of supernatural. Thus, these items became the reference point when Native Americans discussed Europeans. The Narragansetts of Rhode Island called their Europeans *coatmen* or *swordsmen*. Similarly, the Indians of Virginia called the British and later the Americans *longknives*.[52]

So too must Indian women have viewed these pale-skinned alien invaders with a mixture of fear and attraction. Yet these invaders, despite their strangeness, were bringers of wonder in the form of myriad desirable trade items. While Indian males wanted guns and ammunition, women longed for metal cookware, bright paints, trade beads and European clothing. In addition, the inclusive nature of Native American culture meant that strangers, unless totally intractable, were to be incorporated into society, not kept at arm's length. Most European powers initially established all-male outposts. The natural sexual urges of these men so far from home, combined with the relative ease of establishing a relationship in Native American society, meant that sexual unions would soon follow initial contact between the two ethnic groups.

Sexuality is a subject rarely discussed in journals and reports during America's colonial period. Yet, its undertone is quite apparent in the earliest recorded contacts between Native American and Euroamerican peoples. During Amerigo Vespucci's exploration of the New World, he reported that the people "showed themselves desirous of copulating with us Christians."[53] Though military reports and personal journals rarely show it, a fair amount of time was devoted to securing Indian women as sexual partners for European men.

The practice of attacking Indian towns for women began soon after Spain made a bridgehead in North America. From here, the process was enlarged to a virtual slave trade trafficking in Native Americans. A native woman captured by a conquistador would first be branded with an iron for identification. Then, she and others like her would be distributed among the soldiers. In 1538, Pope Paul III forbade Indian enslavement. Later, the Spanish monarch Charles V, at the urging of Father Bartolome de las Casas, issued the Leyes Nueves, which recognized the humanity of the Indians and extended the Spanish crown's protection to them.[54]

French colonizers likewise trafficked in Native American women. France's Royal Council declared such a practice legal in Canada in 1709 and legal in Louisiana in 1745. French slavery was considerably milder than its Spanish counterpart and often ended in marriage between a native woman and a Euroamerican man.[55] Of the three groups of aggressive colonizers, it was the French who, as one author noted, possessed a special empathy with native peoples. "They cheerfully married into the tribes, lived as the Indians did, spoke their language, took the warpath with them and raised a brood of half-breed children."[56] In the fur trading regions of French Canada, marriages between Indian women and Euroamerican men were quite frequent. A woman so married to a chief factor of the fur trade was, "first lady of the post. It made no difference whether she was Indian, half Indian, or white; she met and entertained the aristocracy of the country and presided over a gentleman's house."[57] What cost the French their superior influence among Native American tribes was trade. The British simply offered better liquor and cheaper trade goods.

Of the major colonizing powers, the British are the most silent about mixed unions with Native Americans. Yet, given the fact that an outpost like the Roanoke settlement had only seventeen females among ninety-one males, it is highly probable that mixed unions existed. Even those standard bearers of morality the Puritans admitted to sexual relations with Indian women.[58] Yet not all British explorers and settlers were immediately taken with Indians. A variety of accounts and journals record differing opinions on matters of Indian origin, behavior and appearance. Euroamericans frequently failed to see beauty in Native American women because they did not conform to European standards. Yet, many other Euroamericans did find native women attractive in their own right. When mixed-blood offspring sporting features that did conform to European standards of beauty began to appear, even more Euroamericans found native women desirable.

Gilbert Imlay was a citizen of the United States of America in the late eighteenth century. In publishing his recollections about the backcountry, he found it difficult to believe that Indians were not born white. He surmised that they further attempted to darken their skins with grease while lying in the sun. In all, he found them a pleasant looking lot, especially their women. Imlay also observed that Indians were not ignorant, as some believed, but actually quite bright.[59] William Byrd II, the master of Westover Plantation in Virginia, wrote in 1728, "all nations of men have the same natural dignity, and we all know that very bright talents may be lodged under a very dark skin."[60] Byrd ventured further to say that "Indian women would have made altogether as honest wives for the first planters as the damsels they used to purchase from aboard the ships."[61] Byrd's seemingly open-minded attitude had its limits, however, and ulterior motives. He perceived the natives of Virginia to be tall and well proportioned, a factor which he believed compensated for their dark complexion. He chastised early British explorers for their hesitation in taking Indian wives. Byrd believed that such "intermixtures" would have made Virginia Indians early converts to Christianity. In addition, he felt that the Indians " would have had less reason to complain that the English took away their land if they [the English] had received it by way of a portion with their daughters."[62] If such intermarriages had been practiced, Byrd believed, much bloodshed could have been prevented. Yet, the ultimate goal of his plan was not cultural preservation for native peoples but amalgamation within the dominant culture. Using the earliest European contacts with Indians as a point of reference, he observed that by his own time, 1728, there would have been no Indian problems as he believed that "if a Moor may be washed white in three generations, surely an Indian might have been blanched in two."[63]

In 1727, Byrd had the opportunity to observe Native Americans at close range. In that year, King George II ordered the governor and Council of Virginia to dispatch surveyors to demarcate a clear border with the neighboring colony of North Carolina. William Byrd was part of the team that surveyed that boundary throughout the spring and fall of 1728. In the course of his mission, he journeyed to a village of Nottoway Indians. There he noted that the women wore necklaces and bracelets to adorn themselves. Byrd described their physical complexion as "sad-coloured" and noted that the women were seldom handsome, though he described them as innocent and bashful-looking. Byrd hinted that the men of his party would have been attracted to these native women but for the fact that "the whole winter's soil was so crusted on the skins of those dark angels that it required a very strong appetite to approach them."[64] Unlike Gilbert Imlay, Byrd correctly assessed the reason for the dingy skin. Indians applied animal oils to their skin to protect it from insect bites, though the oil attracted and held dirt. Even so, Byrd's negative judgments about native women were insufficient to dissuade his often amorous nature. An entry dated seventeen years earlier than his survey mission mentioned a visit to a nearby village, marked by native hunting contests and dance exhibitions. After dark, Byrd wrote that "Jenny, an Indian girl, had got drunk and made us good sport."[65]

Indeed, many Euroamericans found native women in the Southeast attractive by European standards. At the turn of the eighteenth century, John Lawson set out from Britain for Carolina, where he arrived in the fall of 1700. In December of that year, the Lord Proprietors of Carolina appointed Lawson to make a reconnaissance survey of the interior of the colony, where he came into contact with various groups of Indians such as the Santees and the Waxhaws. During that original expedition, Lawson took time to write about the Congarees, noting that their women were "as handsome as most I have met withal, being several fine-finger'd Brounetto's amongst them."[66] Lawson, unlike most visitors, made observations on the customs and habits of the peoples he encountered, not just the number of gun men (warriors) they possessed. He observed that Congaree women were free to enjoy multiple sexual partners and actually settled down with mates when they were only twelve or fourteen years of age.[67]

Lawson observed similar customs among the Wateree. In his own style, he observed that the years of sexual freedom were, in actuality, a growing period for a woman "till a greater number of years has made her capable of managing domestick [sic] affairs, and she hath try'd [sic] the vigour of most of the nation she belongs to."[68] Of the Native American women Lawson encountered, he gave the now familiar description of them as well shaped and proportioned, describing their complexions as tawny and their eyes as "brisk and amorous," matched by pleasant smiles. Lawson found their skin smooth, not dingy, and noted the women were experts in the art of love.[69]

Bernard Romans was another Euroamerican traveler in southern North America in the eighteenth century. Born in Holland about 1720, Romans was educated in Britain and sent to America as a civil engineer in 1755. He became the deputy surveyor of Georgia between 1760 and 1770 and later the surveyor of Lord Egmont's estates on Amelia Island and the St. John's River. His work kept him in the vicinity of St. Augustine, Florida, and so his observations dwelt on the Creeks, Choctaws and Chickasaws. Romans wrote a history of the dual provinces of Florida and in it noted that the period term used for Native Americans, savage, was without a doubt a correct one. He found the people of the various societies with which he came in contact to be incapable of civilization. Further, he believed that the natives were contemptuous of every aspect of Euroamerican society and were, in fact, born possessing a natural opposition to the customs of the intruding society. As proof, he noted that unlike Euroamericans, native men urinated in a sitting posture whereas native women urinated standing.[70]

With respect to general physical attributes, Romans was somewhat kinder. He commented, like so many Euroamericans, on the unusually good posture of most natives. Probably as a result of restraining infants on cradle boards, he observed, deformed or otherwise lame individuals were a rarity. With regard to skin tone, Romans described the Native Americans as having a copperish cast similar to the color of cinnamon. Romans oddly believed that these peoples were born white but were darkened through their own doing.[71] Many Euroamericans attributed the skin darkening to the aforementioned use of animal oil. They mistakenly thought oil was used solely to darken the skin, rather than protect it from insects. Romans' observations on the relative attractiveness of native women were begrudgingly complimentary. He noted that they were "handsome, well made, only wanting the colour and cleanliness of our ladies."[72]

Comments on the racial features of specific tribes followed along the lines set out in Romans' more general comments. The issue of cleanliness as defined by Euroamerican standards was a key determinant of beauty. He found Choctaw women quite handsome, when they practiced "cleanly" habits.[73] Romans found Creek women to be handsome as well as hospitable, and many of them, he observed, were even clean![74]

In terms of sexuality, Romans generally observed that unmated Indian girls were free to pursue multiple partners and for that reason he labeled them as promiscuous. He noted that such behavior in mated females often brought swift and severe punishment but failed to acknowledge or record that the sexual norms for the two different states of female life were perfectly natural in native society. Since Euroamerican women were supposed to be chaste and pure when single and models of piety and propriety as married women, many Euroamericans, like Romans, labeled Indian women as lascivious. Speaking specifically of the Creeks, he noted that young women were notorious flirts who would not hesitate to sell their bodies. Yet, Romans refuted the long-held Euroamerican belief that native men forced their women to have sexual relations with intruding Whites.[75] Unlike their Euroamerican counterparts, single Native American women were able to experiment with whomever they chose, free from patriarchal control. Many of them chose Euroamerican traders and Indian agents for temporary or often permanent mates for material benefits.

William Bartram, perhaps one of the more famous Euroamerican visitors to the American Southeast, explored the region noting its indigenous flora and fauna in 1765 and 1773. Bartram was also a rarity for the open mind he kept with regard to the various customs he encountered among Native American peoples. During the first trip to a series of trading outposts along the Georgia-Florida border, he was introduced to a Euroamerican trader with a Seminole wife. Speaking about this woman, Bartram observed that she had every characteristic necessary "to render a man happy. Her features are beautiful, and manners engaging. Innocence, modesty, and love appear to a stranger in every action and movement."[76]

During a 1773 trip along the St. John's River on the Georgia-Florida border, Bartram praised the charms of Seminole women and found them sufficient to entice both Native American and Euroamerican men.[77] Later, traveling along the Tallapoosa River, he encountered a mated Creek woman whom he described as of "a very amiable and worthy character and disposition, industrious, prudent and affectionate."[78] The Muskoghee peoples were one of the numerous groups located around either the Flint and Chattahoochee Rivers of western Georgia or the Coosa and Tallapoosa rivers of eastern Alabama, all generically termed Creeks. Bartram observed that the Muskoghee women were short of stature but well formed and possessing attractive features, as well as being bashful and modest.[79]

Bartram traveled still farther into the backcountry, where he encountered the neighbors and frequent enemies of the Creeks--the Cherokees. He wrote, "the women of the Cherokees are tall, slender, erect and of delicate frame; their features formed with perfect symmetry, their countenance cheerful and friendly, and they move with a becoming grace and dignity."[80]   While Euroamerican standards of beauty, cleanliness and hygiene prevented many travelers from perceiving native women as attractive, such standards did not deter others, who were quite taken with the women according to their descriptions of them.

Evidence indicates that many Euroamerican men did much more than admire native women from afar. Just as Indian women often experimented sexually with Euroamerican men, such men, mostly fur traders and Indian agents, often took native women as mates. Such unions were much more than merely advantageous; they were critical to ensure the success of these men in their occupation as fur trader or Indian agent. When a Euroamerican man operating as either a trader or an Indian agent was successful, he more than likely had an influential native mate from a respected clan.

A tale told by John Lawson about a sexual encounter reveals what native women gained from such a union. Lawson recalled that on an expedition to the Congarees of South Carolina one of his fellows communicated to their guide that he desired a woman for the night. The guide procured an attractive young woman for the man, but, before they settled down to the business at hand, Lawson noted in his own style that the woman indicated to her client that he " was to pay the hire, before he rode the hackney."[81]   The man then displayed a collection of beads and various trinkets which satisfied the woman. The Congarees then performed a ceremony that Lawson termed a "Winchester-Wedding" and left the couple to retire for the night. Lawson awoke the next morning to find his disgruntled companion wandering the village. The companion's hired woman had awakened before him, picked his pocket of all the trade items she had been shown and then taken everything else he owned and departed.[82]   As established earlier, native women in the period before European intrusion had an affinity for jewelry, fragrances and cosmetics. Further, in Indian society, the value of potential unions was judged on the basis of gifts given by the male to the female's family. Euroamericans had access not only to gifts, but to gifts of a foreign and superior technology whose introduction was not unlike that of a new, highly addictive drug. Women, whose lives revolved around food production, child care and ceremonial duties, quickly became adept at using the metal needles, scissors, knives and hoes which revolutionized their lives. Once introduced, these items became such a part of native culture that when damaged or lost, they were replaced at all cost.[83]   Finally, there is evidence at the beginning of the historic period, that various tribes attached status to mixed unions and their bicultural offspring. Women involved in such a mixed union enjoyed a higher status as well as having access to trade items.[84]

Native American cultures as small group societies were characterized by a certain dynamic. Everyone within a village was needed to cooperate to facilitate food procurement and satisfy protection and general survival needs. Yet, one could only function within native society with clan affiliation. Traders came as strangers among the Indians and many tribes believed strangers and recluses were witches. Thus traders had to find an avenue of acceptance into the tribes in which they lived and worked. Intermarriage with native women provided that bridge of acceptance and inevitably produced children who had maternal clan affiliation. The traders provided the prestige of a foreign mate, the prestige of mixed-blood children and, most of all, trade goods.

John Lawson observed that Carolina traders in 1700 almost always had an Indian "bed-fellow" for many reasons. First, since traders were located at such a great distance from Euroamerican towns and cities, such alliances and the clan protection they brought enhanced the safety of otherwise vulnerable men. Further, Native American women fulfilled for Euroamerican men an absolutely vital prerequisite--instruction in native language and customs. Lawson's opinion, borrowed from an unknown French traveler among the southeastern Indians, stated that by comparison " an English wife teaches her [non-English speaking] husband more English in one night, than a school master can in a week."[85] The language skills of Indian women were such that they were occasionally hired outright as interpreters. During a November 1716 meeting of the South Carolina Board of Indian Commissioners, an agency created to regulate that colony's Indian trade, the council noted the need for a "linguister" by the agent at Savano Town and so authorized the hiring of an Indian woman for that purpose.[86] In May 1717, the board discussed two Wateree women who served the British as translators among the Catawbas.[87] Women also were prized for their skill in the preparation of local foods.

A note of clarification is necessary in discussing the usefulness of Indian women, often listed as wives. First, few Euroamericans actually married Indian women--they cohabited with them during their tenure on the frontier. Traders sometimes cohabited with Indian women while maintaining Euroamerican wives back in colonial towns and cities. Second, Euroamericans, like Lawson, almost universally believed that Native Americans viewed paired unions as temporary, transient matters. Lawson noted that the relationships were "no farther binding, than the man and woman agree together. Either of them has liberty to leave the other, upon any frivolous excuse they can make."[88] This perception of the experimental period allotted young women no doubt eased the minds of frontier traders and agents who had legal wives back at home. Thus, the records of men like Lawson and James Adair invariably refer to such unions as temporary marriages. The average trader or Indian agent was, most likely, pleased with the fluidity of relationships when he chose to leave the frontier.

An appropriate question to explore, after examining why Euroamerican men virtually had to have native mates, is what those native women received in return. First, during the early years of European and Native American contact, there is evidence that Indians generally viewed everything connected with Europeans as supernatural. When the Delaware Indians, who formerly lived along the New York and New Jersey coast, first spied Dutch ships in nearby waters, they assumed such vessels were moving houses of the Mannitto, or Supreme Being.[89] When finally convinced these men were not gods, Indians concluded that they were demigods of sorts. Most native societies recognized the existence of shamans, men of superior spiritual power able to mediate elements in the physical world. The foreign nature of Europeans made this perception of them quite easy and their superior technology further reinforced this conclusion. When French explorers traveled in Wisconsin during the mid-1600s, the Indians there blew sacred smoke over their iron weaponry and stated that the existence of such devices had convinced them that the supreme being had sent the Europeans among them as the natural leaders of the Native Americans.[90]

When native women offered themselves to European men, many tribes believed that such a union captured the essence of this "superior" spirit and enabled the woman to transmit it to members of her community.[91] Having mixed-blood offspring became a vehicle to higher prestige for women in some tribes. Second, since many tribes viewed mating as a union of the fortunes of two families, not just two lives, the pairing of a native woman and Euroamerican man brought the woman's father a certain amount of prestige. Her father's influence and power could easily be enhanced by a close alliance with a trader who could provide everything from beads and baubles to arms and ammunition. The status and prestige of her male relatives similarly were increased. The woman's own economic and social position improved as well. She had ready access to the foreign equivalents of the cosmetics, perfumes and jewelry with which she had been socialized to identify. Further, she had access to those manufactured items which revolutionized Native American life. Beyond her immediate needs, she could procure such items for her family and friends as well, sometimes too well. During his 1766 excursion up the St. John's River, near modern Jacksonville, Florida, William Bartram encountered a trader with a Seminole mate. The trader had come to the Georgia backcountry from North Carolina and had made a comfortable living for himself. Though he loved his native wife, her behavior distressed him greatly, for Bartram noted the woman virtually had bankrupted her mate by giving away his trade goods among members of her own family. When Bartram arrived at the trader's store, the woman's whole family was encamped directly adjacent to the store.[92] One such disastrous choice in a mate could not typify all such arrangements. The simple manner of dissolving unions with native women, so often noted by Euroamerican observers, would have precluded widespread retention of spendthrift wives.

The incidence of mixed unions between Native American women and Euroamerican men in the eighteenth century was neither as scarce as the fleeting reports of it would suggest nor confined to any one class of men. Since native women came from preliterate societies, they left behind no records or diaries detailing their lives with Euroamerican men. Our images of them are reflected through the often biased accounts written by Euroamerican men. Indian wives, when they are noted, generally are mentioned, as Bartram did, with only the appellation of "Seminole woman." To discuss them, one must discuss their husbands and surroundings.

From the founding of British colonies in North America, the first Europeans to have prolonged contact with Native Americans were the traders who lived among them. Initially, the traders were free agents operating without either restriction or protection. Gradually, colonial supervisory trade boards and governors assumed control over these frontiersmen. In 1751 a New Yorker named

Archibald Kennedy proposed the creation of the position of Superintendent of Indian Affairs to Governor Cadwallader Colden of New York. Colden in turn submitted the idea to the Board of Trade.[93] As originally planned, the superintendent would address Indian grievances, supply them with craftsmen and missionaries and enforce fair trade practices within the various tribes. In 1754, William Johnson presented a paper at the Albany Congress again calling for such a position. In addition, a delegation of members of the Iroquois Confederacy appeared at the Congress and also appealed for such a position.[94] Secretary of State for the Southern Department Lord Halifax approved the position or rather positions. He divided North America into two districts, each of which would have its own superintendent. These officials were to possess the sole right to issue licenses to trade among the Indians and they were to mediate disputes between Native Americans and Euroamericans. They would be assigned subordinates, who would carry these policies into the various tribes to which they were assigned.[95] British General Edward Braddock named William Johnson to serve as Superintendent for the Northern District and Edmund Atkin for the Southern District. William Johnson was the husband of Molly Brant, a Mohawk woman. After her death, he eventually took two more wives--both Native American women.[96]

Braddock named Edmund Atkin to head the Southern District, assisted by John Stuart. Atkin died not long after he assumed the position which was filled by Stuart in January 1762.[97] John Stuart was born in Inverness, Scotland, on 28 September 1718. As a young man, Stuart joined the Royal Navy in 1740 and signed aboard a ship commissioned to plunder Spanish shipping. Through such means, he accumulated enough capital to emigrate from Scotland to Charles Town, South Carolina, where many friends and family members had relocated to seek their fortune. By the time of his appointment as superintendent, Stuart had filled a number of roles, including that of firemaster, tax assessor and assembly member. He also had been an officer in the St. Andrew's Society.[98]

Initially, Stuart operated his post from Charles Town, where he resided with his wife, Sarah, and their four children. By 1775, Stuart's position had become anathema to American Patriots there, who surmised that Stuart would use it to antagonize the southern Indians to the Patriots' detriment. Stuart eventually relocated to St. Augustine, Florida, though Sarah Stuart and her children remained as hostages in South Carolina until 1777.[99]

John Stuart was held in high esteem by many tribes, especially by the Cherokees who named him "Bushyhead," for an apparently thick head of hair.[100] The British military assigned Captain Stuart to Fort Loudoun [found in modern eastern Tennessee] in 1760 when it was besieged by Cherokee forces. Indian women who had relationships with the soldiers of the fort risked their lives taking food and supplies to them. A quarter-blood Cherokee woman, Susannah Emory, took food to John Stuart.[101] Emory was the granddaughter of Ludovic Grant, a Euroamerican trader, who married a full-blood Cherokee of the Long Hair Clan. Their union produced a half-blood daughter who married William Emory. Susannah had one child by Stuart, Oo-no-do-tu. Because Stuart had a tightly packed head of hair, the Cherokee later coined the name Bushyhead as a surname used by his descendants. The name became a prestigious one in the tribe.[102]

Stuart was well represented among the Cherokees by two deputies-- Alexander Cameron and John McDonald, both from Scotland. McDonald was from Inverness also, like Stuart. Cameron, called "Scotchie" by the Cherokees, arrived in Cherokee lands as a deputy in 1766 and settled near modern-day Abbeville, South Carolina. He married a Cherokee woman, who bore him a son.[103] Years later he used this marriage to claim land the Cherokees were willing to cede him as a reward for his service and paternity. Occonostota, a headman among the Cherokees, wrote to Stuart justifying the cession to Cameron, saying he had treated them justly, told them the truth and was beloved by them. Occonostota also acknowledged Cameron's mixed-blood Cherokee son.[104] No doubt, it was this unnamed Cherokee woman who instructed Cameron so well that his performance earned him the affection of Occonostota and the Cherokees.

John McDonald emigrated from Scotland at age nineteen. He began trading with Indians in Georgia and was sent to Fort Loudoun to trade with the Cherokees. He married Anna Shorey, a mixed-blood daughter of an Indian trader, William Shorey, and they settled near Lookout Mountain, Tennessee. Shorey bore McDonald a quarter-blood daughter named Molly.[105] Historians speculate that such mixed unions between Cherokees and Euroamericans peaked in the 1750s.

As noted, Indian traders had beaten the Indian agents to the altar, so to speak. The traders had predated the Indian agents in the southern backcountry by more than half a century. Thus it is not surprising that the mixed blood women who settled down with the Indian agents of midcentury were the daughters and granddaughters of traders. Bernard Romans noted that before the arrival of a permanent group of British traders, there were few mixed bloods within the southern tribes. Afterwards, Romans noted such bicultural progeny abounded in the backcountry.[106] The traders served many roles. Before the advent of the Indian agents, they were the eyes, ears and mouths of those decentralized agencies which regulated the trade with various groups before the creation of the superintendency. William Shorey was a trader and an interpreter in Cherokee lands in 1760. He married Ghigooie, a member of the Bird Clan.[107] The couple had a daughter named Anna, who married John Stuart's deputy to the Cherokees, John McDonald. John Adair, a traveler from Ireland, lived among the Cherokees and married a Cherokee woman, Mrs. Ge-ho-ga Foster, of the Deer Clan. Nathaniel Gist, a scion of an influential Virginia family, engaged in a relationship with Wurteh, the sister to Cherokee chiefs Doublehead, Onitositah and Pumpkinhead. Gist abandoned the woman around 1760 although she gave birth to his child, whom she raised alone.[108]

Edward Graves, prior to the American Revolution, married a Cherokee woman named Lah-to-tau-yie. The dual nature of native women as cultural bridges is well exemplified in this instance. Graves converted her to Christianity and she, in turn, taught others, offering prayer services from her cabin. He introduced the woman to European clothing which she wore to please him. Graves taught his mate the art of spinning and weaving cloth on a hand-made loom and a spinning wheel imported from Britain.[109] Lah-to-tau-yie introduced new styles of clothing, new work skills and a new religion to her people. Such cultural transmissions cannot be dismissed lightly. The powerful effect of such cultural infusions can be studied by a similar incident among the Creeks where new work skills were adapted to traditional life.

LeClerc Milfort journeyed to America from France in 1775. He arrived in Connecticut but later entered the backcountry of Georgia and Carolina. By May 1776, he had arrived at the Chattahoochee River and the town of Coweta. Milfort soon developed a marked fondness for the Creek people and determined to remain among them as a trader.[110] He observed that the Creek chiefs originally opposed the introduction of new skills among their women for fear that the economic independence they would give them would undermine traditional life. Milfort noted, however, that a small group of women began processing cloth and not only outfitted themselves and their families, but were able to sell their handiwork as well. Soon, they earned enough to buy hogs and cattle, which launched them on a second economic innovation--pastoral farming. Milfort noted that the success of the small group had become so widely known that a much larger group had gone " to the agents of the English trading post to ask them for a hundred pairs of wire-toothed brushes for carding cotton and eighty spinning wheels."[111] This change allowed them to remain home-based providers while earning more.[112]

As among the Cherokees, Indian agents, soldiers and traders spread out among the Creeks as well. Milfort's best friend among the Creeks was Alexander McGillivray, the famous Creek leader . McGillivray's father, Lachlan, had come to America from Inverness when several years of poor crops persuaded the young man to immigrate to the Georgia-Carolina backcountry in 1735 to seek his fortune. With relatives already engaged there in the Indian trade, Lachlan's choice of that profession was not surprising, especially since it was widely considered in its day as a sure way to obtain riches.[113]

Lachlan McGillivray had been recruited to emigrate from Scotland by an agent of Georgia's founder James Oglethorpe. In a report to the trustees of that colony at the end of 1736, an official stated that all the backcountry Indian traders had native wives. Further, the official estimated that they had fathered upward of four hundred mixed-blood children.[114] In 1743 McGillivray, along with a trader named Patrick Brown, began trading with the Upper Creeks, who lived near the Coosa and Tallapoosa rivers. John Rea and George Galphin traded with the Lower Creeks, clustered around the Chattahoochee and Flint rivers.[115] Galphin, in particular, is an example of an expediency-minded Euroamerican working among the Indians. He had several wives back home in Ireland, at least one wife back at his plantation of Silver Bluff (near present-day Augusta, Georgia) and several Indian wives in the backcountry.[116]

Lachlan McGillivray found a mate in Sehoy Marchand, the mixed-blood daughter of a Creek woman, also named Sehoy, and a French officer, Captain Marchand. The somewhat confusing genealogy of the Sehoy-McGillivray family is a perfect example of the invisible web of intermarriage in the Georgia-Carolina backcountry. The first Sehoy, hereafter referred to as Sehoy I, was a full-blood leader among a group of Muskoghees. Sehoy I married a member of the Alabama tribe and had a daughter, referred to as Sehoy II. By 1714, the Alibamas were at war with the British and so turned to the French, asking them to build a fort within their lands to frustrate their enemies. The French built Fort Toulouse on the Coosa River, one mile above its confluence with the Tallapoosa River. A Captain Marchand was dispatched to the fort to act as second in command. Here he met Sehoy II and the two began a relationship in 1720.[117]

When the Royal Bank of France failed, the colony of Louisiana began to suffer dire consequences. Soldiers in Mobile and Biloxi were discharged and stranded in America. In the resulting confusion, the soldiers at Fort Toulouse mutinied in August 1722 and Marchand was killed. Sehoy II was left a widow at a young age but with a daughter by Marchand whom she also named Sehoy, referred to here as Sehoy III. Her mother, Sehoy II, settled down with a Creek man after the death of her Euroamerican husband and bore two full-blood children by him--a son named Red Shoes and a daughter. The full-blood daughter of Sehoy II married a half-blood Scotch-Irish trader named David Francis. Francis was also a silversmith and worked out of Autauga Town.[118]

The young Sehoy III became the object of attention among several British traders in her land in 1735. Trader Malcom McPherson had been among the tribe since 1716 and was well established. A Euroamerican settler named James McQueen was also an early inhabitant of Creek lands. Together, they were fighting to keep the Creeks firmly attached to the British and prevent them from aligning with the Spanish who were threatening the colony. Both men believed that a "marriage alliance" with Sehoy III of the Wind Clan would accomplish their goals and so McPherson was given the task of wooing the Creek woman. McPherson's newly-arrived assistant, Lachlan McGillivray, accompanied McPherson into Creek lands as a packhorseman.

It was McGillivray, not McPherson, who settled down with Sehoy III in the 1740s on the east bank of the Coosa River at Little Talassie. Unlike George Galphin, McGillivray did not maintain women throughout the backcountry--only Sehoy. There is evidence of affection between the two as he filled their home with furniture sent from Dummaglass, Scotland. In order to delight Sehoy III, McGillivray planted an apple orchard there for her. Apple trees were a rarity in the backcountry and highly prized. In his line of work, McGillivray had to speak a semblance of several languages, including French and Spanish, since rival traders from those powers were constantly seeking to supplant the British traders and the influence they held among the Creeks. Sehoy III's fluency in five Creek dialects extended McGillivray's range and influence among the tribe as well.[119]

McGillivray prospered financially and personally. In the course of their union, Sehoy III bore him three children. Sophia was born around 1747, Alexander in December 1750 and Jennet sometime thereafter. In 1776 the mixed-blood Sophia married Benjamin Durant, a Huguenot who made his living initially as a boxer in the backcountry. After their marriage, they settled in Savannah, Georgia, and Sophia eventually had a son, whom she named Lachlan.[120] Lachlan, despite his prosperity, was one Euroamerican who could not be permanently absorbed into backcountry life. He dreamed of attaining a place in colonial administration and, after 1756, McGillivray ceased living with Sehoy III at the "Apple Grove" and relocated to Georgia. Sehoy III, still a young woman, caught the eye of a full-blood named Eagle Wings, who lived a short distance from Little Talassie at Tuckabatchee. A daughter was born of the union and Sehoy III passed on her name to the child, hereafter referred to as Sehoy IV. Unfortunately for the hapless Sehoy III, Eagle Wings was killed on a hunting trip, leaving her single once more.[121] Like the traders, the Indian agents were no strangers to mixed unions with native women. David Taitt, a Scot who immigrated to America, served as a surveyor in West Florida from 1764 until 1767. After a two-year stay in Britain, Taitt returned to the southern backcountry and became John Stuart's deputy among the Creek tribe in the early 1770s. During the turbulent American Revolution, Taitt stayed on among the Creeks struggling to prevent the encroachment of American Indian agents and traders in their affections. It was he who took Sehoy III as his mate and the union resulted in the birth of a son, also named David. Ultimately Taitt abandoned the Indian country and Sehoy III, though she settled down yet another time, with Charles Weatherford. Sehoy III bore him the famous Red Eagle, who fought against Andrew Jackson in the War of 1812.[122] Thus the Sehoy-McGillivray lineage exemplifies several advantages of the mixed union trend. British traders sought Sehoy III, the mixed-blood daughter of the full-blood Creek Sehoy II and the French officer Marchand, as a vehicle through which to keep the Creeks firmly aligned with Britain and prevent them from drifting into the French orbit. Her marriage to Lachlan McGillivray accomplished that, but also gave him prestige and status within her tribe since her clan was influential. Further, she no doubt instructed him, if only through example, in the rules of Creek culture. McGillivray utilized her fluency in Creek dialects which no doubt prompted his success as a trader in Creek lands, as well. After McGillivray abandoned Sehoy III, three other men, only one of whom was Native American, sought her. Both David Taitt and Charles Weatherford obviously had need of an Indian mate and the advantages such a mate brought. Sehoy III herself may have become accustomed to Euroamerican mates and the obvious material benefits they carried.

The majority of unions between Native American women and Euroamerican men are nearly invisible in the pages of history. Their unions, when mentioned, are subordinated to reams of military correspondence of how best to utilize the southern tribes to British advantage in the colonial period. Likewise, the majority of the women involved are nameless, faceless and seldom remembered in the histories of eighteenth century Euroamerican males. Yet, no treatment of the effects of trade on native women would be complete without examining the lives of Mary Musgrove Bosomworth and Nancy Ward, the best known Native American women of the Southeast.

NOTES

1.   Mary Beth Norton, *Liberty's Daughters: The Revolutionary Experience of American Women, 1750-1800* (Boston: Little, Brown and Company, 1980), 18.

2.   Elizabeth Fox-Genovese, "Women and the Enlightenment," *Becoming Visible: Women in European History*, Renate Bridenthal, Claudia Koonz and Susan Stuard, eds. (Boston: Houghton Miffin Company, 1987), 259-260.

3.   Ibid., 260.

4.   Ibid., 263.

5.   James Axtell, *The Invasion Within: The Contest of Cultures in Colonial North America* (New York: Oxford University Press, 1985), 153-155. The Senecas, members of the Hodeenosaunee Confederacy, are used for comparison because their economic strategies were similar to those of southeastern tribes, both built upon hunting and agriculture.

6.   John Upton Terrell and Donna M. Terrell, *Indian Women of the Western Morning: Their Life in Early America* (New York: The Dial Press, 1974), 3-4.

7.   Ibid., 23.

8.   Charles B. Hudson, *The Southeastern Indians* (Knoxville: The University of Tennessee Press, 1984), 122.

9.   Henry R. Schoolcraft, *Information Respecting the History, Condition, and Prospects of the Indian Tribes of the United States*, Vol. 5 (Philadelphia: J. B. Lippincott and Co., 1855), 269.

10.   Hudson, *The Southeastern Indians*, 128.

11.   John Reed Swanton, *The Indians of the Southeastern United States* (Grosse Pointe, Michigan: Scholarly Press, 1969), 715-716. In prehistory, the Chickasaws were found as far east as Alabama; in the historic period they resided in northern Mississippi.

12.   John Reed Swanton, *Social Organization and Social Usages of the Creek Confederacy* (New York: Johnson Reprint Corporation, 1977), 386. Creek is a generic name English colonists gave to tribes like the Alibamas and Hitchitis of eastern Alabama and Western Georgia.

13.   Swanton, *The Indians*, 715-716.

14.   Swanton, *Social Organization and Social Usages*, 363.

15.   James Adair, *Adair's History of the American Indians*, Samuel Cole Williams, ed. (Johnson City, Tennessee: The Watauga Press, 1930), 460.

16.   Jean Bernard Bossu, *Travels in the Interior of North America 1751-1762*, Seymour Feiler, trans. (Norman: University of Oklahoma Press, 1962), 134.

17.   Swanton, *The Indians*, 709.

18.   Bossu, *Travels in the Interior, 131.*

19.   Bernard Romans, *A Concise Natural History of East and West Florida* (New Orleans: Pelican Publishing Company, 1961), 58-59. The Choctaws of the historic period lived in southern Mississippi.

20.   Charles Colcock Jones, Jr., *Antiquities of the Southern Indians, Particularly of the Georgia Tribes* (New York: A.M.S. Press, 1973), 269.

21.   Swanton, *The Indians*, 705.

22.   Bossu, *Travels in the Interior*, 132-133.

23.   William Bartram, *Travels Through North and South Carolina, Georgia, East and West Florida,* (Savannah: The Beehive Press, 1973), 242.

24.   Bossu, *Travels in the Interior, 133.*

25. Hudson, *The Southeastern Indians,* 201. In the historic period, the Cherokees were found in northern Alabama and Georgia, southwestern South Carolina, western North Carolina, eastern Tennessee and western Virginia.

26. George Stiggins, *George Stiggins,* Virginia Pounds Brown, ed. (Birmingham: Birmingham Public Library, 1989), 59.

27. Ibid.

28. Hudson, *The Southeastern Indians,* 320.

29. Ibid., 319-320.

30. Swanton, *Social Organizations and Social Usages,* 360-361.

31. Hudson, *The Southeastern Indians,* 320.

32. David C. Corkran, *The Creek Frontier 1540-1783* (Norman: University of Oklahoma Press, 1967)

33. Hudson, *The Southeastern Indians,* 231.

34. Ibid., 193.

35. Terrell and Terrell, *Indian Women,* 25.

36. Ibid.

37. Ibid., 30-33.

38. Richebourg Gaillard McWilliams, trans. and ed., *Fleur de Lys and Calumet: Being the Penicaut Narrative of French Adventure in Louisiana* (Baton Rouge: Louisiana State University Press, 1953), 35.

39. Terrell and Terrell, *Indian Women,* 53.

40. Ibid., 45.

41. Ibid., 45-46.

42. Ibid., 103-104.

43. Jordan Paper, *Offering Smoke: The Sacred Pipe and Native American Religion* (Moscow: The University of Idaho Press, 1988), 37-38.

44. General Louis Milfort, *Memoirs of a Quick Glance at My Various Travels and My Sojourn in the Creek Nation,*Ben C. McClary trans. and ed. (Kennesaw, Georgia: Continental Book Company, 1959), 200.

45. Terrell and Terrell, *Indian Women,* 110.

46. Ibid.

47. Ibid., 111.

48. James Axtell, *After Columbus: Essays in the Ethnohistory of Colonial North America,* (New York: Oxford University Press, 1988), 130.

49. Ibid., 132.

50. Ibid.

51. Ibid., 133.

52. Ibid., 136.

53. Walter O'Meara, *Daughters of the Country: The Women of the Fur Traders and Mountain Men* (New York: Harcourt, Brace & World, Inc., 1968), 19.

54. Ibid., 123.

55. Ibid.

56. Ibid., 197-198.

57. Ibid., 188.

58. Ibid., 15-16.

59. Gilbert Imlay, *A Topographical Description of the Western Territory of North America* (New York: Augustus M. Kelley, Publishers, 1964), 369. Many of North America's native peoples applied animal or plant fat to their skin for protection from the

elements or insects. The coatings attracted dirt and led to the stereotype of the "dirty" Indian--ironic since most bathed daily.

60. William Byrd, *The Prose Works of William Byrd of Westover: Narratives of a Colonial Virginian,* Louis B. Wright, ed. (Cambridge: Belknap Press, 1966), 26.

61. Ibid.

62. Ibid., 160.

63. Ibid., 160-161.

64. Byrd, *Prose Works,* 218.

65. William Byrd, *The London Diary (1717-1721) and Other Writings,* Louis B. Wright and Marion Tinling, eds. (New York: Oxford University Press, 1958), 424.

66. John Lawson, *A New Voyage to Carolina*, Hugh Talmadge Lefler, ed. (Chapel Hill: The University of North Carolina Press, 1967), 35.

67. Ibid.

68. Ibid., 40.

69. Ibid., 189.

70. Romans, *A Concise Natural History,* 27-28.

71. Ibid., 28-29.

72. Ibid., 29.

73. Ibid., 55-56.

74. Ibid., 63.

75. Ibid., 67.

76. Bartram, *Travels,* 110.

77. Ibid., 192-193.

78. Ibid., 448.

79. Ibid., 482.

80. Ibid., 481-482.

81. Lawson, *A New Voyage,* 46.

82. Ibid., 46-47.

83. Wilbur R. Jacobs, "Unsavory Sidelights on the Colonial Fur Trade," *Indians and Europeans: Selected Articles on Indian-White Relations in Colonial North America,* Charles P. Hoffer, ed. (New York: Garland Publishing, Inc., 1988), 137.

84. Lawson, *A New Voyage,* 35.

85. Ibid., 35-36.

86. Board of Commissioners Meeting, 16 November 1716, *Colonial Records of South Carolina: Journals of the Commissioners of the Indian Trade, September 20, 1710-August 29, 1718,* William L. McDowell, ed. (Columbia: South Carolina Archives Department, 1955), 127. Hereafter referred to as Indian Book 1. Savano Town was located on the east bank of the Savannah River, about six miles below modern Augusta, Georgia. See Newton G. Mereness, *Travels in the American Colonies.* (New York: Antiquarian Press, Ltd., 1961), 133, ftn. 1.

87. Board of Commissioners Meeting, 9 May 1717, 177-178.

88. Lawson, *A New Voyage,* 193.

89. Axtell, *After Columbus,* 131.

90. Ibid., 134.

91. O'Meara, *Daughters of the Country,* 147.

92. Bartram, *Travels,* 109-110.

93.   Richard Alden, "The Albany Congress and the Creation of the Indian Superintendencies," *The Mississippi Valley Historical Review,* 27 (September 1940): 193-195.

94.   Ibid., 196-200.

95.   Ibid., 200-201.

96.   Wilbur R. Jacobs, "British-Colonial Attitudes and Policies Toward the Indian in the American Colonies," *Attitudes of Colonial Powers Toward the American Indian,* Charles Gibson and Howard Peckham, eds. (Salt Lake City: University of Utah Press, 1969), 87-90.

97.   Alden, "The Albany Congress," 208. For the latest work on Stuart's career as superintendent, see J. Russell Snapp, *John Stuart and the Struggle for Empire on the Southern Frontier* (Baton Rouge: Louisiana State University Press, 1996).

98.   Richard Alden, *John Stuart and the Southern Colonial Frontier* (New York: Gordian Press, 1966), 165-166.

99.   Ibid., 171-172.

100.   Grace Steele Woodward, *The Cherokees* (Norman: University of Oklahoma Press, 1984), 76.

101.   Emmet Starr, *History of the Cherokee Indians and Their Legends and Folk Lore* (New York: Kraus Reprint Company, 1969), 30.

102.   Ibid., 466-467.

103.   Woodward, *The Cherokees,* 84.

104.   Great Britain Public Records Office, Kew, Oconostota, Headman of the Cherokee at the Congress of Hard Labour Creek, 15 October 1768, C05/74: 39.

105.   Woodward, *The Cherokees,* 84.

106.   Romans, *A Concise Natural History,* 56.

107.   Woodward, *The Cherokees,* 76.

108.   Ibid., 85-86. Wurteh's son grew up to become the famous Sequoyah, author of the Cherokee syllabary.

109.   Ibid., 85.

110.   Milfort, *Memoirs,* viii-x.

111.   Ibid., 45-46.

112.   Joel Martin, *Sacred Revolt: The Muskoghee's Struggle for a New World* (Boston: Beacon Press, 1991), 106.

113.   Edward J. Cashin, *Lachlan McGillivray, Indian Trader: The Shaping of the Southern Colonial Frontier* (Athens: The University of Georgia Press, 1992), 12-17. This is the most up-to-date, thorough work on McGillivray.

114.   Ibid., 19.

115.   Ibid., 46-48.

116.   Ibid., 72.

117.   Lyn Hastie Thompson, *William Weatherford: His Country and His People* (Bay Minette, Alabama: Lavender Publishing Company, 1991), 1-2. This is a genealogical treasure for intermarriage information.

118.   Ibid., 5-6.

119.   Ibid., 11.

120.   Ibid., 16-17.

121.   Ibid., 14.

122.   Cashin, *Lachlan McGillivray,* 77.

3

Mary Musgrove and Nancy Ward: Beloved Women of the Southern Indians

Mary Musgrove and Nancy Ward fully illustrate the ignored contributions of native women to Euroamerican society, even as it sought to disempower them. Both these mixed-blood women were in prestigious clans and Euroamerican men sought them for their power and influence. Though they contributed as much to the survival of Britain's colonies as any European male, history labeled them Indian "queens" and "princesses" and promptly forgot them.

Tales of Mary Musgrove abound in the history of Georgia. She is most often referred to as the "Creek princess" but is more properly known as Coosaponakeesa, born in 1700 in the Lower Creek town of Coweta in Alabama. Her mother was the sister of two powerful brothers--the Creek leader Brims and his war chief Chekilli.[1] Information on her parentage is unclear, but stories stated her father was either a British or Scottish trader. It is not surprising that Mary's first husband was an Indian trader as well.

The colony of South Carolina employed some two hundred traders in the Georgia-Carolina backcountry. Colonel John Musgrove, Sr., was one such trader, albeit slightly more well connected than most. He was a member of the Carolina Assembly in addition to his career as a trader. He became fluent enough in Creek dialects to serve also as an interpreter.[2]

After the disastrous Yamassee War of 1715, South Carolina sought to prevent more Indian troubles by dispatching an expedition, headed by Colonel

General Oglethorpe. Courtesy of Hargrett Rare Book and Manuscript Library/University of Georgia Libraries.

Musgrove, to secure Carolina's isolated and vulnerable trading stations in the backcountry and also to secure a treaty with the Creek leader, Brims. To that end, Musgrove headed a group of thirty men and a packhorse train of presents. In addition, he took along his son, John Musgrove, Jr., the product of Colonel Musgrove's union with an unnamed Indian woman. The mixed-blood son, John, was educated in Euroamerican society.[3] Not surprisingly, well-to-do men often educated their mixed-blood sons, like Musgrove, Jr., and Alexander McGillivray, in their own culture while mixed-blood daughters grew up in their mothers' society.

The two cultures were able to reach an agreement, and to bind both sides to it, Brims gave Mary in marriage to John Musgrove, Jr. After their union the couple traveled among the Creeks for seven years and Mary used the time to hone her skills in Creek dialects. After the birth of their first child, they settled on Musgrove land in Pomponne in 1723. They maintained contact with their Native American relatives; Johnny's uncle, Willimico, lived with them.[4]

Mary's relationship with Johnny gave him status among the Creeks due to her powerful uncles. It enhanced the prestige he enjoyed as a successful trader, like his father, among the Creeks. In fact, in 1732 the Creek people requested that the Musgroves be allowed to establish a trading house near the future site of Savannah, Georgia. Governor Nathaniel Johnson consented and the post was established, placing the couple at a propitious location for the advent of a thirteenth British colony.

When General James Oglethorpe (Figure 1) arrived in Georgia, it is not surprising that Mary Musgrove was one of the first people he met. He was impressed by her intelligence and her ability to speak English as well as several Creek dialects. Oglethorpe asked Mary to act as his interpreter for the sum of £100 per annum. Further, the Musgrove trading post was optimally located to help supply the infant colony with food.

The relationship between the Musgroves and the colony of Georgia was initially quite beneficial for both sides. Oglethorpe and his colonists made purchases from her trading post. They were, for a time, dependent on the beef purchased from Mary's herd of cattle.[5] In addition, Mary was to receive a salary as an interpreter. From Mary's perspective, she gained status in the eyes of her own people by being the close aide to such a powerful Euroamerican as Oglethorpe. She interpreted all of his talks to the Creeks and likewise participated in the making of treaties.[6] (Figure 2) From Oglethorpe's perspective, he had access to a powerfully connected Indian liaison who was skilled in Creek dialects and yet familiar with Euroamerican culture. Mary's language skills were such that she was known for her ability to express Creek nuances faithfully in English, a difficult feat between any two languages.[7] The Musgroves were so cooperative that when Oglethorpe needed a monitoring outpost closer to Spanish Florida, they opened Mount Venture at the forks of the Altamaha River.[8] The erection of such an outpost so close to Spanish territory was a risky move. During the War of Jenkins's Ear, Oglethorpe was unable to spare troops to defend it. Though guarded by a group of amateur soldiers led by Musgrove, the outpost was burned to the ground by Spanish Indians. Mary was not repaid for the loss of the outpost or its trade goods.[9]   It was here that Johnny

General Oglethorpe negotiating treaties with Creek Indians. Courtesy of Hargrett Rare Book and Manuscript Library/University of Georgia Libraries.

Musgrove contracted a fever of unknown origin. The couple returned to Savannah, where Johnny died, leaving Mary the richest woman in the colony. She had a successful trading business between the two cultures, a five hundred acre plantation known as Grantham, a cattle range known as the Cow Pen, a large herd of cattle and ten indentured servants to help her.[10]

Despite the death of Johnny Musgrove, Mary continued to bridge the gap between the two cultures. The Salzburger pastors Bolzius and Granau approached her about instruction in native dialect. The Methodist minister John Wesley and a Mr. Ingham likewise asked Mary to instruct them; Ingham offered to teach her children to read as well as paying her. When Oglethorpe held meetings with the Creeks and Chickasaws in the summer of 1736, Mary was his voice.[11]

Mary did not remain a widow for the rest of her life. Oglethorpe had authorized Musgrove to enlist his own soldiers at the Mount Venture Trading Post when Oglethorpe could not spare any of his own. Jacob Matthews, an indentured servant of Johnny Musgrove, Jr., was the head of that unit. Matthews sought Mary's hand in marriage; unlike so many backcountry unions, the couple was married Euroamerican style in 1737 by a minister.[12]

Mary continued to occupy an important position as mediator between the two cultures. When the leaders of Georgia's Moravian community decided their land was too infertile and malaria-ridden, they appealed to Mary to put their request for a land transfer before Mico [Chief] Tomochichi, and she did (Figure 3). The Creeks complied with the transfer request and the exchange proceeded smoothly. Mary often served the colony of Georgia to the detriment of her own financial situation. Most colonists disliked the idea of Indians walking into towns to transact business. They much preferred that Indians meet them at prearranged spots away from towns. Mary and Jacob often entertained up to fifty Indian representatives at the Cow Pen, saving Savannah the cost of such expense.[13]

In 1737, the reputation of the ever-useful Mary began to tarnish in the eyes of the colonists. In December of that year, Tomochichi started transferring tracts of land to Mary. Treaties with the Creeks in both 1733 and 1735 had acknowledged the existence of land solely reserved for Creek use and recognized the right to transfer nonreserved land to the British crown.[14] Despite her service to the colony, the trustees refused to acknowledge an internal transfer. Most native cultures had a difficult time with the concept of mortal beings spending their lives in a frenetic rush to acquire land which would exist long after they were gone. The Creeks certainly would not have accepted the right of the British government to interfere with internal cessions of land, especially when someone as famous as Mary was involved. The transfer consisted of the Musgrove Plantation and the Georgia Sea Islands of Sapelo, St. Catherine and Ossabaw. Though Oglethorpe may have led Mary to believe the trustees would support her claim, they did not.

Mary continued, however, to serve the interests of Georgia and Oglethorpe. When he held a council of 7000 warriors in Coweta in 1739, Mary

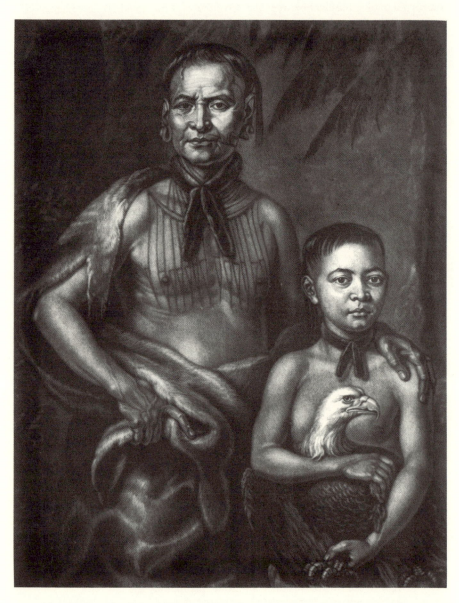

Mico [Chief] Tomochichi and his nephew. Courtesy of Hargrett Rare Book and Manuscript Library/University of Georgia Libraries.

accompanied him as linguist. The ten day cession concluded on August 21, 1739 with a reaffirmation by the Creeks of their grants of land to Georgia in 1733 and with a promise by the Georgians to respect the boundaries of the land reserved solely for Creek use.[15]

With the advent of the War of Jenkins's Ear, Oglethorpe asked Mary to send Creek warriors to assist British forces against the Spanish, promising to reimburse the Creek woman for the cost of such measures.[16] After Oglethorpe left the colony, his successor, Major William Horton, continued to ask Mary for all the help she could send him.[17] At the conclusion of hostilities, the Creek warriors encamped near Fort Frederica, awaiting the customary presents for their service. When a drunken colonist named Jones began to stir the Creeks up, Horton quickly called for Mary to quiet them. Horton wrote to Thomas Bosomworth of Mary's efforts, "before she came I was harassed to death, [by the warriors] & all I could do fell quite short of their expectations."[18]

When Oglethorpe left the colony in July of 1743, he gave Mary a diamond ring, £200 and a promise of forthcoming payment for her services.[19] Jacob Matthews had died in June 1742. Mary was widowed once more, and Oglethorpe, her biggest supporter, was no longer physically present in the colony. By this time, Mary seemed accustomed to Euroamerican mates. She became acquainted with Thomas Bosomworth, who arrived in Georgia in September, 1741 to serve a colonist, William Stephens as a clerk. When the colony pastor, the Reverend Christopher Orton, died of plague less than a year after his arrival, Bosomworth decided to return to Britain for religious instruction in November 1742; he returned to Georgia in December 1743. Upon his return, Bosomworth served as chaplain to Oglethorpe's regiments at Savannah and Fort Frederica. Two brothers, Abraham and Adam, were also present in Georgia. Abraham eventually represented the colony of South Carolina as agent in the distribution of Indian gifts.[20]

Widowed twice and only forty-four years old, Mary married Thomas Bosomworth in July 1744. Despite his vocation as chaplain, Bosomworth was somewhat of an adventurer and fortune hunter and Mary's vast land and livestock holdings may have been the true object of his desire. Still, she continued to be an invaluable asset to Georgia. President Stephens recorded in his journal that no "talk" could be held with Georgia's Indians without her and summoning them to aid in the colony's defense was impossible without Mary's influence. When foreign powers tried to lure the Creeks away from British interests, it was Mary who thwarted their efforts.[21] Though absent from the colony, Oglethorpe tried to bolster Mary's position there by reminding Georgia officials of her worth. In November 1745, he wrote to William Horton that Mary should be helped and supported because of the help and support she had given both Georgia and its founder. He noted that the Spanish were intent on destroying her precisely because she was a person of influence among the Creeks and had used that power in behalf of the British Crown.[22] Likewise, Oglethorpe wrote to Georgia public store-keeper, Thomas Causton, asking him to assist Mary and her husband in their affairs with the colony. He noted that Georgia's welfare was tied to the proper treatment of Mary and her people.[23]

In December of 1745, the Georgia trustees received a notice from Mary Bosomworth requesting recognition of Tomochichi's cession of the Yamacraw tract of land to her. She also requested back payment of £1,200 for the twelve years she had served the colony as interpreter, £100 per annum, as Oglethorpe had stated. In addition, she also requested the payment of bounties promised by the trustees for growing wheat and corn but never paid. In response, the trustees stated that they had never promised to pay Mary as an interpreter nor had any bounties been previously requested from her. They did note, however, that her second husband, Jacob Matthews, owed a debt of £114 and if Mary were due anything, she would get it after this debt was paid. As for Mary's land claims, the trustees refused outright to honor Tomochichi's cession to Mary.[24]

Mary continued to battle the Georgia trustees while serving their colony. In January of 1747, she persuaded her cousin, Malatchi, a leader among the Lower Creeks, to cede her the islands of Ossabaw, Sapelo and St. Catherine. In that same year, the relationship between the Creeks and the colonials of Georgia and South Carolina broke down. Georgia leaders enlisted Mary's help in an expedition to ameliorate the dispute, though Euroamerican custom dictated that the mission be commanded by a man. While helping the colonials, Mary was being disempowered by them. Abraham Bosomworth was put in charge of the mission, though it was Mary who supplied £300 worth of presents requisite for any such meeting.[25] Lieutenant Colonel Alexander Heron replaced William Horton as commander of Oglethorpe's regiment in Georgia in June 1747. He wrote to Mary in July 1747 acknowledging her years of service to the colony and pleading with her to use her influence to prevent the Creeks from attacking either Georgia or South Carolina. At the same time, Heron told her he could not provide the salary she had been promised. He did assure her, however, that he regularly reminded his superiors of the necessity of treating the Indians generously to keep them aligned with Britain.[26]

Malatchi granted Abraham Bosomworth an audience because of his family ties to Mary. Abraham asked the Creek leader to make a trip to Fort Frederica to affirm his friendship with the British; in return, Malatchi asked Bosomworth to go to Britain and ask King George II directly for presents for Malatchi's people. The real loser in Abraham Bosomworth's mission was Mary. Alexander Heron told her he was unable to reimburse her for the £300 worth of presents.[27]

Malatchi meanwhile made good on his pledge to visit Frederica, with a group of sixteen *micos,* or chiefs, and more than one hundred other Creek delegates. It was Mary who met them there and passed out gifts among them. Seven different towns acknowledged both Malatchi's leadership and loyalty to the British crown. Finally, they reaffirmed their intent to retain Mary Bosomworth as their adviser and counselor. Upon her death, they would look to Thomas for such guidance.[28]

To his credit, Heron tried to arrange payment for Mary. In December 1747, he wrote to Andrew Stone, deputy secretary of state, that he was impressed by her service to the colony, much of it performed at her own expense. He observed that Mary was perceived by the Creeks as a "princess" and so any injury done to her would offend that tribe. He asked Stone to place Mary's case before the Duke of Newcastle, for, if Mary were denied much longer, Heron felt he could not maintain the safety of the colony.[29]

Heron was not the only petitioner for Mary Bosomworth. The same month, twenty of the officers and inhabitants of Fort Frederica sent a letter to the home government attesting to Mary's good character and service. They observed that she was a powerful leader among the Creeks, who often had used her position to further His Majesty's policies. They noted that she had soothed the disputes between them and the Creeks and had even enlisted Creek warriors to fight against Britain's enemies. In general, they believed her to be a loyal British subject who had proved her devotion to His Majesty repeatedly over the years.[30]

Such glowing character references accomplished little. Faced with a total inability to receive payment for every service she rendered the colony, Mary and Abraham decided to travel to Britain and confront the Trustees directly for compensation for past supplies, service and for acknowledgment of her claims to the Georgia Sea Islands. To that end, she summoned a conference with her people to explain the purpose of her journey, expounding on the great injuries they had all experienced because of the British. Focusing on the lands swallowed up by the colonists, Mary aroused anger among her people and a commitment on their part to take arms in her behalf to defend her claims against the British.[31] In a conference with the South Carolina governor, James Glen, Malatchi reaffirmed Mary's claim to the land, stating that it was he and the other headmen of the tribe who advised Mary to take her case to Britain.[32]

Unfortunately, rumors sprang up in the Creek lands that Mary was traveling to Britain under duress--in fact in chains. Malatchi especially became concerned for the safety of his kinswoman and journeyed to Savannah on the night of 21 July 1749 to check on Mary's status for himself. Another, larger body of Creeks departed shortly after Malatchi's small party. This group was traveling to Savannah in hopes of intercepting the returning Abraham Bosomworth and the presents from King George II. When Malatchi informed the colony's president, William Stephens, of the impending visit of the second group, Stephens panicked. Henry Parker, a member of the colony council, decided that so powerful an Indian leader as Malatchi would not have made such a trip for so trivial a reason as to check on Mary. He decided the second group was coming to force the colony to accede to Mary's land claims. Thus, the Georgia Council opted to ignore Malatchi's arrival. Rather than entertaining him lavishly as Euroamericans had learned to do from the Native Americans, they let him wait several days; that, from the native perspective, was an insult to his position as leader.[33] Malatchi later told James Glen that he was received, "in a very rude and uncivil manner, more like enemies than friends, upon which I told them that I expected other sort of treatment."[34] Fear borne of mistrust had led the colony leaders unintentionally to insult the Creek leader. While many of the fears of the officials were without substance, they did learn that if the trustees continued to oppose Mary's land claims, the Creek chiefs would confine Euroamerican settlement to the coastal region while enforcing Mary's land claims themselves. Despite the intransigence of the colony's trustees and officials, it is not surprising to whom they turned for linguistic skills during Malatchi's visit. Mary chastised colonial officials for the insult given the Creek leader and reminded them that they never had been received among the Creeks in such a manner. She conveyed Malatchi's hope that the group following him would be well provided for and her own note that the cost of such treatment, often borne by her in the past, was now too great for any private person to absorb.[35]

Colonial policy had always been to prevent Indians from entering Euroamerican towns. Now Stephens and the council wanted the larger body of approaching Creeks to be housed on Grantham, the old Musgrove plantation six miles from Savannah. The council, still wary of surprise attacks, ordered woodcutters to clear a path from Grantham into Savannah. In the course of their task, the artisans crossed onto Mary's property, and she sent a slave to disperse them. When they did not, Mary and a group of Creeks confronted them, though the workers still refused to retreat without council orders. The Creeks then seized their tools and threw them back across Mary's property line.[36]

The board was both alarmed and surprised by Mary's actions and mobilized the militia, sending it to Grantham with an order for the Indians to surrender their weapons and return to William Stephens' home. As they marched into Savannah, a drummer played (Figure 4). From the Euroamerican perspective, the natives were under house arrest. From the hapless Malatchi's point of view, he was now receiving the triumphal march he had been denied earlier.[37] The leaders were treated to a dinner at which Mary Bosomworth was present. During the course of the meal, she announced to the Georgia officials that she was "Empress" and "Queen" of the Lower Creeks. She was, in her opinion, an ally of the British crown and not a subject as the colonials considered her because of the nationality of her father.[38] In a later petition to the crown, Mary disparagingly asked whether she was to forfeit her Creek inheritance because, "one of his Majestys [sic] subjects violated the laws of God and man?"[39] When officials refused to acknowledge her claim, she left the gathering with Malatchi in tow.[40]

He and others retired to Mary's house, where they continued drinking the wine they had begun at dinner. Fairly mellow after a time, Malatchi decided to take a bottle of wine to the colony president's home with a companion playing a drum en route. This gesture frightened the panic-stricken colonists, who assumed the worst and began rounding up the Creeks. In the ensuing melee, someone ran to get Mary Bosomworth. Enraged by the incident, Mary confronted the military official who mistakenly arrested her kinsman. In the heat of anger, she told him that his people did not own a foot of land in Georgia and that even the land they were presently standing on belonged to her.[41] On 17 August 1749, Malatchi and the other Creeks were summoned to the president's house, where they presented a paper written by Thomas Bosomworth stating that leaders like Malatchi accepted Mary as their queen. The council replied that she, " was just an insignificant squaw whom Oglethorpe found in poor circumstances at Yamacraw Bluff and had raised to her present importance."[42] During the meeting, Mary rushed in and threatened to

Mary (Musgrove) and Thomas Bosomworth. Courtesy of Hargrett Rare Book and Manuscript Library/University of Georgia Libraries.

mobilize the Creeks to destroy the colony if her claims were not met. When asked to leave the room, Mary refused and began shouting. When a constable began to remove her forcibly from the room, Malatchi motioned for the Creeks to respond. Meanwhile, a Creek alerted the main body of warriors back at Grantham to paint and arm for war. When ready, groups of Indians began pouring into Savannah as the town alarm was struck. The militia arrived and began arresting the Creeks and imprisoning them.[43] Of the incident, Malatchi stated, "they carried Mrs. Bosomworth from us a prisoner. The house was surrounded with armed men, so that we really began to think that they had evil designs against us."[44]

Thomas Bosomworth later appealed to the council to excuse his wife's conduct. The president and his assistants reprimanded both the Bosomworths and had them apologize for their behavior in front of the Creek delegation. Eventually, Mary and her husband moved to St. Catherine's Island with plans to develop all three islands into large cattle ranches. Mary continued visiting Creek towns to solicit support for her claims. Thomas still planned to make a direct appeal to the British government for Mary's claims, and such support from the Creek people would be an invaluable bargaining chip. When the Bosomworths traveled to Charles Town in 1752, ready at last to embark on their mission to Britain, they found the colony embroiled in Indian troubles once more. Creek warriors had attacked a group of Cherokees and Indian traders leaving Charles Town after scheduled meetings, resulting in the death of one of the Cherokees.[45] Now, South Carolina would have to seek justice for the Cherokees or risk incurring their wrath. Glen approached various agents about undertaking the mission but could find no one to accept it.[46]

In June 1753, Mary volunteered her services for that assignment. In a letter to Glen, Mary stated that she had heard she was the unanimous choice of Glen and his council to act as a representative to the Creeks. She reminded them that she had served the Carolina government well enough to be recommended to the service of Oglethorpe when he came, and, after Oglethorpe, Horton and Heron both used her to tend to government business with the Creeks. She was a natural leader among the Creeks, she told Glen, by the "laws of God and nature."[47] She offered the South Carolina government her services in exchange for its help with her husband's creditors in order to prevent his arrest for debt. Mary blamed their financial state solely on her past sacrifices as an Indian agent for the Georgia and Carolina governments.[48]

Though Mary Bosomworth was the true Indian agent and had openly requested the mission, the Carolina government nominated Thomas Bosomworth as its agent to the Creeks. His instructions required him to seek retribution for the slain member of the Cherokee delegation and to complain of robberies committed by the Creeks against traders in the Cherokee homelands.[49] By nominating Thomas instead of Mary, the Carolina government refused to accord her the political power she wielded among her own people. Yet, subsequent instructions to Thomas casually mentioned that he probably would want to include Mary on the mission because she was reported to have some influence with the Creeks and was skilled in their language.[50]

Thomas and Mary's first stop on their mission for South Carolina was Coweta Town. There, Chekilli announced their arrival to the Cowetas, stating that while he did not know the nature of the Bosomworth mission, he believed it important for Mary to have traveled so far during the summer's heat. Thomas initiated negotiations with the Creeks but had difficulty explaining the import of the crimes committed in Charles Town; Chekilli could not comprehend the logic of being punished for fighting the enemies of his people, wherever he found them.[51] Then Mary took over the negotiations. She assailed them with lengthy arguments and tear-filled eyes stating that "nothing but the blood of some of the offenders would make satisfaction to the English."[52]

Initially, Mary's request for the death of the Creek who had murdered the Cherokee delegate in Charles Town was so unexpected that Chekilli replied that the matter would require further deliberation. At a later meeting of all headmen with the Bosomworths, Thomas again began preliminary negotiations. After he failed to achieve results, Mary took over. She reiterated that the motive behind her mission was the welfare of the Creek people. Mary assured them that any call for the execution of one of her people was not made lightly, but in the interest of preventing British retaliation against the Creeks. When the headmen continued to resist the notion of surrendering the criminal or an acceptable substitute, Mary told them bluntly that only by sacrificing the guilty party would the Creeks be spared.[53] She then used the most powerful weapon at her disposal--she told the headmen that the British, if angered, would recall the traders from the Creeks. Thomas Bosomworth noted that avaricious traders already had told the headmen that if South Carolina cut off their trade, Georgia traders would be ready and willing to supply them instead.[54] Trader rivalry had been and would continue to be a detriment to diplomatic relations between the two cultures.

The trader's ability to instigate trouble will be discussed more widely in a later chapter; the Bosomworth mission is a perfect example of the potential problems backcountry merchants could cause in Anglo-Indian relations. Thomas noted that a man named Kennard was spreading a rumor among the Creeks that the demand of blood for blood was ridiculous and that the government of South Carolina had not even authorized the Bosomworth mission. Kennard told the Creeks that Mary and Thomas had contrived the whole mission to secure money from Governor Glen of South Carolina. According to the story, they were impoverished and hoped to receive pay for killing off Indians. Thomas noted that such rumors were not only an impediment to the mission, but a threat to their very lives as well.[55]

Ultimately, Mary succeeded in her mission. Early one morning, an Indian entered the Bosomworth campsite to tell Mary that Acorn Whistler, the murderer of the Cherokee delegate to Charles Town, was dead.[56] Having accomplished their first task, Thomas and Mary turned to their second and third tasks--to seek reparation for robberies by the Creeks of British traders in Cherokee lands and to arrange a peace between the Creeks and Cherokees. In May 1751, forty Creeks attacked some British traders at the town of Cheowie, where they stole horses, saddles, guns and leather goods.[57] In October 1752, Thomas notified Governor Glen that fifteen Cherokee horses were being paid to the traders and that most of the stolen goods were being returned to them. He further noted that both the Upper and Lower Creeks were desirous of a peace with the Cherokees and that Glen only had to set the date for such a meeting. Finally, Thomas credited Mary for the success of the venture: "I must likewise declare that the merit of the whole is chiefly due to her and . . . I hope some reward will be allowed her."[58] It was indeed Mary's efforts which bridged the impasse in negotiations, no doubt aided by her threats concerning trade, though hampered by avaricious traders.

Having accomplished their mission, Thomas and Mary returned to Charles Town to await their pay. In March 1753, Thomas complained to Governor Glen of the delay in payment, attributing financial difficulties to the outlay of money they had expended in public service.[59] The next month, Thomas sent a follow-up request, noting that he and his wife had gone almost four months without pay. Thomas also observed that the South Carolina Assembly was questioning the need for the mission and had thus rejected the couple's requests for payment.[60] By September 1753, the Bosomworths still had not been paid. Thomas again wrote to Glen, stating that the Bosomworths had money for their trip when they arrived in Charles Town, but had expended it upon the mission. Thomas found it curious that the assembly was impeding their pay request when it had unanimously supported the mission originally. Both he and Mary had accepted the mission in good faith, expecting payment upon its successful completion. Now, eight months had passed and Thomas requested Glen refer their case to the home government and defray their passage to Britain.[61]

Mary's attempt to obtain payment for their mission made the couple anathema in Charles Town.[62] On 23 June 1752, the control of the colony of Georgia passed from the trustees to the crown. Mary Bosomworth's claims remained unsettled there though she finally did address the Board of Trade in London on 30 June 1755. Mary told the board that before the arrival of the Europeans, her people had been free and had owed allegiance to no other nation. She told them that, by her culture's maternal line of reckoning, she was a natural leader of her people and legally entitled to the lands she claimed. It was through her intervention that Oglethorpe was ceded the land for his colony. After his departure, Mary had served the colonial governments on many occasions but had never been paid. Mary chastised them, saying that she might have expected such roughshod treatment had the Creeks been aligned with a despotic power, but not from the British government.[63] The board deliberated upon Mary's case, then sidestepped the issue by saying that only royal governors could deal with matters involving Indians. Mary would have to present her claims in Georgia's courts and, if she did not receive satisfaction, make an appeal to the Privy Council.[64]

Not until 23 July 1759 did Mary Bosomworth's battle with Georgia end. On that date the governor in council offered her £2,100 sterling for past services to be paid to her in exchange for the sale of the islands of Ossabaw and Sapelo to Georgia. She would be allowed to retain a grant of land on St. Catherine's Island, however, and the offer was indeed a final one. Mary Bosomworth accepted it, though it was a small fraction of her original claim.[65]

The other major figure in the history of native women in the southern backcountry is Nancy Ward. Nancy was born in 1738, in the Cherokee capital of Chota on the Little Tennessee River near the reconstructed site of Fort Loudoun. (Figure 5) Her true name, Nan-ye-hi, was anglicized to the more familiar Nancy. Like Mary Musgrove Bosomworth, Nancy Ward was powerfully connected among her people. Her mother was Tame Doe, a member of the Wolf Clan and sister of the powerful chief Attakullakulla, who had visited Britain in 1730.[66] He was also the man responsible for rescuing John Stuart during the Cherokee attack on Fort Loudoun in 1760.

In the early 1750s, Nancy entered a relationship with a full-blood Cherokee, Kingfisher, of the Deer Clan. These were turbulent times for the Cherokee people, as they were engaged in a fierce struggle with the Creeks. In 1755, the Cherokees reached the pinnacle of this long struggle when they fought and won the decisive battle of Taliwa, near modern Canton, Georgia. Nancy accompanied her husband in that battle; as he fired on the Creeks, Nancy chewed the bullets so they would tear the flesh more upon entering enemy bodies. When Kingfisher was mortally wounded, Nancy took his gun and continued fighting as a warrior throughout the rest of the conflict. This act won her great approbation among the Cherokee people.[67] After the Creeks were defeated, Nancy's people rewarded her: at the battle site, they gave her the black slave of a vanquished Creek opponent, then they elevated her to the high office of Ghighau, or "Beloved Woman," which carried great political power. The Cherokees believed that the Supreme Being spoke to them through such women and thus revered them highly.

As a Ghighau, Nancy was the leader of the Woman's Council that was composed of members of each clan. The function of that body was to voice concerns affecting village life from the woman's point of view, and it often opposed those decisions made by the ruling headmen.[68] Further, because Nancy was also a voting member of the Council of Chiefs, she was able to make decisions about matters of war or peace. Finally, her position gave her the sole authority to pardon prisoners of war--something even the powerful headmen could not do.[69]

In 1757, Nancy's uncle, Attakullakulla, requested that the colony of South Carolina construct a fort in the backcountry to draw the highly desirable trade in Euroamerican merchandise to the Cherokee people. In response, South Carolina, partially to strengthen Britain's hold on the backcountry Indians, constructed Fort Loudoun in modern eastern Tennessee near the town of the same name. After-wards, Indian traders quickly moved into the region of the fort and aligned themselves with Indian women who could give them access to the Cherokee people.[70]

Nancy was a widow when British traders began moving into the Cherokee homelands. From her union with Kingfisher, she had two children--Little Fellow and Catherine. Bryan Ward was a widower who entered the backcountry with a son and a desire to become an Indian trader. Nancy joined the invisible web of

Map of the Cherokee Homelands. Courtesy of Hargrett Rare Book and Manuscript Library/
University of Georgia Libraries.

intermarriage when she began a relationship with Bryan Ward in the 1750s. Some sources indicated that Nancy and Bryan actually were married in a civil ceremony.[71]

Nancy's children and stepchildren also became a part of that invisible web. Bryan's son, John, married Catherine McDaniel, a half-blood Cherokee, who bore him eight children. Catherine was the daughter of a Scot named McDaniel and a full-blood Cherokee named Granny Hopper.[72] Elizabeth Ward, the only child of Nancy and Bryan, entered unions with not one but two Euroamerican men. Her first husband was General Joseph Martin, North Carolina's agent to the Cherokees. After his death, Elizabeth settled down with an Indian trader named Hughes.[73]

Bryan Ward was not content to remain in the backcountry; he returned to the Pendleton District of South Carolina by 1760. Once there he took a Euroamerican wife and started yet a third family, though he never severed ties with Nancy. William White Martin, Nancy's grandson by Joseph Martin, recalled that Nancy was a frequent visitor among Ward's "white" family.[74]

During the fall of 1759, Anglo-Cherokee relations were strained by a combination of French influence and poor handling of the Cherokee trade by the Carolinians and Virginians. Details of this trade conflict will be discussed in a later chapter but, the Cherokees ultimately attacked and defeated the British military forces at Fort Loudoun, including a young officer stationed there--John Stuart. Once hostilities ceased, Nancy's uncle, Attakullakulla, sought to make peace through the Treaty of Charles Town, signed December 1761.

Throughout the period, Nancy Ward remained an influential figure among the Cherokees and, to some extent, among the colonials as well. In 1772, when Commissioner James Robertson paid a diplomatic call on the Cherokee people he made a courtesy call on Nancy as well. The advent of the American Revolution acted as a catalyst to destabilize Anglo-Cherokee relations though it brought Ward to the forefront of relations between the two cultures in the backcountry.

In March 1775, a group of Cherokees sold land encompassing the future states of Kentucky and Tennessee to the Transylvania Company for £2,000 sterling and £10,000 in trade goods. Obviously, one of the most exasperating problems for Euroamericans in their relationship with Native Americans was the inability to determine one central leader who spoke with true tribal authority. Nancy's uncle, Attakullakulla, favored the sale. Chiefs Savanooka and Occonostota favored it as well. Occonostota had been particularly impressed with a cabin filled to its limits with arms and ammunition which was part of the deal. Many Cherokees disagreed with the sale of such a large tract of land to Richard Henderson and Nathaniel Hart, representing the Transylvania Company.

Dragging Canoe, Nancy's first cousin by Euroamerican reckoning, violently opposed the sale. At the Treaty of Sycamore Shoals, Dragging Canoe exhausted all means at his disposal to prevent his father, Attakullakulla, and Occonostota from signing. In point of fact, the British government had made an agreement in 1730 with the Cherokees similar to the one made with the Creeks. Indian lands could be transferred to the crown, but were not supposed to be sold to private individuals or corporations.[75]

Dragging Canoe gathered supporters and prepared a war party to attack the frontiers of Carolina and Georgia in retaliation. Occonostota and Attakullakulla worked to prevent this, as did John Stuart and his deputy to the Cherokees, Alexander Cameron. To his credit, Cameron vehemently opposed the Sycamore Shoals Treaty, but he was a part of a bureaucracy committed to carrying out government policy. Attakullakulla, Occonostota, John Stuart and Alexander Cameron began making appeals to the war party at least to delay their plans until Stuart and Occonostota could try diplomatic means to get the colonials to vacate Cherokee lands. Another prominent member of this peace party was Nancy Ward.[76]

The war movement was fueled by talks of representatives of northern Indian tribes with Dragging Canoe. John Stuart noted that Nancy Ward, in her capacity as leader of the Women's Council, opposed the mission of these northern Indians.[77] Stuart meanwhile became alarmed at the growing disaffection of the Cherokees over their conflicting land claims with the colonials. He dispatched James Colbert, agent to the Chickasaws, to Pensacola, Florida, to transport one hundred horse loads of ammunition to the colonials in case the conflict with Dragging Canoe erupted into a general Cherokee war.

One of the functions of women in Cherokee society was the preparation of the Black Drink, a ritual beverage made from the leaves of the *Ilex Vomitoria* plant. Women prepared the drink but only warriors and chiefs drank it. On the night of 8 July 1776, Nancy helped prepare the concoction for a meeting of warriors. As Ghighau, she was privy to all council discussions and so learned that Dragging Canoe had organized an attack against multiple targets; he planned to attack Holston Island in Virginia on 20 July 1776. Concurrently, a man named Abram of Chilhowee would strike against the Nolichucky and Watauga River settlements in Tennessee. While the other two attacks proceeded, Raven, a warrior from Chota, planned to attack settlers in Carter's Valley.[78]

Southeastern Indian warriors underwent ritual purification ceremonies before and after battles. Nancy Ward waited until the warriors present at the council began such ceremonies and then took off into the woods, heading for the trading post of Isaac Thomas, Jarrett Williams and William Fawling. She not only disclosed details of the plot to the Euroamerican traders, but helped them escape Chota so that they could warn settlers at the intended targets.[79]

When Dragging Canoe's parties made their move, they found their potential targets had been either militarily reinforced or evacuated. The Holston River settlements were protected by five companies of militia and 175 other frontiersmen. The Watauga settlers all fled to the safety of nearby Fort Caswell. Male settlers in Carter's Valley had relocated to join the defense forces at the Holston River. Their wives and children had evacuated to Wythe County, Virginia. During the initial moments of battle, Dragging Canoe was felled by a shot which pierced both his thighs, forcing his removal from the field.[80]

The entire attack would have been completely routed if not for a foolhardy act practiced by the inhabitants of Fort Caswell and learned by the Cherokees. Women at such forts left their secure confines at daybreak to milk the cows. When the women left Fort Caswell, Old Abram made his move, seizing several prisoners, including a young boy named Samuel Moore and a Mrs. Lydia Bean. As war prisoners, these individuals faced several alternatives; they could have been adopted into the tribe, kept as slaves or ritually tortured and put to death. Samuel Moore was dispatched immediately by being burned at the stake and Mrs. Bean was slated to follow. Tied to a stake and surrounded by growing flames, Lydia Bean appeared to be lost when Nancy Ward intervened, using her power as Ghighau to pardon prisoners of war. Allegedly, Nancy kicked the burning logs away from Lydia Bean as she waved the swan's wings, symbol of her authority. She not only rescued Mrs. Bean, but took her home to Chota. Here as a guest of Nancy Ward, Lydia Bean taught the Cherokee woman the skills of making butter and cheese. Soon after, Mrs. Bean was returned to her home. Later, Nancy Ward procured a herd of cattle to pursue dairy industry.[81] Her exposure to this economic strategy allowed her to adapt pastoral farming, foreign to American Indians, to the home-based provider role traditional to southern Indian women. Ward was reportedly the first Cherokee among her tribe to own cattle.[82] Previously the Cherokees had disapproved of pastoral farming as an occupation.[83]

Nancy Ward's actions could be interpreted as traitorous to her people. Instances abound of native women siding with Euroamerican mates in disputes between the two cultures. For example, Susannah Emory's support of John Stuart at the Cherokee siege of Fort Loudoun typifies many of the decisions Indian women made when faced with taking sides between the two cultures. Most likely, Nancy Ward knew that a short term victory by the Dragging Canoe faction would lead to a greater conflict with the Euroamericans in which many of her people would be killed.[84] Because Ward spared Euroamerican settlements from a surprise attack, Colonel William Christian later spared her town of Chota when he took a force of eighteen hundred Virginians into the Cherokee homelands in an attempt to break the British hold on that Indian tribe.[85] During the King's Mountain campaign of 1780, the Cherokees used the absence of fighting-age men from Euroamerican settlements to attack the Americans in the Watauga area. Again, Nancy Ward dispatched the trader Isaac Thomas with news of the impending attack to warn the Watauga inhabitants. Luckily, the American leader, John Sevier, returned from King's Mountain in time to heed the warning. On 25 December 1780, American forces pursuing the Cherokees camped near Chota. Nancy went out to greet them with a gift of cattle from her herd and with intelligence information. The expedition leader, Colonel Arthur Campbell, wrote to the Virginia governor, Thomas Jefferson, of Ward's efforts, which he noted were made in behalf of several Cherokee chiefs who wished to sue for peace. Campbell noted that the Cherokee dissidents were located mainly in Hiwassee and Chistowee, yet on 28 December 1780 he destroyed the town of Chota. Nancy Ward lost her home and was taken into protective custody by U.S. officials.[86]

Representatives of the Cherokee people were ordered to meet John Sevier and his followers on 20 July 1781 to conclude a permanent peace. Nancy Ward represented her people at that meeting, to the surprise of American military officials. The nature of her address was unique by Euroamerican standards; by Cherokee tradition her address was quite in keeping with the position of Ghighau. "Our cry is all for peace; let it continue. This peace must last forever. Let your women hear our words," she declared.[87] She addressed the Americans as she would have any group--from the woman's point of view.

The Americans wrought heavy destruction upon the Cherokee people because they sided with the British in the American Revolution. Both the British and the Americans had tried to manipulate the various Indian tribes with threats, rewards and lies. Southern tribes aligned themselves with the power they had known longest--the British. After the British defeat, the Americans could view the Indians only as traitorous allies of a despotic, colonial power. Amidst all this, Nancy Ward continued to act as a mediator between Indian culture and the new dominant power of North America--the United States of America. In 1783, two American traders went into the Cherokee lands with concealed weapons; when the Indians discovered the weapons they became incensed. Ward acted to soothe both sides and the traders completed their transactions without incident. When the Cherokees were forced to cede more land with the Treaty of Hopewell in 1785, Nancy Ward addressed the American commissioners, reiterating the need for peace. She offered them a string of beads which she likened to a chain of friendship between their two worlds.[88]

In accepting elements of Euroamerican culture and diffusing them among her people, Nancy contributed to the demise of traditional Cherokee culture, to be replaced by a fusion culture which bore aspects of the old combined with Euroamerican traits. In that culture, native women like Nancy were disempowered because women in the dominant intruding culture were subordinate to men, not equal. Native men relegated their own women to subordinate positions as did Euroamerican men.

By the turn of the nineteenth century, Nancy Ward was more properly known as "Granny" Ward. Concurrently, the men of the Cherokee tribe were no longer hunters and warriors, but pastoral farmers. The traditional clan-dominated government was superseded by a call for a republican form of government based on the Euroamerican model. In May 1817, Nancy Ward attended the Amovey Council session by proxy. Instead of her swan's wings, she sent her walking cane as a symbol of her authority. The Cherokee people were debating the merits of creating a government similar to that of the United States--an idea of which Nancy approved. Her message to the council was, of course, from the woman's point of view, but it carried a warning as well.[89]

Nancy's speech was addressed to her people's children, their headmen and their warriors. She reminded them gently that they all had been raised by women-- not an unusual tactic by the head of the Women's Council. Unlike in previous attempts to mediate between the cultures, she strongly urged her people to refuse further land cessions to the Americans. While some members of the tribe wanted to accept offers of the American government to remove to western lands, Ward noted that this would be like "destroying your mothers."[90] She stated, "your mothers, your sisters ask and beg of you not to part with any more of our lands."[91]

Ward could now only urge the male members of her culture to make decisions she favored. Yet, in pleading for the retention of tribal lands, Ward urged her people to fix themselves upon the land by enlarging their farms and learning to grow corn and cotton--Euroamerican economic strategies. While they did this, Nancy promised that the women would spin cloth and make clothes, another Euroamerican adaption.[92] These were also the activities which Euroamerican men thought fitting pursuits for women. When the U.S. government purchased the Hiwassee lands in 1819, all Cherokees living north of the Hiwassee River were forced to sell out and move. Nancy Ward moved to the present town of Benton and ran an inn there until she died in 1822.[93]

The lives and careers of both Coosaponakeesa and Nan-ye-hi, Mary Musgrove and Nancy Ward, fully illustrate the role of cultural mediator played by native women in the historic period. Mary was the mixed-blood daughter of a British trader and an Indian woman. Both she and Nancy Ward were part of powerful, important families. Mary was the niece of the Creek leaders Brims and Chekilli, while Nancy was the niece of Attakullakulla. As a mixed-blood, Mary already had contact with both the Native American and Euroamerican worlds, a fact which would make her attractive to Euroamerican men. Both women's powerful family connections would have proved valuable to Euroamerican men seeking acceptance by the backcountry tribes. Both women and their children became a part of the invisible web of intermarriage in the backcountry. Mary's first marriage was to another of mixed-blood, a trader's son who became a trader. After Johnny Musgrove's death, Mary married two more Euroamerican men. Nancy Ward's first husband, Kingfisher, was a full-blood Cherokee; she married the trader, Bryan Ward, after Kingfisher died. Nancy's stepson, John Ward, married a mixed-blood woman himself. Nancy's daughter by Ward, Elizabeth, first married the North Carolina Indian agent Joseph Martin, then, after his death, an Indian trader named Hughes.

As cultural instructors, Indian women both taught and learned. Mary's family connections and linguistic skill enabled her first husband to become a successful fur trader. Other Euroamericans sought her skill as a linguist: James Oglethorpe, William Horton, Alexander Heron, the Salzburger pastors Bolzius and Granau, John Wesley, a Mr. Ingham, the colony president William Stephens and the South Carolina governor James Glen. From Euroamerican culture, both she and Nancy Ward learned pastoral farming, an innovation not practiced by their own societies. Nancy Ward noted that Cherokee women spun thread and made clothes by the early 1800s. Thus Indian women also learned from Euroamerican men and transmitted the information to their people.

Perhaps most importantly, both women held high status in their own cultures. Nancy Ward was a Beloved Woman, a free and valued participant in Cherokee political life. Mary Musgrove was a Creek woman of high rank--called a queen by her own people. While most Indian women helped the fur traders through acculturation, Mary went a step further. She was an active partner in her own trading firm. Creek pressure paved the way for Mary and her first husband to open a trading house near the future site of Savannah. Both Oglethorpe and the colonists made purchases from the Bosomworth firm. Mary also supplied various government missions with trade goods, for which she was seldom reimbursed.

Both women were politically active. James Oglethorpe and William Stephens regularly employed Mary as a diplomatic aide and translator. Mary was a mediator with the Creeks over land issues, helping the Moravians obtain an alternate tract of land from the Creeks when their own proved unsuitable. Mary also procured military assistance for Georgia during time of crisis. She performed similar services for James Glen and the colony of South Carolina. During a Creek-Cherokee crisis in the 1750s, Mary stepped in when no other agent would undertake a seemingly impossible mission.

Nancy Ward also provided diplomatic assistance. When the Cherokees threatened to go to war over an unpopular land deal with the Transylvania Company, Ward opposed the war party and spoke against representatives from northern tribes who tried to persuade the Cherokees to go to war. When it appeared that the war party, led by her own relative, Dragging Canoe, would strike against the colonials, Nancy risked her own life to warn nearby Euroamerican traders of the impending attack. When the Cherokees struck multiple targets, they found all had been forewarned, thanks to Nancy's efforts. Later as the Cherokees prepared to execute the few prisoners they had taken, Ward intervened once more, using her authority as a Beloved Woman to prevent the execution of a Euroamerican woman.

During the American Revolution, Nancy Ward again risked her own life to notify a trader who warned settlers in the Watauga area of the impending attack. When the Cherokees concluded a peace treaty with the Americans under John Sevier, Ward addressed both sides with a call for peace. The Cherokee woman worked to eliminate conflicts both great and small between the two cultures. At the Treaty of Hopewell in 1785, Nancy Ward again spoke in favor of peace between the two groups. She remained visible as a political figure till 1817, when the Cherokees were considering the creation of a democratic government. Nancy favored the idea but warned her people to cede no more land to the Americans.

Both Musgrove and Ward often sided with Euroamerican culture in conflicts with their own people. Their family connection, linguistic skills and diplomatic talents promoted the success of not only their husbands, but surrounding colonies. The colonies of Georgia, South Carolina and North Carolina enjoyed the stability they did in part as a result of the efforts of both women. Through their interactions with Euroamericans, they absorbed ideas and skills from the intruding culture even as they taught fundamental concepts from their own. When they were exposed to obviously beneficial innovations, they adapted them to traditional life.

There is another issue related to the effect of trade on Native American women's lives. The more deeply native women came into contact with elements of Euroamerican culture, the more they found their own traditional authority diminished. They held a higher status within their own cultures because of the less stratified nature of Native American society when compared with Euroamerican society. They were accorded that higher status in acknowledgment of the role women played in society as food producers and mothers, as well as in ceremonial functions, such as the Woman's Dance at the Creek Busk, or Green Corn Ceremony. In Cherokee society, war women sometimes called pretty women traditionally attended all war councils and were revered both for performing heroic acts in battle and for being the mothers of future warriors. They sat in a "holy area" and advised war chiefs on intimate details of battle strategy.[94]

Euroamericans steadily opposed the traditions of native culture which empowered Indian women. James Adair, the British traveler who marveled at many aspects of native culture, deplored the Cherokees' custom of admitting women to war councils and accused the Cherokee men of living under "petticoat govern-ments." Lieutenant Henry Timberlake, a British military officer sent on a mission among the Cherokees, mused that Cherokee war women were the Amazons of mythology.[95] Euroamericans blatantly and subtly disempowered native women by refusing to treat with them. Indians as a whole, fearful of the termination of trade or attack, began to imitate the conventions of the more male-oriented Euroamerican society.

Though Nancy Ward worked to inform, assist and save colonials living in her homelands, she was rewarded by her exclusion from them eventually. The new Cherokee government created in the early nineteenth century was a true replica of its American model--it held no active place for women. Mary Musgrove's experience with the colonials is a fitting commentary on the treatment of native women. Though not bound to either Oglethorpe or colony president Stephens by a physical relationship, she utilized her skills in their behalf as native women did their Euroamerican mates. When she finally challenged Stephens and his council in 1749 after years of unpaid service as a linguist and diplomat, they dismissed her as "just an insignificant squaw whom Oglethorpe found in poor circumstances."[96] Though Governor Glen of Carolina needed her help during a Creek diplomatic crisis, he dealt with Mary only through her husband, Thomas.

Since Mary Musgrove and Nancy Ward were women and members of a culture deemed "uncivilized" by the intruding European culture, their contributions have been forgotten. Both have been swept from the pages of history to the forgotten corners of folk culture. Labeled as "queens" and "princesses" they were quietly dismissed though it is quite possible that, without Mary Musgrove's help, the colony of Georgia would have failed and South Carolina's Indian conflicts would have been even bloodier. The backcountry of modern Georgia, North Carolina and Tennessee would have been a great deal more violent without the efforts of Nancy Ward. While both women illustrate the concept of Indian women as "cultural bridges," transmitting information both ways, they represent an even greater invisible army of Indian women who performed these same functions in the southern backcountry during the eighteenth century.

NOTES

1. Helen Todd, *Mary Musgrove: Georgia Indian Princess* (Chicago: Adams Press, 1981), 18.

2. Ibid., 26.

3. Ibid., 37.

4. Ibid., 39-40.

5. Ibid., 48.

6. Marion E. Gridley, *American Indian Women,* (New York: Hawthorn Books, 1974), 34.

7. Todd, *Mary Musgrove, 55.*

8. Gridley, *American Indian Women, 35.*

9. Kenneth Coleman, ed., *The Colonial Records of the State of Georgia: Original Papers of Governor John Reynolds 1754-1756,* Vol. 27 (Athens: University of Georgia Press, 1977), 1-2. See NB 2. Hereafter referred to as the *Colonial Records of Georgia.*

10. Todd, *Mary Musgrove, 55.*

11. Ibid., 59-61.

12. Ibid., 63.

13. Ibid., 64.

14. Ibid.

15. Ibid., 70-72.

16. Oglethorpe to Mary Matthews, 13 July 1742 *Colonial Records of Georgia,* 3.

17. Major William Horton to Mary Matthews, 23 July 1743, ibid., 6.

18. Horton to Mary Matthews Bosomworth, 8 October 1744, ibid., 8.

19. Todd, *Mary Musgrove,* 81.

20. Narrative by Thomas Bosomworth, n.d. *Colonial Records of Georgia,* 155.

21. Todd, *Mary Musgrove,* 88.

22. Oglethorpe to Horton, 13 November 1745, *Colonial Records of Georgia,*9.

23. Oglethorpe to Thomas Causton, 13 November 1745, ibid., 9.

24. Todd, *Mary Musgrove,* 90.

25. Ibid., 94.

26. Alexander Heron to Mary Bosomworth, 8 July 1747, *Colonial Records of Georgia,* 10-11.

27. Heron to Mary Bosomworth, 31 August 1747, ibid., 15.

28. Todd, *Mary Musgrove,* 96.

29. Heron to Andrew Stone, 8 December 1747, *Colonial Records of Georgia,* 16.

30. Statement of the Officers and Inhabitants of Frederica, 17 December 1747, Ibid., 17.

31. Todd, *Mary Musgrove,* 91.

32. Malatchi in Conference with Governor James Glen, 2 June 1753, *Colonial Records of South Carolina: Documents Relating to Indian Affairs: May 21, 1750-August 7, 1754,* William L. McDowell, ed. (Columbia: South Carolina Archives Department, 1958), 404. Hereafter referred to as Indian Book 2.

33. Cashin, *Lachlan McGillivray,* 112.

34. Malatchi to Glen, 2 June 1753, ibid., 404.

35. Todd, *Mary Musgrove,* 100.

36. Cashin, *Lachlan McGillivray,* 112-113.

37. Ibid., 113.

38. Todd, *Mary Musgrove,* 104.

39. Memorial of Cousaponakeesa (Mary Bosomworth) to the Lords Justices of Council, 30 June 1755, Indian Book 2: 68.

40. Todd, *Mary Musgrove,* 104.

41. Ibid., 104-105.

42. Ibid., 109.

43. Todd, *Mary Musgrove,* 110.

44. Malatchi in Conference with Governor James Glen, 2 June 1753, Indian Book 2: 404.

45. Instructions to Thomas Bosomworth, n.d., Indian Book 2: 344.

46. Memorial of Reverend Thomas Bosomworth, 3 September 1753, ibid., 386.

47. Mary Bosomworth to Governor Glen, 1 June 1753, ibid., 264.

48. Ibid.

49. Commission to Thomas Bosomworth, 2 July 1752, ibid., 267-268.

50. Instructions to Thomas Bosomworth for the Mission, n.d., ibid., 343-344.

51. Journal of Thomas Bosomworth, 25 July 1752, ibid., 270-274.

52. Ibid., 275.

53. Ibid., 276-278.

54. Ibid., 277-278.

55. Ibid., 280-281.

56. Ibid., 282.

57. Ibid., 346.

58. Instructions to Thomas Bosomworth, n.d., ibid., 348-350.

59. Memorial of Thomas Bosomworth to Governor James Glen, 27 March 1753, ibid., 369.

60. Memorial of Thomas Bosomworth, 19 April 1753, ibid., 376-377.

61. Reverend Thomas Bosomworth to Governor Glen, 3 September 1753, Ibid., 385-387.

62. Todd, *Mary Musgrove,* 121.

63. The Memorial and Representation of Cousaponakeesa, 30 June 1755, *Colonial Records of Georgia,* 67-70.

64. Todd, *Mary Musgrove,* 121-123.

65. Ibid., 127.

66. Ben Harris McClary, "Nancy Ward: The Last Beloved Woman of the Cherokees," *Tennessee Historical Quarterly* 21 (December 1962): 353.

67. Emmet Starr, *History of the Cherokee Indians and Their Legends and Folklore,* (New York: Kraus Reprint Company, 1969), 468.

68. Pat Alderman, *Nancy Ward: Cherokee Chieftainess* (Johnson City, Tennessee: The Overmountain Press, 1978), 3.

69. Starr, *History of the Cherokee,* 468.

70. McClary, "Nancy Ward," 354-355.

71. Alderman, *Nancy Ward,* 4.

72. Ibid., 27.

73. Starr, *History of the Cherokee,* 468.

74. McClary, "Nancy Ward," 355.

75. Woodward, *The Cherokees,* 88-89.

76. Ibid., 90-91.

77. Ibid., 92.

78. Ibid., 94.

79. Ibid.

80. Ibid., 95-96.

81. McClary, "Nancy Ward," 357.

82. Woodward, *The Cherokees,* 96.

83. McClary, "Nancy Ward," 357.

84. Ibid.

85. Ibid., 357-358.

86. Ibid., 358.

87. Ibid., 359.

88. Ibid., 359-360.

89. Ibid., 361.

90. Alderman, *Nancy Ward,* 80.

91. Ibid.

92. Ibid.

93. McClary, "Nancy Ward," 361.

94. Woodward, *The Cherokees,* 43.

95. Henry Timberlake, *Lieutenant Henry Timberlake's Memoirs 1756-1765,* Samuel Cole Williams, ed. (Marietta, Georgia: Continental Book Company, 1948), 93.

96. Todd, *Mary Musgrove,* 109.

4

Trade and Indian Women in Southeastern America, 1700–1783

The vast majority of native women are not remembered by history. Most are mentioned briefly in passing: many are nameless and unrecognized for their contributions in the histories of both cultures. Instead of references to Nancy Ward, one is more likely to encounter references to women like "Indian Nancy" and "Indian Peggy." Because these women are scarcely mentioned in white men's records, history has forgotten them. Yet, their efforts contributed to the success of European culture in America and their story is the story of many relatively unknown women.

In November 1716, the records for the South Carolina Board of Indian Commissioners noted that a woman named "Indian Peggy" had shown friendship toward the British and was to be rewarded with clothing.[1] A second discussion of Indian Peggy by the board concluded that she was a valuable friend to the British, especially since she had brought in a French man, captured by the Cherokees. Evidently no fool, Peggy exchanged the man for a trading gun and the board gave both her and her son a suit of calico clothing.[2]

In December 1756, Captain Raymond Demeré, a British commander in charge of construction of Fort Loudoun in the Cherokee homelands, noted he was receiving intelligence reports from a woman known only as "Indian Nancy." Demeré was receiving these reports during the turbulent years of the Great War for

Empire when the Cherokee people were close to breaking ties with the British. In her first report, Indian Nancy had discovered in a conversation with an elderly War Woman that a Cherokee leader, Man Killer, expected a group of French in Tellico bearing thirty horse-loads of ammunition.[3]

Eight days later, Nancy offered information that Man Killer actually was working for the French. His recent visit to Fort Loudoun had been to reconnoiter the fort for a future attack, prompted by French backing.[4] A few days later, Demeré employed her to obtain more information about these plots from a headman's wife. Demeré believed that Nancy "got a true and exact account of her."[5]

Many Indian women, both mixed-blood and full-blood, contributed to British success in the settlement of the backcountry. Sophia Durant, the mixed-blood daughter of Lachlan McGillivray and the Creek woman Sehoy III, learned in the summer of 1790 that a faction among the Creeks planned to attack a mixed-blood settlement at Tensaw. Her brother, the Creek leader Alexander, was away and so Sophia traveled sixty miles on horseback for four days to reach a ceremonial meeting place, Hickory Ground. There, she called a meeting of headmen and persuaded them to arrest the conspirators planning the attack. At the time, Sophia Durant was in a late stage of pregnancy; she gave birth to twins at Hickory Ground two weeks later.[6] Further, while Alexander is remembered as the influential mixed-blood Creek leader, it was Sophia McGillivray Durant who served as linguist for her brother.[7] At his father's insistence, Alexander had been sent to Charles Town for a Euroamerican education and did not speak the Creek language as well as sisters Sophia and Jennet.

Other members of the McGillivray-Sehoy family joined the invisible web of intermarriage in the backcountry. LeClerc Milfort arrived there in 1775 and became a close friend to Alexander McGillivray. Milfort noted, somewhat boastfully that after a period of sexual abstinence during his visit in the Creek lands he was lured into the loft of a very attractive young woman's home. Climbing the ladder to the loft, he found not one but four women who had taken it upon themselves, according to Milfort, to determine why he had slept with none of the women of their tribe. He noted with pride that he, "came out of combat with honor, and my adventure was soon generally known."[8] As trivial as such a matter might seem, McGillivray interpreted Milfort's combat as an act of extreme friendship toward the Creek people. He then offered Milfort his sister Jennet in marriage, telling him "she knows the English language and that of the savages, and thus will be able, to be sometimes of assistance to you, and serve as an interpreter for you."[9] LeClerc and Jennet lived with Alexander initially, but then moved to the Alabama town of Pakana on the north bank of the Tallapoosa River near the location of old Fort Toulouse.[10] Finally, Lachlan Durant, the son of Benjamin and Sophia Durant, married the mixed-blood daughter of a trader, Richard Bailey, and a Creek woman.[11] Thus mixed-blood offspring often sought each other for intermarriage in the backcountry.

Most mixed unions in the southern backcountry were between relatively unknown men and women whose obscurity precludes a detailed knowledge of their lives. The lack of intimate knowledge about these couples does not reflect the pervasiveness of the mixed unions, which are mentioned briefly in a great majority of the accounts of the southern backcountry. Nor does the lack of in-depth knowledge mean that these lesser known native women performed cultural services any less valuable to their mates or their tribes than those of the better known women.

In June of 1751, James Maxwell, a South Carolina Indian agent stationed among the Cherokees, reported to the Carolina Board of Indian Commissioners a tale of heroism involving Indian women. When a Cherokee man killed a trader, Daniel Murphy, an Indian woman warned other Euroamericans of the deed and told them to beware the Cherokee murderer. When the nameless woman learned the Cherokee man planned to attack another trader, Bernard Hughs, she warned him of the threat. Hughs, however, would not abandon his trading post until he saw his assailants approaching; his decision led to his capture and death.[12] Maxwell noted that all the traders were warned of the danger by their Indian mates.[13] Most Indian women helped their Euroamerican husbands in a less dramatic fashion. The Dutch trader William Dixon Moniac was a relatively obscure figure in the backcountry. Moniac had a relationship with Polly Colbert, the daughter of the Creek chief, William Colbert.[14] William Colbert was, himself, the son of a Scot trader, Logan Colbert, and a Chickasaw woman he took as a mate.[15] Moniac's relationship with Polly brought him acceptance within the tribe in which he worked and probably gave him status as well since Polly's father was a chief. Moniac also worked as a linguist for Alexander McGillivray.[16] His instruction, most likely, came from Peggy Colbert.

In 1783, Moravian missionaries were dispatched from Pennsylvania on conversion missions among the Cherokees. One, Brother Martin Schneider, was escorted by Colonel Joseph Martin, Indian agent for North Carolina, among the Cherokees and Chickamaugas. In a town of the latter, Martin took Brother Schneider to the home of James McCormick, an Indian trader who had lived previously among the Cherokees for thirty years. Schneider noted that the trader had an Indian woman for a wife. McCormick, not surprisingly, served as interpreter during Schneider's visit.[17] Martin took Schneider onward to the town of Chota, where he found four Indian traders--all with Indian mates.[18]

Ludovic Grant was a Scot who entered the backcountry in 1720 and operated as a trader out of Tellico in the Cherokee lands. Not surprisingly, Grant took a Cherokee woman as mate. He became well known for his longevity in the backcountry as well as his fluency in the Cherokee language.[19] In a speech to the governor of South Carolina, Grant stated that he knew the headmen of the Cherokee country and was frequently consulted by them in their dealings with Euroamericans because he knew their language.[20] Grant would not have been accepted into tribal life without an Indian wife and it was she who probably instructed him in the language which made him so useful to both cultures.

For every trader like Grant whose name appears in numerous journals about the backcountry, there are dozens who were forgotten in the crucible of colliding cultures. Yet wherever important Indian towns existed, Euroamerican traders were sure to be found. More times than not, they had Indian mates who acted as bridges between cultures, transmitting information both ways. The people who lived in this crucible of contact and fusion often assimilated more aspects of the foreign culture than they retained of their own. A British trader settling among the Creeks in modern Coosa County, Alabama, went by the appellation "Woccocoie Clarke," and he called his Creek mate "Queen Anne."[21]

While the cultural assistance provided by Indian women helped Euroamerican Indian agents and fur traders succeed, it also helped backcountry scoundrels and rebels as well. William Augustus Bowles was a Loyalist born in America on the Maryland frontier. He left his regiment when it was stationed in Pensacola in 1778 after he clashed with a superior officer. From Florida, he traveled in the Lower Creek country, where he eventually acquired two native wives. One was a Chickamauga woman; while the other was a daughter of a Creek Chief.[22] When the fall of British Florida to Spain seemed imminent in the American Revolution, Bowles rejoined Loyalist forces. After the war, he relocated to the Bahamas, like many Loyalists, though he actually traveled back and forth between the Caribbean and the southern backcountry.

In the later 1780s Bowles tried to foster an Indian confederation as a threat to the infant United States. To that end, he traveled to the principal town of Coweta in the Creek homelands with presents and tried to enlist Alexander McGillivray in his scheme.[23] When that approach did not work, Bowles began assaults in 1788 on the Scottish-based trading firm Panton, Leslie and Company, which dominated the Indian trade from Spanish Florida. Now a true outlaw, Bowles fled first to the Bahamas and then to Britain. Once in London, he found Home Secretary William Grenville sympathetic to the idea of British protection for the Cherokee and Creek tribes in return for Indian support of British ventures in North America. In fact, Bowles announced to the world the creation of the Creek state of Muskoghee with himself as director general.[24] He then tried to break the hold of the more well known leader Alexander McGillivray on the Creek people. He held a grand council at Coweta, which was attended by both Upper and Lower Creek officials, as well as by representatives of the Chickamaugas and Seminoles. Bowles told the Indians that McGillivray had betrayed them by siding with the Americans in their bid for Creek lands.[25]

Bowles ultimately continued his career as a backcountry rabble-rouser until incarcerated by the Spanish government, which shipped him to Spain and later the Philippines. By 1798 he made his way back to Britain where he continued to lobby for the resurrection of the independent state of Muskogee.

While many native women who had contact with Euroamericans were serial monogamists, a separate group charged for their sexual services. These backcountry courtesans were known as "trading girls," clearly suggesting one effect of commerce on native cultures. According to John Lawson, some tribes designated their youngest and most attractive women as trading girls.[26] In eighteenth century North Carolina, they were distinguished from other women by a certain hairstyle they wore to designate their profession.[27] Lawson believed the trading girls gave their village chiefs the goods they received in payment for their services.[28] He also noted that the trading girls knew how to prevent pregnancies during their working years, for very few had children and those who did were ridiculed. Many trading girls eventually wearied of their life-style and settled down, their past profession having made them more highly prized by potential mates.[29]

Native American women contributed to the successful ventures of Euroamerican men who traveled to the southern backcountry as Indian traders and agents. Once linked to these men by sexual relationships, the women participated in a cultural exchange which initially brought them higher status and material prosperity, though the ultimate price they paid was the eventual diminution of their own power.

NOTES

1. Board of Commissioners Meeting, 16 November 1716, Indian Book 1: 125.

2. Ibid., 126-128. The British sold the Indians firearms whose defects made them unacceptable to colonials. These faulty weapons were known as trading guns.

3. Intelligence from Indian Nancy to Captain Raymond Demeré, 12 December 1756, Indian Book 2: 269.

4. Intelligence from Nancy Butler to Captain Raymond Demeré, 20 December 1756, ibid., 276.

5. Captain Raymond Demeré to Governor William H. Lyttelton, 23 December 1756, ibid., 281-282.

6. Lyn Hastie Thompson, *William Weatherford: His Country and His People,* (Bay Minette, Alabama: Lavender Publishing Company, 1991), 55.

7. Albert James Picket, *History of Alabama and Incidently of Georgia and Mississippi: From the Earliest Period* (Tuscaloosa: Willo Publishing Company, 1962), 419. The Tensaw settlement today is better known as Stockton, Alabama.

8. Milfort, *Memoirs,* 201.

9. Ibid., 202. Milfort's term "savage" probably was not derisive since he evidently liked the Creeks well enough to live among them for twenty years.

10. Thompson, *William Weatherford,* 19.

11. Ibid., 140.

12. Deposition of James Maxwell, 7 May 1751, Indian Book 2: 117.

13. Affidavit of James Maxwell, 12 June 1751, ibid., 70.

14. Ibid., 21.

15. Samuel Cole Williams, ed., *Early Travels in the Tennessee Country 1540-1800* (Johnson City, Tennessee: The Watauga Press, 1928), 376, f.n. 1.

16. Thompson, *William Weatherford,* 49.

17. Williams, *Early Travels,* 256-258.

18. Ibid., 262.

19. Starr, *History of the Cherokees,* 25.

20. Ludovic Grant, "Historical Relation of Facts etc.," *South Carolina Historical and Genealogical Magazine* (10): 54.

21. Picket, *A History of Alabama,* 422.

22. William S. Coker and Thomas D. Watson, *Indian Traders of the Spanish Borderlands: Panton, Leslie and Company and John Forbes and Company 1783-1847* (Pensacola: University of West Florida Press, 1986), 114.

23. Ibid., 114-116.

24. Ibid., 149-150.

25. Ibid., 149-150.

26. Lawson, *A New Voyage,* 41.

27. Ibid., 190.

28. Randolph F. Randolph, *British Travelers Among the Southern Indians, 1660-1763* (Norman: University of Oklahoma Press, 1973), 84.

29. Lawson, *A New Voyage,* 194.

5

Fur Traders and Indian Agents

Historians traditionally preferred to discuss European exploration of North America and contact with its indigenous peoples through references to elite European males. In discussing Virginia, conversations soon turn to John Smith and his adventures among the Powhatan Indians. For Puritan New England, no proper review would be complete without mention of Plymouth's William Bradford and Massachusetts Bay's John Winthrop. In Georgia, James Oglethorpe is the standard reference for early contact between native peoples and Europeans.

Yet, how limiting is this practice! It ignores the influence, good and bad, that an army of fur traders and Indian agents had on relationships with Native American peoples. These men, most of whom were not members of the cultural elite, chose occupations which brought them into direct daily contact with American Indians in the southern backcountry. Most of these men, especially the fur traders, share a certain amount of anonymity with the Indian women with whom they cohabited, in that history has likewise assigned little or no importance to their roles. Years before the implementation of the British Indian superintendencies, however, the fur traders were the eyes and ears of the colonial governments, which often needed the trade with Native American peoples in order to survive. Colonial settlements, fearing for their safety, felt bound to monitor the various activities of surrounding Indian tribes. Colonial governments first carried out their Indian policies through individual fur traders, who made reports to and received orders from governors. Few European males could have had greater contact with Native Americans or more influence over relationships between the two cultures than these forgotten men. When the British government tried to implement a comprehensive colonial policy over subject Indian peoples in the 1750s, the Indian agents superseded the fur traders as messengers of colonial will. Like the fur traders, they resided in the backcountry as mediators between British policy and the day-to-day realities of Indian life. Freed to some extent from the profit motive which drove the fur traders, the Indian agents were more directly concerned with tribal loyalties during the numerous great power confrontations in North America among Spain, France and Britain. Despite the more military nature of their mission, trade was a nonetheless pervasive element in relationships between Euroamericans and Native Americans. It was the tool employed by the fur traders and Indian agents to try to redirect Indian behavior into desired channels. Thus they wielded great power among the Indians with whom they dwelled. As such, the fur traders and Indian agents were indeed the bringers of wonder to Indian peoples of the southern backcountry.

Images of the Indian trade might bring to mind crude, ill-fashioned objects which no "civilized" European might want. Yet, how many colonies survived physically because of produce and game sold them by Indians? The Indian trade was one reason American colonials achieved a higher standard of living than their British counterparts. With respect to South Carolina, the Indian trade allowed businessmen to develop the wealth they later invested in rice and indigo plantations and the slave trade business.[1] The colony of South Carolina received an impressive profit from the trade in white tail deerskins from earliest times. From 1699 until 1715, South Carolina exported approximately 54,000 skins per annum. After South Carolina's crippling war with the Yamassees in 1715, the trade went into a slump from 1716 till 1730. However, for the subsequent twenty years, it experienced a golden age. In 1748 alone, the colony exported 160,000 skins.[2] The price of the 1747/1748 exported skins translated to values of £250,000-£300,000.[3] Items produced or processed by Native Americans were not only necessitiess but often luxury items desired by cultural elites. In September 1710, Virginia's William Byrd II noted that he had bought his wife Indian goods to the value of £4 10s.[4] Shortly after the establishment of British colonies, individuals were needed to deal in the Indian trade.

As stated previously, when British settlers began to occupy North America they found a tradition of gift giving among Native American peoples. They also inherited a legacy of trade already established by aggressive European colonizers. James Needham and Gabriel Arthur, early British traders among the Cherokees, found that those people had previously traded with the Spanish in Florida for a long time. The British travelers also found trade connections to Virginia suppliers, through an intermediate group of Indians, the Occoneechees. Interestingly enough, when Needham attempted to supplant the Occoneechees' position as middlemen, they had him killed in September 1673.[5] During Robert La Salle's 1882 trip down the Mississippi River, he encountered utensils and clothing of European origin which he surmised had come west from trade with Carolina.[6]

Though South Carolina tribes were eager to establish trade ties with colonial powers, they paid a heavy price for that trade in many ways. With trade came disease, often borne on the very articles for which native peoples of the Southeast traded. James Adair, an eighteenth century southern trader, noted the degree to which smallpox affected tribes with whom he traded. He noted the Cherokees, whom he considered a proud people, sometimes committed suicide rather than live with the lasting disfigurement of smallpox scars.[7] Beyond the psychological discomfort of survivable diseases, lay the insurmountable damage of social devastation as entire communities were eliminated by more virulent diseases passed through trade. Even simple diplomatic negotiations between native peoples and colonials opened with an exchange of gifts between the two peoples and always carried an unforeseen but deadly risk.[8]

The Indian trade quickly became an avenue through which Europeans sought to find easy wealth. As noted earlier, men like Lachlan McGillivray emigrated from Scotland during harsh economic times to seek their fortunes in the southern backcountry as Indian traders. McGillivray is a fitting example from which to create a model. The fur traders were, in the majority, Scots, Irish or Scotch-Irish.[9] William Byrd II of Westover Plantation in Virginia further defines the model by noting that such men got their start by sending to Britain for trade goods either in payment of cash if they had it or on credit to be paid with skins bartered from the Indians. Writing in the year 1728, Byrd observed such wares might include, first and foremost, guns and ammunition. After those items, Indians desired such things as hatchets, knives, vermilion, duffield blankets, calico cloth, hats, broadcloth coats and girdles.[10] Once procured, these items were loaded onto packhorses in amounts from 150 to 200 pounds. Near the beginning of the eighteenth century, Byrd noted that horse caravans often consisted of up to one hundred animals accompanied by fifteen to sixteen people. By 1728, however, he estimated that such horse trains seldom reached half the number of animals or men.[11]

Indians hunted during the winter months on forays lasting weeks at a time. After killing the animals, they skinned them in hunting lodges in the woods. It was not until late spring that these hunting parties returned to their villages. There, the traders were waiting for them in order to receive payment for the previous year's debt and ideally to accumulate one for the next year. The skins were tied into bundles and loaded onto horses for a return trip to towns like Charles Town, where the trader often had his own creditor waiting. Traders of various tribes often formed a single caravan as they journeyed out of the backcountry and returned to Euroamerican towns. By late summer or early fall, they had acquired new goods and returned to the backcountry to start the cycle again.[12]

Traders often located permanently among Indian peoples in those towns which produced the most skins.[13] This practice left some towns undersupplied, often contributing to jealousy and an upsurge in disputes between the cultures. Compared to the material scarcity of the surrounding Indians, they backcountry bourgeois lived lives of comfort in homes tended by their Indian mates, filled with mixed-blood children. Their smokehouses were usually stocked with preserved

Charles Town Harbor. Courtesy of South Carolina Archives History Center.

venison and bear meat as well as with dried fruits, nuts and vegetables. This diet was enhanced by tea, sugar, salt, and spices bought from Charles Town (Figure 6). The dwelling necessarily contained store rooms for their trade goods. The traders also introduced pastoral farming to the towns in which they lived.[14]

Once the trader was established in a village and accepted by the Indians through intermarriage, or at least through sexual relationships with native women, and through evidence of fair trade practices, a prominent warrior often chose him as a special friend. The identification often involved a complete exchange of clothing and of names. It was a permanent relationship, and the native man often took a second name to identify him as the trader's friend. Thus, the great Cherokee warrior Ostenaco was also known as Judd's Friend.[15]

While the Indian trade could provide a comfortable living, it was a financial gamble involving an intricate credit structure somewhat analogous to that of the antebellum cotton planter. Often the agency supplying trade goods was based in London. It provided wares on credit to a colonial merchant in places like Charles Town; that merchant then supplied the trader with the Indian goods needed for the backcountry trade. In trading with the Indians, the fur trader was taking payment in skins for goods purchased the previous year and selling goods to be paid for with the next winter's hunt.[16] Most likely, a communal preliterate society would have encountered difficulty in fully grasping concepts like credit and accumulated debt. The obvious alternative of purchasing only with furs would have been impossible to implement because of the addictive nature of European goods. Without the use of credit, tribes who ran short of guns and ammunition in June would have to wait until the following spring to buy new ones. Tribes considered the option of returning to projectile-point spear tips in the interim as unacceptable. A lack of guns and ammunition might preclude the possibility of having a successful hunt and being able to purchase items at all. Finally, the lack of advanced trade would have left Indian groups at the mercy of other tribes who could afford guns and ammunition. Hence, if a tribe's hunters fared poorly one winter, they were unable to pay their debts. Likewise if they were engaged in warfare and unable to hunt, their debts went unpaid and they incurred the wrath of the trader and his creditors.[17]

While the deer skin trade was a financial gamble for Euroamericans, it wreaked cultural havoc with the life style of American Indians. Native crafts had to compete with the often more durable mass-produced goods of Europe. Since calico cloth and metal skillets were more utilitarian than animal skins and wooden or stone bowls, America's native peoples allowed some craft skills to atrophy while they absorbed the European wares. Adaptation, in many cases, led to dependence and often made the tribes vulnerable to diplomatic pressures from colonial governments.[18] As Indian communities of the Southeast experienced a growing need for trade with Euroamerican culture, competition among the traders themselves, often escalating to a violent end, affected Anglo-Indian relations as well. Writing about competing Georgia Indian traders in 1752, the Carolina Indian trader Ludovic Grant described them as "a monstrous sett [sic] of rogues for the major part of whom the gallows groans."[19] Though borne of the jealousy of competition, Grant's statement sadly reflects the disposition and intent of a significant number of Euroamerican men who had an important part in shaping the relationship between the two cultures in the backcountry. The Indian trader James Adair was told by the Creeks that the Choctaw word for traders was derisive; when translated it meant something akin to "contemptible heterogenous animal."[20] Bernard Romans, a traveler in lower Georgia and upper Florida in the early 1770s, harshly characterized the Indian traders as "those monsters in human form, the very scum and out cast of the earth, [who] are always more prone to savage barbarity than the savages themselves."[21] Romans went on to state that the traders had been a dissolute and indecent lot during the initial contact period between the British and the Indians and were still so during his own time.[22]

In colonial Carolina, Indian traders had long been members of a powerful group. Colony proprietors wrote to one early governor with disturbing reports that Carolina Indian traders bragged they could "with a bowl of punch get who they would chosen to the parliament and afterwards who they would chosen to the Grand Council."[23] At the very least, traders were men of influence, often called to the colonial assembly to advise about situations on borders shared with the Spanish or French.[24] Because they possessed such power and influence, their character and morals determined whether their influence would be beneficial or disruptive to colonial relations with backcountry tribes. As one colonial governor noted, the Indian traders could often be "a set of abandoned wretches."[25] They easily could be as violent and "uncivilized" by their own culture's standards as the Indians were perceived to be. More dangerous perhaps than their wildness was their business acumen. Where colonial governments failed to regulate the trade, some dishonest traders knew no bounds of decency in outselling rival traders.[26] In November 1751, the veteran Indian traders Robert Bunning, Cornelius Dougherty, James Beamer and Ludovic Grant wrote to the governor and council of South Carolina complaining about such men among the Cherokees. They noted that up to that point the Indian trade had "been carried on after a most licentious, lawless and irregular manner much to the prejudice of the same, and to the dissatisfaction of the Indians."[27] Traders of this ilk coined the phrase "it's no crime to cheat and gull an Indian."[28] Those who most influenced Indian relations were often the worst ambassadors of their culture.

Where commerce and corruption flourished, government regulation was sure to follow. The imposition of rules and regulations over the Indian trade in the southern backcountry suggests three beliefs on the part of colonial governments. First, it meant that the Indian trade was valuable. Edward McCrady, an early historian of South Carolina, noted that all the family fortunes in colonial Carolina were based on the Indian trade. In 1708, South Carolina alone was exporting fifty thousand pounds of skins per year.[29] Second, the establishment of trade guidelines meant that the relationship between a colony and surrounding tribes could be dangerous, even fatal. South Carolinians acknowledged this fact with an early article in the *South Carolina Gazette,* stating that the Indian trade was "the means by which we keep and maintain the several nations of the Indians surrounding this province in amity and friendship with us, and thereby [prevent] their falling into the interest of France or Spain."[30] Finally, the creation of a public regulatory system was proof that free traders were jeopardizing that relationship.

South Carolina was uniquely situated. Like the colony of Virginia, it had contact with multiple Native American groups, such as the Congarees, Peadees, Waterees, Santees and Catawbas who were located near Euroamerican settlements like Charles Town. To the south and west it had contact with members of the Creek Confederacy, including the Muskoghees, Alibamas and Uchees. It also had access to the Cherokees to the north and west. It is not surprising then that one of the earliest public attempts to regulate contact and trade between Native American and Euroamerican culture occurred in South Carolina, where the assembly enacted a law in 1707 creating a Board of Indian Commissioners, nine in all, to license and regulate traders going into Indian lands. The act provided for a superintendent assigned to live among each of the tribes in order to enforce fair trade practices decided by the commissioners. Traders had to purchase an annual license for £8 and give a bond of £100 to guarantee compliance with the new trade rules. Traders were not to seize free Indians and sell them as slaves[31] to cancel Indian debts nor to force native peoples to trade furs under threat of physical violence. While they could sell arms and ammunition to Indians who had treaties with the government of Carolina, they were not to trade with so-called enemy Indians who were aligned with either France or Spain. Finally, they were not to give or to sell rum to the Indians.[32] Such a noble effort immediately met with opposition from the heretofore free traders who had done as they pleased in the anonymity of the backcountry.

In August 1711, the Indian commissioners of South Carolina reprimanded a trader named Frazier for selling an Indian boy. Further, Frazier was guilty of trading without a license. His punishment was to forfeit his £100 bond, to discharge the debt owed him by Indians for rum and to release those Indians indebted to him through debts of their relatives.[33] Four days later, the commissioners decided to look into two cases of abduction. Cornelius McCarty was being investigated for taking an Indian man's wife and child while the man was away at war. George Wright was being investigated for abducting a free Indian woman from her home in Tomatly.[34]

Such abductions are indicative of the general lawlessness of some Indian traders, but they touch upon the subject of Indian slavery. Historian Theda Perdue has observed that tribes such as the Cherokees practiced a form of slavery prior to European contact, although the differences between Indian bondage and European bondage were notable. These people were obtained in warfare and the purpose of their bondage was punishment, not profit. The entire aim of warfare among groups like the Cherokees was vengeance. Cherokee warriors sought to kill a number of their enemies, equivalent to their own losses in prior conflicts.[35]

Sometimes enemies were not put to death but rather ransomed for trade goods or saved for ritual torture. Those who met neither fate were either adopted by a clan and incorporated into village life or made bondsmen. As a bondsman, one existed within Cherokee society but, without clan membership, enjoyed no rights and privileges. While a stranger who had been adopted into the tribe held the same rights as a birth member, a slave was the exclusive property of his owner.[36] First and foremost, native bondsmen served as tools of vengeance. In a broader sense, their undesirable condition served Native American society as disempowered minorities do in all societies. As visible models of "what not to be," they provided social cohesion among the majority.[37]

With the introduction of Europeans and their goods to Indian society, the nature of Indian bondage changed. Indian captives became the viable alternative to deer skins as an exchange medium for the much-prized trade goods; the labor shortage which so plagued transplanted Europeans provided a ready market for these slaves. While the Cherokees did not use their own bondsmen the way Europeans did, they changed from subsistence slavers to commercial slavers, and, since slaves were obtained through warfare, trade increased the incidence of intertribal conflict.[38]

The goal of warfare changed from vengeance to slave procurement. As the Cherokees grew more dependent on European goods, traders began to wield more influence, often encouraging intertribal war to obtain slaves. In 1714, Alexander Long and Eleazar Wiggan incited the Cherokees to raid the Yuchis for slaves.[39] Colonial officials, likewise, used the slave trade to further their own interests. Governor James Moore of South Carolina prompted attacks on the Appalachee Indians of Florida so that captives might be sold.[40] The introduction of European trade altered the purpose of bondage in native society, changing occasional slave owners into professional slave hunters.

In September 1711, the South Carolina Indian Board met and issued fifteen new trader licenses and sets of guidelines. It also discussed the incidence of rum being sold to Indians by Edmund Ellis, John Cochran, William Ford, Samuel Hilden and Nicholas Day.[41] Most items of European trade created a psychological "addiction"; rum was a trade item which promoted physical addiction as well. Travelers in the backcountry reported finding Indian bodies piled in the forest--dead and reeking of alcohol. By altering perception and judgment, rum and its illegal trafficking in the backcountry further exacerbated relationships between the two cultures. Unscrupulous traders often intercepted warriors returning home from a hunt before they reached their village, offering these men a free drink of rum and then insisting on trading. Drinking continued past the first, friendly drink until the warriors were drunk, and, in such a state, they were easy prey for the traders.[42] Since the Indians procured skins to pay the previous year's debt, they incurred the wrath of their own creditors when they returned empty-handed. Indian debts began to accumulate while the Indians became victims of substance abuse. John Lawson reported that the traders sold the Indians rum by the mouthful in exchange for buckskins. However unhygienic the measuring may have been, the Indians soon learned to take to the negotiating table the man with the biggest mouth in the village.[43]

Native Americans generally seemed highly susceptible to alcohol dependency, more so than their European business partners. Explanations for the phenomenon cover a broad spectrum. Some sources identify excessive alcohol consumption as a communal expression of being Indian. Others link alcohol consumption with cultural decline. The Iroquois were given to brief bouts of intoxication before Europeans controlled North America. By the 1790s, alcohol abuse had become a critical social problem. Since drunkenness carried no social stigma in Indian society, its progress was unimpeded.

Once introduced, alcohol was quickly integrated into tribal life. Certainly, genetic factors play a part in this vulnerability. Studies done on the Tarahumara Indians of Mexico show that their metabolism was geared for the highly specialized extraction of protein from their traditional foods of beans and Indian corn. Once exposed to the protein and sugar-rich foods of the Europeans, the Tarahumara fell prey to obesity, diabetes and heart disease.[44] With respect solely to alcohol consumption, Peter H. Wolff observed that alcohol affected Mongoloid populations, including American Indians, more than Caucasoid groups. Wolff noted that test subjects experienced facial flushing after consuming only small quantities. Their body required more time to metabolize the alcohol consumed and thus experienced intoxication longer than that of their Caucasoid counterparts.[45] Most likely, a combination of all these factors predisposed Native Americans to dependency on the liquor sold in their lands.

The Carolina Board of Commissioners tried to regulate this traffic. In August of 1713, they notified the traders of the Savannah and Yamassee Indian settlements of reports of large amounts of rum being shipped into their territories; they ordered these agents to seek out and destroy the contraband.[46] The ability of the board to deal with such matters had always been tenuous as they were far removed from the day-to-day dealings with Native Americans. They might order free traders to carry out certain edicts, but in the expanse of the backcountry, their only means of enforcing these policies was their agent. Part of the original act of 1707 called for the creation of an Indian agent to spend at least ten months of the year in the Indian homelands. Carolina's first was Thomas Nairne, who was followed later by John Wright.[47] The agent received a salary of £250 and was charged with visiting all major Indian settlements, handling Indian complaints and generally managing the trade.[48] Nairne, a wealthy businessman, had supported the 1707 bill which created a protrader public Indian commission.[49] After traveling among the Yamassees near Port Royal Sound, Wright traveled among the Savannah Indians at the modern location of Augusta, Georgia. In March 1712, he told the board that none of the traders he met was licensed.[50]

Nairne first appeared in South Carolina in 1695, as an immigrant from Scotland. He quickly established himself as a military figure, beginning in 1702, when he led Indian and Euroamerican troops on a military raid against St. Augustine which was intended to procure slaves from among the Spanish Indians. Nairne repeated the venture in 1704, engaging the Appalachee Indians for profit.[51] One of Nairne's initial tasks as South Carolina's first Indian agent, was to arrest James Child for leading Cherokees on a slave raid against pro-British Indians, which netted 160 captives.[52] In 1712, Nairne was made a commissioner to the Yamassee and Palachocola Indians, and he came into conflict with his replacement, John Wright, over jurisdiction. Wright's office ultimately was given superior authority, but Nairne returned to the office as Indian agent later the same year, displacing Wright.[53] In August of 1714, the board authorized Nairne to arrest

Wright, its own former agent, for rum trafficking in the Indian lands.[54] Thus the loyalty of the board's own employees was questionable, as was its efficacy in regulating the Indian trade.

Along with skins, lawless traders often intercepted warriors returning home with slaves taken in raids to sell. These slaves were usually members of other tribes taken in raids, but Indians also trafficked in Africans. In April 1712, the board was notified that a trader named Hilden had intercepted a group of Indians and forced them to exchange their slaves for trade items. Wenoya, an Indian man, noted that Hilden had forced him to trade a slave for items worth 160 skins.[55] The next month, the board received complaints that William Bray, Daniel Callahaun and John Frazer forced Indians returning to Pocotalligo Town to sell their slaves.[56]

Members of various tribes began to register complaints. Indian head men vainly sought stricter regulation of rum smuggling in their homelands, telling colonial officials that it was the source of much dissension between their people and the colonials.[57] In April 1715, the Board of Commissioners was notified that the Creek Indians were dissatisfied with the traders among them, especially one John Jones. They warned the board that they had made several complaints without satisfaction. Any further offenses by any of the traders would provoke retaliation against all of them.[58]

In addition to the liquor trade, the introduction of Euroamerican guns into native societies of the Southeast markedly changed those societies. Like more mundane items, guns radically changed culture. They increased the efficacy of native hunters in their struggle against the white-tailed deer. The race to collect more deer skins in order to buy both rum and guns led southeastern Indians to exhaust their game reserves. Parallel to this trend to commercial hunting was a waning respect for native religious practices which limited kills, motivated by respect for the animals' spirits and by of respect the benevolent supreme being in whom they believed.[59]

Gun technology also contributed to native dependency on Euroamerican trade. In addition to its greater killing power than that of the bow and arrow, the gun's loud shot helped to frighten enemies. Gun wounds were often more serious than those of arrows for critical complications could develop. Guns also changed the traditional Indian reasons to make war--to seek revenge and/or achieve honor. Now, Indians of the Southeast sought conflicts to dominate Euroamerican trade lines, to seize more fertile hunting grounds of neighboring tribes or to secure slaves to sell to Euroamerican traders.[60] Indeed, contact with Euroamerican culture completely changed the style and duration of Indian warfare, as native peoples turned to the practice of "total war," sparing no prisoners, destroying an enemy's food resources and practicing siege tactics.[61] While Euroamerican trade items were indirectly changing native lifeways, traders were deliberately changing those same traditions.

Despite the growing tension between southeastern tribes and traders, new traders flocked to the profession. Only a few months before spring 1715, twenty-three men took out licenses to trade.[62] Thus the potentially dangerous relationship between Native Americans and colonials was reaching a critical stage. Critical mass was reached on 14 April 1715, when William Bray and Samuel Warner met Nairne at Pocotalligo Town, southwest of modern Charleston near the Coosawatchie River, pursuant to a mission to head off an impending attack by the Yamassees. The Yamassees had become accustomed to slave hunting to pay their trade debts and had habitually preyed upon the Appalachee Indians of northern Florida. Numerous raids had depleted the ranks of the Florida tribes, however. Lacking the means to pay but still harassed by their creditors, the Yamassees turned on them on 15 April, killing Bray and Warner and torturing Nairne for three days before he died. The Yamassee uprising lasted two years and threatened the survival of South Carolina.[63]

In 1716, the government of South Carolina assumed a public monopoly over the fur trade with the backcountry. Official representatives or factors would replace the old agent and would be stationed at designated points among the tribes aligned with Carolina. Their duty was to take direct charge of the trading goods sent up by the board and exchange them for the skins and slaves previously bought from licensed, but ungovernable traders.[64] Carolina planters who dabbled in the Indian trade had fully advocated the new system for some time prior to implementation. Career merchants opposed it, viewing it as a serious threat to profit margins.[65] Like their predecessors, the factors could sell arms and ammunition to aligned tribes but not to those known to deal with the Spanish or French. They were also forbidden to enslave free Indians from tribes aligned with Britain. Addressing the issue of accumulated Indian debts, the board forbade the factors to extend credit to the Indians even for as little as one skin's value. The factors were not to trade with the Indians on a private basis, only to represent the public trade. They were supposed to mark items bartered from the Indians with a particular brand and were to maintain the pack animals and other conveyances used in the trade in a proper manner. The factors were to keep an "exact" journal to record not only information related to the Indian trade but all proceedings within their assigned tribe.[66]

Factors were to note the deaths of any prominent Indians, especially those who held commissions from the government of Carolina. In such an event, the board expected the factor to make a recommendation on a suitable successor. The factors were to report the incidence of murder among their hosts, as well as to note that tribe's policy toward other Indians. They were to note the departure and arrival of other tribesmen, as well as of emissaries of other colonial powers. Factors were to keep accounts of the number of fighting men in their tribe and be able to identify them as headmen, warriors or Beloved Men.[67] Thus, the factors were becoming true backcountry diplomats to many diverse Indian groups and modifying their culture through the imposition of foreign hierarchical systems like the commissions.

The factors were to remain dependent officials, however, lacking the power to invoke the word of colonial government without authorization from the board. One of their functions was to see that Indians stayed away from towns, where they might cause mischief and incur diplomatic expenses. Indians were to become accustomed to trading with the factor at his factory. Of seventeen points of instruction, trade guidelines dominated the first twelve entries. Guideline number thirteen did charge the factors to maintain friendly relations with the Indians by striving to end abuses by colonials.[68] Nonetheless, the prioritization of points indicates that Indian abuse was viewed mainly as an impediment to trade, despite the threat to Euroamerican settlers.

Wages for the factors and their assistants varied. Initially, Theophilus Hastings, factor to the Cherokees, received £9 per month while Major Blakewey, factor at Savano Town, received £4 per month. Hastings was allowed two assistants; John Sharp and Samuel Muckleroy were to receive £1 10s per month for working under Hastings. Blakewey had one assistant, Charlesworth Glover, who received £3 per month, nearly as much as Blakewey. All factors and assistants had to take an oath and give bond that they would carry out the wishes of the board.[69] Two weeks later, the board met and advanced Hastings' salary to £25 per month and that of his assistants to £8.4 (£102 per year).[70] Quickly, new factors were appointed to all those tribes aligned with the colony of Carolina. William Watis, Sr., was appointed factor for the Northward Indians (Wackamaws, Wawees and Peadees) of the Wineau Bay area.[71]

Other officials were involved as well. Thomas Barton served as storekeeper for the Board of Indian Commissioners. In keeping the repository of trade goods, Barton had to take an oath of service, swearing not to embezzle the goods, nor trade directly with the Indians.[72] Obviously, the 1716 Act for the Better Regulation of the Indian Trade intended to eliminate one official--the independent trader. The threat posed by the actions of unscrupulous traders was worthy of such attention. The act also sought to eliminate the competition posed by free traders, whose growing numbers effectively lowered the profit of all and encouraged baser behavior by some of them to make a living. Any private trader arrested under the act would pay the rather exorbitant fine of £500 while his goods were liable to be sold by the factor for the public trade.[73] Such stiff penalties and the curtailment of free enterprise were bound to arouse the ire of many of the Scotch-Irish free traders.

While the profession of Indian trader was often a temporary one for many adventurous souls in the backcountry, it was a lifetime profession for several as well. The Carolina Trade Act of 1716 posed a great threat to men like Eleazar Wiggan and Ludovic Grant. Wiggan had entered the Overhill Cherokee country around 1711. In 1715, the South Carolina government employed him to enlist the Cherokees' aid for the colony during the Yamassee attack. He also escorted military officials, like Colonel George Chicken, on missions into the backcountry.[74] Samuel Cole Williams, historian of early Tennessee, noted Grant was a descendant of the Grant family of Dalvey, Scotland, headed by a Sir Ludovic Grant. Young Ludovic came to America in the early 1700s and became a resident of the Cherokee homelands about 1726, serving as a trader from his home base of Great Tellico, located on the Tellico River in modern Monroe County, Tennessee. By midcentury, he was living on the Hiwassee River in service to South Carolina's governor, James Glen, as a peacekeeper and an informant about backcountry happenings.[75] A contemporary of both men, Robert Bunning, arrived there in 1714. Cornelius Dougherty began the Indian trade in modern Tennessee even earlier, around 1690.[76] As a result of the imposition of government regulation, such men would have to decide whether to quit their profession, be absorbed by the new system and become public traders or live beyond the law and take their chances.

The case of Eleazar Wiggan will serve to illustrate how one private trader dealt with the changing system. Though Wiggan provided Cherokee warriors for a South Carolina besieged by the Yamassees, in July 1716 the board chastised him for his failure to comply with the new law. They acknowledged that they had given him permission previously to pursue his small trade but stated they had never intended that trade to go on so long. The board could not allow his efforts to clash with the public trade and so gave him six days to evacuate Cherokee lands. The new public trader, Theophilus Hastings, was ordered to seize his goods if he did not comply.[77]

In October 1716, Wiggan's name was back before the board as it issued orders that he be prosecuted. He evidently had departed the Cherokee lands but had taken up a trade with the Catawba people, again without a position as public trader.[78] Ultimately Wiggan was absorbed by the new system, for in January 1717 the board accepted him as a factor to the Catawba people.[79] In such a position, he proved a valuable servant to the board over the years. As expected, the new system carried a specific set of trade equivalents, though the amounts varied from tribe to tribe. An examination of price tables used among the Congarees is necessary to chart a decline in prices charged. In 1716, the Congarees accepted the price schedule in Table 1 from Carolina traders.

Table 1: Price Rates for Congarees. . .[80]

Item	Number of Skins
1 gun	35
1 yard strouds	8
1 white duffield blanket	16
1 narrow hoe	3
30 bullets	1
1 knife	1
1 laced broadcloth coat	30
1 ax	5
1 sword	10
1 calico petticoat	14

As Native Americans of the Southeast became more dependent upon European goods, they grew more vocal in their demands about trade practices. The imposition of a government monopoly over the trade did not solve many preexisting problems, but it allowed for more efficient reporting of Indian grievances.

Soon after the imposition of these prices, various tribes began to protest. In a November 1716 session of the board, a letter from the factor Theophilus Hastings noted that the Cherokees considered the prices charged for certain items, like strouds, too costly.[81] Scarcely six days later, the board moved to reduce their cost of strouds from eight skins per yard to seven.[82] By the end of that same month, a letter to Charlesworth Glover, a factor at Savano Town, indicated that the price of strouds had been dropped once more to six skins per yard.[83] Such price rollbacks illustrate colonial fears that the Indians would turn violent or align with other powers. In 1717, the factors encountered what they most feared--traders of rival powers. If the Indian tribes had been isolated, their demands for cheaper goods would have fallen on deaf ears. Alternative suppliers, however, meant threats to Carolina's hegemony, and the suppliers were not always French or Spanish.

In May 1717, the board wrote to Meredith Hughes, factor to the Wineaus, that the Virginians were encroaching upon what Carolina had considered its preserve--trade with the southeastern Indians.[84] Scarcely a week later, Eleazar Wiggan, firmly reestablished in the Indian trade as a factor to the Catawbas, reported that his hosts spoke of an impending visit by Virginia traders, with whom they promised not to trade.[85] Virginia traders threatened the hegemony of Carolina over the southern Indians, increased the numbers of an already glutted profession and threatened to create a price war for customers. In September 1717, the board noted a report from Wiggan that the Virginia traders intimated they would undersell Carolina traders in order to secure tribal loyalty. The board directed Wiggan to provide them with detailed reports concerning these rivals, including their prices and ordered him to do whatever was necessary to keep the Catawbas aligned with Carolina, including drastic cuts of merchandise prices to match Virginia trade prices.[86]

It is not surprising, then, that the board responded to Indian complaints about rates of exchange by lowering prices. In a schedule issued in April 1718, the price of one gun was lowered from thirty-five skins to sixteen. The price of a hatchet was lowered from three to two skins, and that of a yard of strouds from eight skins to only four. A white duffield blanket cost eight skins in 1718; it had cost sixteen in 1716.[87] With the influx of more traders into the backcountry, the competition lowered the profit for all. Traders began to locate in native towns with the most hunters, and such towns were oversupplied with goods while smaller towns often went undersupplied. Yet various tribes began to wield the bargaining power they held over the Carolina government with more finesse. In May 1718, Eleazar Wiggan reported that the Catawbas felt they were not supplied with sufficient goods. They also complained of the colonial practice of using Indian males as burdeners to transport wares to and from the East. The Catawbas cited the Virginians as proper trading partners to Wiggan; they had brought great quantities of goods, which they had sold more cheaply than Carolina factors. Finally, the merchandise had been shipped on packhorses.[88] In response, the board sent Wiggan presents for the Catawba headman and his sister. They told Wiggan to notify the Catawbas to expect the arrival of a proper load of merchandise--on packhorses. The board also created a new backcountry official, the packhorseman, and assigned several to the various tribes much as it had assigned the factors. The packhorsemen were, like the traders and Indian agents, directly involved in daily life in the Indian lands and helped shape the relationship between the Native American and Euroamerican cultures. Some, like Lachlan McGillivray, advanced from the job of packhorseman to that of trader.[89] Salaries for the post were nearly as high as those originally paid the factors and more than that paid their assistants. The board hired Joseph Ponder as a packhorseman at a monthly wage of £10 with an expense account of seven shillings and six pence per day.[90] In June 1718, the board noted that Jack Coleman had been appointed chief of a train of thirteen packhorses bound for Cherokee lands. Interestingly, Coleman had five men to assist him in his mission. Once among the Indian tribes, the packhorsemen passed from the jurisdiction of the board to that of the factors.[91]

When these backwoodsmen were of good character, they were of invaluable aid to the colonial governments. George Galphin, an Indian trader based at Augusta, Georgia, reported to the commissioners in the fall of 1749 that he had tried unsuccessfully to stop a party of Cussita (Creek) Indians from making war on the Cherokees. Galphin also reported to the South Carolina government that the French were trying to make inroads among the Cowetas. He noted that the Cowetas invited him into the square of their town, but he refused because they were flying French colors; in fact, Galphin refused to act as a mediator for them until they displayed proper British colors.[92] Galphin, a partner in the trading firm of Brown, Rea and Company, illustrates how influential traders could be. Born in Tullamore County, Ireland, in the early 1700s, he left in 1737 for the American colonies. By 1745 he was employed by South Carolina as an interpreter.[93]

His first posting by Carolina was among the Creeks, keeping the government well informed about their activities. While among the Lower Creeks he cohabited with a woman, Metawney, and had children.[94] Galphin's service was not always above reproach; when he presented a bill for £467 to the South Carolina Assembly for Indian trade goods, that body found his estimate overcharged by £114. Upon further study, the assembly found he had spent another £83 to supply the Creeks with rum, an expense they did not reimburse.[95]

In the 1740s, Galphin joined the Augusta-based trading firm of Brown, Rea and Company, a company begun earlier in the century by Archibald McGillivray, ancestor of Lachlan McGillivray. Daniel Clark, Jeremiah Knott, William Sludders and George Cussings were also original partners. The company employed about 20 packhorsemen and owned 123 horses as well.[96] After 1741, the company was controlled by both Patrick Brown, licensed to trade with the Upper Creek towns, and John Rea, licensed to trade among the Lower Creeks along with Galphin.[97]

John Rea, also from Ireland, immigrated to America around 1730 and by 1734 made his way to Georgia where he began running a trading boat from Augusta to Charles Town. By 1750, he had entered into partnership with Patrick Brown to create Brown, Rea and Company.[98]

Besides his trading firm, his most ambitious scheme was one which brought him together with the Indian trader George Galphin in an effort to sponsor Irish immigrants to America with government assistance. In 1761, Rea along with ten others petitioned South Carolina for a grant of forty thousand acres to be used for townships for Irish settlers. When immigration enticements in that colony expired in 1765, Rea and Galphin began similar efforts in Georgia.[99]

They petitioned that colony for a bounty payment to cover passage and settlement, plus exemption from taxes and rents for a ten-year period. Galphin purchased fifteen hundred acres on the Ogeechee River at the boundary of Indian territory. He established a herd of cattle and a trading post there and called the site "Galphin's Old Town."[100] Settlers began to arrive in 1768 and Governor Wright of Georgia designated their land "Queensborough."[101] Troubled by Indian neighbors and a poorly situated grant, Queensborough barely survived until the American Revolution. The resulting dislocation of the war and sale of Loyalist lands spelled the end of the ill-fated community, though land from a settler was confiscated to build the new state capital, Louisville.[102]

Most traders were not as ambitious as Galphin or Rea, but even the average trader of low character was able to exacerbate tensions between the two cultures. David Dowey was a Euroamerican trader stationed along the Overhill towns of the Cherokee people in modern Monroe County, Tennessee. In a report to the board, he noted that the Indians there were generally helpful to the white traders living among them. It was the traders who disrupted relations with the Indians by spreading both lies and rum among them, in order to attract their business. Dowey noted that a man named William Broadway had recently told the Indians there that " the people of South Carolina were raising an army to cutt [sic] them all to peices, [sic], and to make slaves of their wives and children."[103]

While fur traders manipulated Anglo-Indian diplomacy for better or worse, a fierce battle raged behind the scenes with South Carolina's public trade. Carolina merchants resented the exclusion of free traders from the new public trade. They petitioned the Carolina proprietors to reverse the public monopoly and, in 1718, welcomed the repeal of the public act. Rather than abandon the public system altogether, Carolina government replaced it with a curious hybrid organization that blended public and private elements. The public traders were reorganized into three factors and three subfactors in charge of sixty employees. Public trade continued at designated factories and private traders were prohibited from doing business within twenty miles of such sites. Where the public trade did not exist, private traders were now welcome and public traders could not encroach upon the new private domain. Profits from the public trade funded the upkeep of garrisons and trading forts in the backcountry. Carolina government levied a 10 percent tax on the private trade also to defray costs for public trade.[104]

Whether public or private, the position of trader was not without a certain amount of danger itself. When angered by Euroamericans, various tribes often turned on those representatives closest to them--the traders and their assistants. In December 1749, Governor Glen, in a report to the Board of Trade, mentioned that a group of French influenced Indians had killed a trader named Robert Kelley during a raid on the Overhill Cherokees. Glen felt Kelley's loss was a blow to the government since he had lived among them long enough to learn their language and their customs.[105] James Maxwell, a trader assigned to the Lower Cherokees, near the headwaters of the Savannah and Chattahoochee rivers, reported in June of 1751 that a group of Cherokees went on a rampage and killed a trader named Daniel Murphy and had proceeded on to the store of Bernard Hughs intending to kill its owner, though Hughs had fled. These same Indians declared that the remaining traders and their merchandise would be held as hostages in the Cherokee lands till the Carolina government sent them ammunition.[106] Carolina responded with a very powerful weapon--the cessation of trade. Cornelius Dougherty wrote to Governor Glen in July 1751 that, acting on the governor's orders, he had held a meeting of traders to inform them they were being ordered out of tribal lands until the disruptive faction among the Cherokees could be brought under control. Dougherty told Glen of the many pains he had taken to carry out the governor's wishes. He noted that in 1751, he had been among the Indians for thirty years and that, without seeming immodest, he held no little power over them. To that end, Dougherty also held a meeting with several Cherokee headmen to tell them why the traders were being evacuated. He petitioned Governor Glen to help him with debts he had accrued over the years by being involved with "several great companies." Dougherty intimated that he remained in the backcountry longer than he would have cared to because of these debts, presumably in hopes of paying them off while avoiding prosecution by his creditors.[107]

By the mideighteenth century, the number of Indian factors combined with those illegal independent traders had grown so large that none involved in the trade was making a profit. Cherokee traders Robert Bunning, Cornelius Dougherty, James Beamer and Ludovic Grant petitioned the Carolina government noting that the trade was so low that they could not pay merchants for old debts, much less purchase new goods. They also advocated the creation of a new official who would live among the various tribes with the power to regulate the trade properly. Finally, they suggested the building of British forts throughout the backcountry. Garrisoned with soldiers, these forts would enforce the trade policies so often ignored by wayward traders in the wilds of inland Carolina and Georgia. They would serve also as visible reminders to the Indians of the relationship between them and the British, helping to minimize the influence of traders from other colonies and nations.[108]

The petition by veteran traders like Bunning, Grant, Dougherty and Beamer was accurate in its portrayal of problems between the two cultures and prophetic with regard to some of the solutions. In 1751 a member of the Governor's Council of New York, Archibald Kennedy, proposed the creation of an Indian superintendent. He found an advocate in New York's governor, Cadwallader Colden, who forwarded the idea to the Board of Trade in the fall of 1751.[109] They called for an official who would enforce just treatment of the Indians, mediate their grievances when they had been ill used and supply them with craftsmen and missionaries. Ironically, the source of this official's salary would be the sale of liquor--that trade item which had wreaked so much havoc in relations between the two cultures.[110]

The next call for the creation of such a colonial official came at the Albany Congress of 1754, when William Johnson presented a paper stressing the importance of securing the firm loyalties of America's Indian tribes in light of the impending war with France. Representatives of the six tribes of the Iroquois Confederacy also petitioned the Congress for the creation of such an official, and the Congress, in turn, endorsed the idea to the Secretary of State for the Southern Department on 22 July 1754.[111] Prototype plans to regulate the Indian trade began to appear from various quarters; again South Carolina was in the forefront as its governor, Thomas Boone, offered his own version for the Cherokees.

The blueprint observed that neither the Indians nor the Indian traders could be trusted to manage the relationship between the two cultures. It noted that the traders were the scum of the earth, who would stop at nothing to seek an advantage in that trade, no matter its cost in lives. In short, their behavior had cost them membership in civilized society and had reduced them to life among "savages."[112]

Boone's proposal had several ideas of merit; it proposed that laws concerning Indians should have to be passed by all assemblies in those colonies dealing with the same groups of Indians. It proposed that all trade with Indian tribes be under a colonial monopoly, as was South Carolina's trade. The plan called for the establishment deep within the backcountry of outposts that doubled as garrisons and trading posts. The traders were to be men of good character who would deal in the most popularly requested trade items, including rum, at low prices. In this system, however, Indians could not purchase on credit. The factors in the proposed system would be magistrates with power to stop unauthorized people from trading with the Indians and with power to seize their goods. Punishment for Indian misbehavior was quite harsh; if an Indian killed a Euroamerican, the factors would execute two members of that Indian's tribe. In order to prevent the long, bloody results of retributive justice, all trade would be stopped with that tribe until such time as it agreed to accept the punishment and return to normal relations. Under this system, the government would disallow Indian conferences with their requisite gifts. Boone viewed conferences as disgraceful, highly wasteful of money and the reason Indians made surprise visits to colonial towns. His plan called for contact with Indians to take place in the forts of the backcountry.[113]

Lord Halifax, Secretary of State for the Southern Department, chose to use the plan submitted by the Albany Congress . He proposed to divide North America into two districts presided over by two commissary generals, later called superintendents, regulating diplomatic and trade relations with the various tribes. They, not colonial governments, would issue licenses to traders, thus depriving those governments of expected revenue and power. The commissioners would require assistants in the field, much as the factors employed by the Carolina government had employed assistants; the pay for both would come from a general fund for the government of the colonies.[114]

One of the most frustrating weaknesses of the Indian agents appointed by colonial governments was their lack of ability to enforce policy dictated from colonial centers of power. The new Indian superintendents were placed under the authority of the Commander-in-Chief of British Forces in North America, Major General Edward Braddock, who was instructed to select the agents for both districts. For the North he chose William Johnson and for the South, Edmund Atkin. John Stuart initially assisted Atkin, and upon Atkin's death, Stuart assumed the superintendent's post on 5 January 1762.[115]

The shift from individual colonial control of contiguous tribes to a centralized, bureaucratic effort to regulate relations with America's Indian peoples marked the first stage of home government involvement. The next phase came in 1761, when the superintendents assumed control of the transfer of Indian lands. In 1764, the Board of Trade further defined guidelines for the Indian trade, in connection with the proclamation of 1764.[116]

Various colonial officials offered opinions on the plan, including John Stuart. Stuart opposed continued trader licensing by colonial governors, whose actions only encouraged competition among the colonies for trade. He believed the southern Indians were producing the maximum number of pelts possible; more traders in their lands would increase only the number of trading conflicts.[117] Stuart especially wanted to eliminate the presence of independent colonial agents in the backcountry. He wanted agents of the Indian superintendency to be the only officials there. Stuart saw the danger of intercolonial competition and believed his measures the only way to end the trouble it caused.[118] In fact, he wanted to limit the number of traders to 1 for every 150 gunmen in each tribe. Above all, Stuart considered proper government of the Indians the ultimate goal of his office; regulation of the trade was merely a means to that end. Eliminating the glut in the number of traders was the first step toward regulating the Indian trade.[119]

Colonial government did not welcome the loss of such power. Colonies like Carolina had controlled the trade of nearby tribes for four decades. Now, their power was being usurped by officials like Stuart. In April 1764, Governor Boone of South Carolina wrote to the Board of Trade suggesting his colony was more adept at managing the Indian trade than Stuart, partly because its agents were prepared to insinuate themselves among the Indians. Their men were able not only to observe and report on the behavior of the traders within the backcountry but to distinguish true Indian intentions from false talk.[120] Boone suggested that the superintendent might not be able to deliver the same quality of service in Indian management and asked "whether it might not be proper to make him subordinate to the Governor & Council of each province, where his duty may call him."[121] Claiming that Stuart was very new, that his instructions were vague and that he was far removed from authority should a crisis arise, Boone's suggestion was a thinly veiled attempt to retain power.[122] Smarting from the loss of power, the governors began to oppose Stuart and his goals.

While the Indian trade would now receive thorough scrutiny from a pancolonial perspective, the new administration would struggle with the same problems first experienced by the South Carolina Board of Commissioners and their agents. One historian of the Carolina frontier, Verner Crane, observed that South Carolina's Indian management system was probably the best of any such colonial organization: the only superior organization was that organized by the British government in 1756.[123]

Despite Carolina's Governor Boone's objections, the new superintendent for Indian affairs, armed with supracolonial authority, appeared in the backcountry. Stuart's initial task was to soothe the various tribes there who had been agitated by the Great War for Empire among Britain, France and Spain. While several tribes in the backcountry were firmly aligned with Britain, some had been affiliated with the French and had to be realigned to British Indian policy. He held a series of conferences to that end which also publicized the Proclamation Line of 1763, Britain's pledge to hold its colonial settlements to the general region of the eastern seaboard. To reaffirm established relationships and cement new ones, Secretary of State for the Southern Department Lord Egremont sent £4,000-£5,000 worth of presents to be dispensed at a conference Stuart held at Augusta, Georgia, in November 1763 with the Upper and Lower Creeks and Choctaws.[124]

In 1765, Stuart issued a series of trade guidelines which bear a haunting resemblance to those issued earlier by colonial Carolina. Traders were not to sell liquor, rifles and ammunition to Indians. Attempting to curb the age-old problem of debt accumulation, Stuart imposed limits on the number of deer skins that traders could purchase and limited the amount of credit traders could extend to a value of thirty pounds of skins. He imposed a set of uniform weights and measures on the traders as well as a fixed price for goods. The trade was taxed and was to be confined to the Indian towns. Physical abuse of the Indians was strictly forbidden and traders were not to call Indians together for talks without permission of the superintendent.[125]

Despite final recognition of the need for a comprehensive Indian trade policy, the implementation of such a system was difficult for several reasons. While emissaries of foreign powers traded on the North American continent, opportunities to influence the Indians against British colonials existed. When those emissaries were traders of long standing in various Indian lands, the threat they posed was even more dangerous. In November 1760, Lieutenant Governor Bull of Charles Town wrote to the Board of Trade, warning them of a rogue French trader who was attempting to alienate the Cherokees from the British.

Originally a soldier, the trader Lantagnac got lost on a hunting trip near Fort Toulouse in November 1745. A group of Chickasaws found the thirteen-year-old and turned him over to British officials, who shipped him to South Carolina. After a time, he applied for and received permission from Carolina to trade with the Cherokees. In a letter to French officials, Lantagnac spoke of his sojourn among the Cherokees as a time during which he learned the Cherokee tongue and customs. He also observed how the British tried to turn the Cherokees against the French. Despite abandoning his post, Lantaganac petitioned to rejoin French forces.[126]

Ultimately, he reconciled with them and renewed efforts to alienate the Cherokees from the British, a turn of events which terrified British officials like Lieutenant Governor Bull. In a letter to the Board of Trade, Bull noted that Lantagnac had a Cherokee wife who aided her husband's efforts by relaying promises of French goods to her people. Just prior to Bull's letter, Lantagnac held a conference at Chota, where he distributed presents and tried to incite the Cherokees to attack Fort Prince George, near Pickens, South Carolina.[127] Though the Lantagnacs of the backcountry menaced British interests until the Great War for Empire, the Treaty of Paris of 1763 ended such threats.

Occasionally, Stuart was able to co-opt foreign Indian agents to act in the British. Writing in January 1764, Stuart noted that he traveled to Pensacola to try to engage the services of the Chevalier de Monberaut, a former commander of Fort Toulouse noted for alienating the Creeks from the British. Feeling slighted by the French government with regard to his career, Monberaut switched sides in the postwar years and agreed to become an agent for John Stuart.[128]

Stuart relied upon deputies like Alexander Cameron and John McDonald to carry his policies into the backcountry. Cameron, like Stuart, was born in Scotland: he immigrated to Darien, Georgia, in either 1736 or 1737 with a group of Highlanders. Cameron enlisted in a South Carolina militia known as the Independent Regulars during that colony's conflict with the Cherokees. After the war, Stuart hired him in 1768 and promoted him to deputy superintendent. Cameron was assigned to work among the Cherokees and took one of their women as a mate. In the course of their relationship, she bore him three mixed-blood children. The Cherokees nicknamed Cameron Scotchie, and though he lacked the refinements of education, he reportedly lived in a grand style at this South Carolina estate, Lochaber.[129]

John McDonald was from Inverness, Scotland. Born there in 1747, he migrated to Charles Town in 1756 and applied for a permit to trade with the Cherokees near Fort Loudoun. In 1769 he met and married Anna Shorey, the mixed-blood daughter of William Shorey and a Cherokee mate. Hired by Stuart, McDonald also was assigned to work among the Cherokees. McDonald, a Loyalist in the American Revolution, remained in North America after the conflict, moving to Chickamauga, near Chattanooga, Tennessee. Because he was always a powerful figure among the Cherokees, the Spanish government hired him as their agent among those Indians in the postwar years.[130]

Stuart's deputies supplied him with disturbing intelligence reports from their outposts deep within the backcountry. In a letter to Stuart, Cameron found many old abuses alive and well despite implementation of the new system. The Cherokee agent was appalled to note the "tearing, cheating & horse stealing, that have been committed among the Indians, by the traders & packhorsemen last winter in this Nation."[131] Cameron further observed that with such abusive treatment of the Indians by the British, it was no wonder the Cherokees were siding with the French. Like his colonial predecessors, Cameron dispatched intelligence reports concerning these activities and of rival traders. He alerted Stuart of the arrival in the Cherokee homelands of a Mr. Ross, a public trader from Virginia. Cameron noted that Virginia had voted to subsidize this trade to the amount of £30,000 for a period of seven years. He believed the Virginians were more concerned with securing Cherokee loyalty than in making a profit.[132]

The profession of Indian trader continued to attract men long past the days when it was a guarantee of easy money. By the 1760s, traders scrambled to survive in a glutted market, often resorting to questionable trade practices among the Indians regardless of the difficulties posed for the Indian Department or the sheer cost in human life. Cameron reported in August of 1766 that the traders had started hiring Indian assistants whom they strove to impress at all costs. He noted that such a trader told all manner of lies to impress his assistants and was "indefatigable in striving up against all other white persons, whom he judges his rivals in trade."[133]

Thus a few unscrupulous traders could predispose the Indians to harm all Euroamericans in their lands in a conflict.

Even after the implementation of the Indian superintendency, the trading profession was a dangerous one. Since Indians could not always distinguish a Virginia trader from a Carolina or Georgia trader, they often retaliated against all Euroamerican men in their homelands when the tribes felt slighted. In May 1766, Ensign George Price reported that a Cherokee plot to murder every trader in their country was prevented only by an attack of Shawnees.[134]

Stuart and his associates came to be fairly skilled in achieving smooth, diplomatic relations between the two cultures. They lacked the political force necessary to eliminate problems like the rogue traders, who could, when necessary, disappear into the backcountry at will. Stuart faced competition from colonial governors who were recalcitrant in giving up their old power. In July 1767, he wrote to Secretary of State for the Southern Department Shelburne, noting that he had requested colonial governors within the Southern District to issue Indian trade licenses only in strict conformity with British policy. The licenses were to be issued only to men who could produce witnesses to guarantee their good character. The traders had to obey the orders of both the governors and the Indian superintendent on penalty of paying a £300 fine. Finally, traders were responsible for the behavior of all assistants and packhorsemen in their employ.[135]

Such attempts to regulate the quality of Indian traders and ensure their just treatment of native peoples continued to fall short of desired goals. In May 1767, a group of South Carolina traders complained to Stuart about the falling prices obtainable for Euroamerican goods, which were due to increased numbers of traders in the backcountry. They noted that unscrupulous traders stooped to base behavior in order to secure the Indian trade despite the consequences. Finally, the Carolina traders decried two current trade practices. First, they complained about the practice of lavish treating, claiming it was conducive to many ills. In reality, the traders were acknowledging the age-old fact that whoever supplied the Indians best held their loyalty. If that provider were supplanted by a more able one, the Indians could be expected to shift their loyalty. Second, the traders complained about the restrictions concerning rum sales in tribal lands. If not supplied in the backcountry, the traders noted that the Indians simply would travel to Euroamerican settlements to purchase rum.[136] During the same month, Alexander Cameron issued a report from the Cherokee town of Toqueh indicating that most traders were not obeying the rules and that liquor was being pumped into the area, causing conflict between Indians and colonials.[137]

In 1768, Stuart received a serious setback to the operation of his department. First, the government ordered the evacuation of all army posts in the southern backcountry. Second, it remanded the control of the Indian trade back to the individual colonies which were free to issue licenses and formulate policies favorable to them without regard for the needs of the colonies as a whole.[138] John Stuart continued on as superintendent but retained only two salaried assistants--one in West Florida and one among the Cherokees. Not all colonial governors were pleased with this return of power. Georgia Governor James Wright wrote to Stuart that he wished that all the power to regulate the trade had been stripped from the governors and given to Stuart.[139]   In the fall of 1768, Stuart wrote to ask Hillsborough to require the colonial governors to force the Indian traders to obey Stuart.[140] He also instructed Alexander Cameron to inform the Cherokees that the British pullout was merely an admission the Cherokees could run their own affairs.[141]

The deregulation of the Indian trade did nothing to solve its chronic problems. On the contrary, the absence of trade officials removed the existing restraints on all forms of trade, legal and illegal. Further, members of various tribes had no one conveniently located with whom they could lodge grievances. In December 1770, Stuart wrote to the Earl of Hillsborough that, while he had hoped the colonies would formulate a comprehensive trade policy, they had failed to do so and every Indian tribe in his district was petitioning for restraint against the traders. Stuart suggested an agent be dispatched to the Chickasaws because of their proximity to the French. In addition to gathering intelligence on the French, the agent could regulate the trade with them. Stuart dispatched John McIntosh, their former deputy before the deregulation of 1768.[142]

Stuart also was alarmed by the apparent disaffection of the smaller tribes of the Mississippi River, who were technically located in British territory but were crossing the river to trade with the Spanish. While Stuart wanted no trouble with the Spanish government, he wanted to end such vacillation and so dispatched Lieutenant John Thomas to Manchac.[143] Here, unregulated local traders were more dangerous than agents of the Spanish government. In October 1771, Thomas arrived at Fort Bute on the Iberville River, where he found relatively small tribes existing as remnants of once larger groups. Though diminished in numbers, they were not lacking in savvy, for they used the relative proximity of the Spanish and British to their own advantage by treating with whoever gave gifts and better trade prices.

Thus, it was not Spanish soldiers who were a threat but Spanish traders. One, Jaime Terrasco, told the Mississippi tribes that British goods were shoddy, that the British practiced incest and that Thomas had been sent there to enslave them.[144] As it turned out, however, his worst enemies were the British traders there. One, John Blommart, forcibly took lands belonging to the Tonica Indians and refused to pay them for it. Worse yet, he supplied their Choctaw enemies with great amounts of rum. On one occasion, drunken Indians stormed Thomas' dwelling at midnight brandishing knives and rum bottles. Indeed, local merchants had grown haughty in the absence of British officials. George Harrison and Thomas Bentley used the fort barracks as storehouses at Thomas' expense. When Thomas detained John Clark for possession of goods belonging to a missing trader, Clark escaped during the night but was recaptured. Houma Indians found the missing trader, lost in the woods for seventeen days, and freed Clark of suspicion of foul play.[145] Conflict between Thomas and the traders reached its zenith in 1772 when Thomas began regulating all trader arrivals and departures from Fort Bute. His greatest problem was John Fitzpatrick, who sold the Indians rum, cheated them in trade and smuggled wine from New Orleans to Manchac.[146] While historians traditionally have underestimated the deleterious effects of abusive traders, Thomas exceeded the limits of good judgment in his attempt to control the traders. He tore down their buildings inside the fort and ordered one man out of his home. In March 1772, a group of such merchants petitioned the governor and council of West Florida for relief and John Stuart temporarily suspended his agent.[147]

In response to Stuart's complaints and misgivings about the deregulation of trade, Hillsborough could only state the obvious. In July 1771, he wrote to Stuart that the lack of proper control over the Indian trade was a wellfounded and long-standing complaint. Though the secretary felt this neglect would have dire consequences, he told Stuart that the governors had convinced George III that they were the best judges of trade policies.[148]

Stuart's conflict with the colonial governors continued. He had tried for some time to bolster his position by requesting true military status, believing it might clarify some of the ambiguities and overlapping jurisdiction problems he encountered with the governors.[149] Hillsborough responded that such a move would create even more difficulties but offered Stuart an extra seat on the councils of all the American colonies.[150] These positions again were subordinate to the governors, thus resulting in no change for Stuart.

Neither Hillsborough nor Stuart had to wait long for the disastrous effects of deregulation of the Indian trade. Without someone to monitor the traders or their credit extension practices, trouble soon arose. In January 1772, Hillsborough responded to a warning by Stuart that certain traders had extended so much credit to the Cherokees that their debts could not be repaid. Instead, the Cherokees offered to cede land adjoining Georgia to them to cancel their debts. The prospect of the transfer alarmed Hillsborough, who drafted instructions to Governor James Wright of Georgia to stop the exchange.[151] Stuart acknowledged that extending large amounts of credit to the southern Indians violated several trade regulations which had gone unheeded without the presence of the Indian agents. Stuart further believed the credit balloon was the result of competition among the traders. Adding to the difficulties was a rival claimant to the land in question--the Creeks.

Stuart notified Hillsborough that the Creeks, long enemies of the Cherokees, also claimed the land to be ceded. Given the enmity between the two tribes, the Creeks would certainly not relinquish their claim to the contested land.[152] Stuart quickly directed Alexander Cameron to publish a warning to the traders in the backcountry not to accept land in exchange for debts. Unfortunately, Cameron was attempting to claim Cherokee land as well.[153]

Occonostotah, a headman among the Cherokees, noted that Cameron had lived among his people for quite some time, treated them justly and told them the truth. Thus, he had become a Beloved Man among them. Occonostotah hoped that Stuart would not recall Cameron anytime soon, for without him, the head man felt that his people would be cheated and abused by the traders. Occonostotah stated that Cameron "kept bad white men in order."[154] The Cherokee leader's references about trade indicate trader abuse was still a problem.

Occonostotah also wanted Cameron to receive the land because of his family ties. Of Cameron's three mixed-blood children, one was a son.

Occonostotah wished for Cameron to "educate the boy like the white people, and cause him to read & write, that he may resemble both red & white men & live amongst us when his father is dead."[155] However sincere Occonostotah's wish for peaceful coexistence was, he obviously wanted to retain someone educated in Euroamerican ways, like the mixed-blood son, to help the Cherokees deal with the traders.[156] Such a transfer set a dangerous precedent in relationships between the two cultures. The year after the offer was made to Cameron, Richard Pearis and Jacob Hite both arranged large cessions of land from the Cherokees. Pearis claimed land by his union with a Cherokee woman and the son produced from it. Hite took possession of his lands by fraudulent documents. Though Stuart prosecuted both men, he could not reverse the situation before they sold large tracts to settlers from the northern colonies.[157] Ultimately, Pearis and Hite were brought before the Circuit Court at Ninety-Six, South Carolina, where they relinquished their title to the land.[158] The land cession to his agent was personally embarrassing to Stuart. He wrote to Cameron in December 1770 "the present of land to your son has occasioned much censure to fall upon me it being every where resented as an unrestrained transaction of mine."[159] Stuart told Occonostotah that, as superintendent, he could not interfere in Indian affairs but British subjects could not accept direct transfers of Indian land bypassing the government.[160]

While Cameron may have embarrassed Stuart, the free traders in the backcountry were engaging in unrestrained transactions of their own. Members of this new generation of Indian traders were bold and unabashed in their determination to prosper. In November 1771, the powerful Gentlemen of Augusta, otherwise known as Brown, Rea and Company, got involved in the matter. George Galphin, Robert McKay, James Jackson and Andrew McClean wrote to warn Stuart that the overabundance of Indian traders in the 1760s had ruined the market, and unless it improved, traders would quit the backcountry, leaving the Indians undersupplied. Since trade goods bound the tribes to British policy, diplomatic ties would then break down. After indicating their leverage, they stated their wishes. They noted that the contested land was too close to Euroamerican settlements to be of any use to either Cherokees or Creeks. The traders wanted the government to accept the cession and sell it to a growing number of Virginians who had migrated south in search of fresh farmlands, as their own had been drained by tobacco production.[161]

Independent traders continued to pressure Stuart. In October 1772, John Jamieson, George Baillie and Thomas Netherclift petitioned John Stuart as representatives of the traders in Creek and Cherokee lands. They stated that should the conflicting Creek claim to Cherokee lands halt that intended cession, the traders petitioning Stuart would lose large sums of money. In order to prevent that, they wanted Stuart to use his influence over the Creeks to effect an easy transfer of the land. If Stuart needed presents to achieve that goal, the petitioners were prepared to supply them as well.[162]

The free traders did not confine their activities to writing to Stuart. Stuart notified Hillsborough that David Taitt, his other agent, wrote from the Creeks that traders in both Georgia and South Carolina had been "indefatigable in disposing the minds of the Creeks to acquiesce in the grant of land [from] the Cherokees to their traders."[163] Since trade issues were inexorably bound to diplomatic ones with the southern Indians, unregulated traders were able to escalate Indian debts into diplomatic crises if those traders felt their livelihoods threatened. The Indians often sided with the traders, for it was they who lived among them day to day. Stuart noted that the traders insulted Taitt at a meeting of Upper Creeks to discuss a land cession on the Scambia River. The traders believed Taitt was there to oppose that land cession and so insulted him in front of the Creek headmen, thus lowering Taitt's authority in the Indians' eyes. Stuart noted his own influence over the Indians was weakened by that of such men.[164]

Stuart's power to carry out the duties of his office effectively occasionally was circumvented by internal factors as well as external ones. When the Earl of Dartmouth replaced Hillsborough as Secretary of State for the American Colonies in 1772, Stuart found an opponent to his policies in London. Late in 1772, Governor James Wright of Georgia sent Dartmouth a proposal to exchange more Cherokee lands for Indian trade debts. Though Stuart had warned the secretary against such a move, Dartmouth planned to endorse it.[165] Trader abuses in America meanwhile worsened; offenders progressed from isolated to multiple offenses. Alexander Cameron noted that the month before his court appearance at Ninety-Six for land fraud, Richard Pearis was reported to be selling rum to the Indians for horses.[166]

With the American Revolution, Stuart's job changed quite dramatically. Before the war, the superintendent was in charge of enforcing trade regulations, handling disputes between the two cultures and promoting peaceful relations between the southern tribes and Euroamerican civilization. It should be noted, however, that an intertribal peace was not necessarily part of that goal. From 1765 until 1775, the Creeks and Choctaws were at war. In 1768, hostilities escalated as the Chickasaws joined the Choctaws. By 1770, both of the original belligerents were ready to make peace when a group of Lower Creeks murdered four Choctaws. Before the two sides could once again resume negotiations, Hillsborough became fearful that they would attack West Florida if at peace with each other. He then ordered Stuart to cease all efforts at peacemaking.[167]

After the war began, the superintendent was expected to extinguish tribal conflicts and mobilize the Indians against the colonials, a difficult task after pursuing contrary goals for so long. As negotiations between the colonial officials and the British government deteriorated, colonials began to spread rumors that Stuart was enlisting the help of both the Cherokees and the Catawbas against the colony of South Carolina.[168]

The backcountry had been a training ground for many would-be Indian traders. Given the glut in numbers of traders by petitioners over the years, it is not surprising that many sided with Patriot forces. Like Loyalist Indian traders, they had lived and worked in the backcountry all their lives; when the war came, they utilized their expertise with Native Americans in behalf of their cause, just as the Loyalist Indian traders did. Such conditions posed yet another threat for Stuart. In December 1775, Stuart notified Dartmouth that the Continental Congress had named three former traders to act as superintendents for the Patriot cause in the

Southern District. George Galphin, Edward Wilkinson and John Rea, members of the powerful Brown, Rea and Company had traded in the backcountry for years and were traveling to meet counterparts named as northern Patriot agents.[169]

The Carolinians accused Stuart of manipulating Indians against the colonials in the summer of 1775. In truth, Stuart was not ordered to do so until September of that year by General Thomas Gage, Commander-in-Chief of British forces in America.[170] In December, Stuart passed those orders along to Alexander Cameron. Stuart wrote that he had been ordered to use the various backcountry tribes to distress those colonies in rebellion, but he did not interpret this order as authorization to attack backcountry residents indiscriminately. Rather, the Native American were to be employed in assisting Loyalist forces in direct attacks on Patriots. Stuart went further, saying that over the years Cameron has assured Stuart of his ability to motivate and influence the Cherokee peoples; now the superintendent expected him to mobilize their warriors and have them ready to join either Loyalist forces or other British-aligned tribes. Cameron was to contact the Cherokee headmen, like Attakullakulla, Oustenaka, Kittagusta, the Terrapin and the Great Raven, with this information immediately. Finally, Cameron was given explicit instructions to counter the actions of Galphin, Wilkinson and Rea, the rival Indian agents, at all costs and to apprehend them if possible.[171]

Stuart's apprehension at the threat posed by rogue Indian agents was well founded. Like all who trafficked in the backcountry trade, they knew what best motivated the Indians--the threat of cessation of trade. In fact, in September 1775, George Galphin addressed the Creeks, telling them that the Patriots were fighting the Loyalists because the "Great King" wanted to withdraw the trade from the Indians. Further, Galphin told them that their friend Stuart was old and sick, implying they could not count on him much longer.[172] Stuart felt compelled to employ his own propaganda to offset the Patriot agents.

Through David Taitt, Stuart informed the Creeks that there was indeed a dispute between the Euroamericans in their lands, but that it did not concern their people. Taitt told them that Stuart promised to keep the trade open, but in return, he expected them to remain loyal to the king and to ignore talks given by the Patriot agents.[173] In early September 1775, those agents tried again. Members of the Georgia Council of Safety told the Lower Creeks that the war erupted because the "Great King" demanded more money from the colonists than they could pay and had sent soldiers to collect it.[174] Such a tactic may have tried to strike a sympathetic chord among the Creeks by making Patriot problems analogous to Indian credit problems and forced land cessions. Loyalist agents were not unadept at striking responsive notes among the Indians as well. Alexander Cameron told the Cherokees that had it not been for the British government, the colonial inhabitants would have stripped the Indians completely of their land. The Carolina Patriot, Henry Laurens felt that Cameron could not have selected a more destructive charge against the Patriots and so ordered Edward Wilkinson to do all in his power to counter Cameron's efforts. The intelligence report was provided to Laurens by Richard Pearis,[175] the trader who illegally tried to take Cherokee lands and who also trafficked in rum in their homelands.

In March of 1776, Stuart notified Major General Henry Clinton of the status of Indian affairs in the backcountry. He wrote that the race to control the Indians tribes was a swift one. Patriot Indian agents were just as familiar to the Indians as were his own and were often better supplied with funds with which to treat them. Bitterness crept from between the lines of the letter as Stuart blamed the success of the Patriot agents on the lack of power given his office in the years preceding the war. Speaking of George Galphin, Stuart noted that he had amassed a sizable fortune from trading with the Lower Creeks for many years. Galphin's familiarity with them alone would not have been such a threat in the 1770s had,"he not been employed by Sir James Wright and Lieutenant Governor Bull to interfere in Indian affairs, and to carry whatever point they had in view."[176] Stuart stated that Robert Rea, an Augusta trader licensed by Sir James Wright, was being employed by the Continental Congress to distribute ammunition among the Creeks. Finally, he noted that Edward Wilkinson, a trader of long standing among the Cherokees, had been an employee of Lieutenant Governor Bull.[177] Colonial governors had stubbornly used traders as independent agents for years, now many of them were Patriot agents who employed their expertise against Great Britain.

In January 1777, Stuart, in a letter to George Germain, noted the effects of both competing Indian agents and the war on the backcountry tribes. He observed that the Creeks and the Cherokees were prevented from hunting by rebel incursions into their homelands. Both were unable to pay old debts or purchase new items and had become entirely dependent on the government dole. Stuart's expenses increased as he hired more agents to oppose Patriot agents.[178]

Patriot Indian agents pulled no punches in their attempts to use the Indians against the Loyalists. Lachlan McIntosh told the Creeks that the colonials and Indians should be brothers, especially in the conflict with the British, whom he referred to as the "people over the water." He also said that these people wanted to make slaves out of both the Indians and the colonials. "They pay John Stuart, Governor Tonyn and other bad me to tell you lyes [sic] and cheat you," McIntosh stated, "as they paid our old Governor to cheat us."[179] He told the Creeks that the Cherokees near Virginia had believed Stuart and had warred against the Patriots; now they had been driven from their homes and lost their crops. The British were too far removed to be of help to the Indians and the Patriots were winning the initial conflicts in the colonies.[180] McIntosh tried to sway them by focusing on Patriot success.

Both sides competing for Indian loyalty experienced measures of success. In a letter to George Germain, Stuart noted that despite the efforts of George Galphin in the backcountry, the Loyalists had persuaded a group of Cowetas to harass Patriots on the Georgia frontier, attacking a fort there and driving off a herd of horses. A group of Cherokees as well had gone out to attack the Virginia frontier but had returned home in want of supplies.[181] In September 1777 Alexander McGillivray wrote to Stuart that he had intercepted a group of 120 Creek warriors on their way to the ceremonial spot of Hickory Ground determined to kill Taitt, Cameron and their interpreter, William Dixon Moniac. McGillivray entreated them to abandon their mission and return home, and they did begrudgingly, telling the mixed-blood leader that he had spoiled their fun and cost them an opportunity to obtain needed clothing. Ultimately, the Loyalist McGillivray was unable to sway all of the Creeks; a group of Tallapoosa Indians attacked Cameron and Taitt's outposts but failed to kill them.[182]

The war and concerns of the Indian Department ceased to concern John Stuart on 21 March 1779, when he died. The West Florida governor, Peter Chester, appointed a five man commission to fill Stuart's position temporarily after his death. In the summer of 1779, Germain appointed Alexander Cameron and Lieutenant Colonel Thomas Brown, a Loyalist from Augusta, Georgia, as dual superintendents for West and East Florida, respectively.[183] In September 1780, Cameron wrote to Germain speaking about age-old lessons learned in the Indian trade. He was aware of the great financial burden incurred by the government over the years because of increasing costs of the Indian Department, yet he knew his meetings would have little meaning unless backed by presents. In fact, he termed the task of maintaining their affection as insurmountable without gifts. Cameron noted that the Southeastern Indians had grown to expect abundant presents, "even when their services were not immediately called for, and they now consider as their due what they formerly received as great favors."[184] From East Florida, Thomas Brown reported that the Creeks also had become totally dependent on the British for their livelihood.[185]

By 1779, the creation of two superintendents stationed in the Floridas was quite logical for several reasons. First, there was no one successor capable of filling Stuart's shoes. Second, fleeing Loyalists flooded into East and West Florida, creating the potential for conflict with its more numerous indigenous population. Thus Indian officials were placed there to head off trouble. While Loyalist forces held cities like Savannah and would take Charles Town in 1780, Patriot forces were strong in the backcountry. Ultimately, the southern Indians were unable to secure a Loyalist victory in the South. They were expected to fight according to customs of Euroamerican society, ignoring the seasons and rhythms of their own lives. Naturally they were unable to meet these obligations and often were judged as failures by both Patriots and Loyalists, especially given the expense of supplying them with gifts and trade goods. For example, during the fall and early winter of 1780, the Creeks departed on their customary hunting trips in order to procure deer skins to pay for trade items. In November, General John Campbell told Alexander McGillivray to rally Creek warriors against an expected Spanish invasion of Florida. The warriors had gone hunting, however. McGillivray took to the woods to gather them when Campbell notified him that the Spanish invasion fleet had been destroyed. Then in January 1781, Campbell sent another urgent call for help.[186] Abandoning the winter hunt would have been quite an alien notion to the Creeks and would have increased their indebtedness to the British government as well. Thus, the British would have been displeased either way.

Many of the southern tribes sided with Loyalist forces. Stuart and agents like Alexander Cameron had much to do with that decision, as did the fact that the Loyalists were able to supply the Indians better than the Patriots. With the end of the war, the British Indian agents were given the unenviable task of effecting a withdrawal from the backcountry without arousing the ire of the southern Indians. In June 1783, Thomas Brown wrote to Thomas Townshend that he had received his orders to withdraw; he feared for the safety of the traders, agents and interpreters in the government's employ should groups like the Creeks learn they would be abandoned to the colonials. Brown further noted that a Creek headman had been dispatched to meet with him. The headman stated that the Creeks were determined to follow their British friends. They requested that the British government send ships for them so that they might be relocated close to the British people, with whom they might continue to trade as they did not wish to be sacrificed to the revenge of victorious colonials.[187] In a war in which representatives of both sides were well known to the Indians and often indistinguishable to them, the Indians of North America were perhaps the major losers.

A highly effective method to regulate the behavior of traders among the tribes of the backcountry was never found. These frontier merchants were, in many ways, the only diplomats Native Americans ever knew. When such business men were honest and truthful, they did much to further the relationship between the two cultures. More times than not, they were ruthless adventurers willing to breach either culture's rules in order to make a profit. By the end of the Revolutionary War, most southern tribes were hopelessly dependent on trade items at the expense of traditional ways. They also had to share occupancy of North America with the victors of that revolution, people who now viewed them contemptuously for their choice of allies in the late war.

NOTES

1. Philip M. Brown, "Early Indian Trade in the Development of South Carolina: Politics, Economics, and Social Mobility During the Proprietary Period, 1670-1719," *The South Carolina Historical Magazine,* 76 (1975): 118.

2. W.O. Moore, Jr., "The Largest Exporters of Deerskins from Charles Town, 1735-1775," *The South Carolina Historical Magazine,* 74 (1973): 144-145. Moore noted that the deer skin trade only began to slacken when supplanted by indigo production in the 1740s.

3. Mary U. Rothrock, "Carolina Traders Among the Overhill Cherokees, 1690-1760," *East Tennessee Historical Society's Publications,* 1 (1929): 4.

4. William Byrd, *The London Diary(1717-1721) and Other Writings,* Louis B.Wright and Marion Tinling, eds. (New York: Oxford University Press, 1958), 237.

5. Rothrock, "Carolina Traders," 10. At the time of heaviest contact between the English and the Cherokees, the latter were typically living in modern western South Carolina, western North Carolina, eastern Tennessee, northern Alabama and northern Georgia.

6. Ibid., 5.

7. James L. Axtell, *The European and the Indian: Essays in the Ethnohistory of Colonial North America* (New York: Oxford University Press, 1981), 250.

8. Ibid., 253.

9. Rothrock, "Carolina Traders," 7-8. License records reveal such family names as Campbell, Dougherty, Gillespie, McGillivray, McKinney, McIntosh, MacDonald, McCormick, Millikin and McBain. See Verner W. Crane, *The Southern Frontier: 1670-1732* (Ann Arbor: University of Michigan Press, 1964), 125.

10. Indian Book 1: 89. Hereafter referred to as Indian Book 1 (out of 3). Vermilion or red paint was a popular trade item, often used by tribes in body adornment. Unfortunately for native peoples, it often had a lead base, further contributing to health problems incurred from trade contact with Euroamerican colonists.

11. William Byrd, *The Prose Works of William Byrd of Westover: Narratives of a Colonial Virginian,* Louis B. Wright, ed. (Cambridge: Belknap Press, 1966) , 308.

12. Rothrock, "Carolina Traders," 13.

13. Ibid., 16.

14. Ibid., 15-16.

15. Ibid., 16.

16. Ibid., 9.

17. Ibid., 10.

18. Axtell, *The European and the Indian,* 255.

19. Ludovic Grant to Governor Glen, 3 May 1752, Indian Book 1: 263.

20. Adair, *The History of the American Indians,* 2.

21. Romans, *A Concise Natural History,* 40-41.

22. Ibid.

23. Brown," Early Indian Trade," 119.

24. Crane, *The Southern Frontier,* 108-109.

25. Wilbur R. Jacobs, "Unsavory Sidelights on the Colonial Fur Trade," *Indians and Europeans: Selected Articles on Indian White Relations in Colonial North America,* Peter Charles Hoffer, ed. (New York: Garland Publishing, 1988), 135.

26. Ibid.

27. Memorial of Robert Bunning and Others, 22 November 1751, Indian Book 2: 150.

28. Jacobs, "Unsavory Sidelights," 136.

29. Rothrock, "Carolina Traders," 10.

30. Crane, *The Southern Frontier*, 115.

31. Gary B. Nash notes that Carolina merchants made alliances with coastal Indian tribes and convinced them to hunt other tribes for slaves in exchange for European goods. Once brought to Charles Town, Nash notes the enslaved Indians began a "middle passage" of sorts, ultimately bound for the West Indies, New York and New England. See Nash, *Red, White and Black,* 132-133.

32. Rothrock, "Carolina Traders," 6. Both South Carolina and Virginia were pioneers in the field of Anglo-Indian trade management. In 1714, Virginia investors organized the Virginia Indian Company, a private monopoly whose board of directors fixed trade rates and hired appropriate personnel. See James H. Merrell, *The Indians' New World: Catawbas and Their Neighbors from European Contact through the Era of Removal* (Chapel Hill: University of North Carolina Press, 1989), 80-81.

33. Board of Commissioners Meeting, 2 August 1711, Indian Book 1: 13.

34. Board of Commissioners Meeting, 15 August 1711, ibid., 17. Tomatly was located at the modern site of Tomatola in Cherokee County, North Carolina.

35. Theda Perdue, *Slavery and the Evolution of Cherokee Society 1540-1866,* (Knoxville: The University of Tennessee Press, 1979), 4. The Cherokees called their bondsmen *atsi nahas'i* which means "one who is owned."

36. Ibid., 11-12. Euroamerican slavery existed to increase the wealth of slaveowners. Simply purchasing the slave enhanced the financial worth of the buyer, who naturally assumed that slave would add to the owner's productivity. The Cherokees, like other tribes before heavy dependence upon trade, did not keep slaves for wealth. Cherokee society prevented large accumulations of goods through ritual sharing with unfortunates and through

dispersal at the annual Green Corn Ceremony. At death, a person's material possessions were destroyed, not passed to beneficiaries. Cultural norms among southeastern tribes like the Cherokee prevented the use of slaves in the same manner as the Euroamericans with whom they traded. See Perdue, *Slavery,* 12-13.

37. Ibid., 17-18.

38. Ibid., 19.

39. Ibid., 23.

40. Ibid., 25.

41. Board of Commissioners Meeting, 13 September 1711, ibid., 18.

42. Jacobs, "Unsavory Sidelights," 138.

43. Rothrock, "Carolina Traders," 13.

44. Ibid., 109-110.

45.   Peter H. Wolf, "Vasomotor Sensitivity to Alcohol in Diverse Mongoloid Populations," *American Journal of Human Genetics,* 25 (1973): 193-199.

46. Board of Commissioners Meeting, 19 August 1713, Indian Book 1: 49-50.

47. Indian Book 1: viii-ix.

48. Crane, *The Southern Frontier,* 150.

49. Brown, "Early Indian Trade," 121.

50. Board of Commissioners Meeting, 21 March 1711/1712, ibid., 20.

51.   Alexander Moore. ed.. *Nairne's Muskhogean Journals: The 1708 Expedition to the Mississippi River* (Jackson: University Press of Mississippi, 1988), 7-9.

52. Ibid., 13.

53. Indian Book 1: viii-ix.

54. Board of Commissioners Meeting, 31 August 1714, ibid., 59.

55. Board of Commissioners Meeting, 17 April 1712, ibid., 23.

56. Board of Commissioners Meeting, 17 May 1712, ibid., 25.

57. Rothrock, "Carolina Traders," 14.

58. Board of Commissioners Meeting, 12 April 1715, ibid., 65.

59. Axtell, *The European and the Indian,* 260-61, *Nash, Red, White and Black,* 241.

60. Ibid., 262.

61. Nash, *Red, White and Black,* 242.

62. Board of Commissioners Meeting, 24 November 1714, ibid., 63.

63.   Moore, *Nairne's Muskhogean Journals,* 20. For more on Florida Indians, see Jerald T. Milanich, *Florida Indians and the Invasion from Europe* (Gainesville: University Press of Florida, 1995).

64.   Rothrock, "Carolina Traders," 6-7. Economic motives undoubtedly influenced the regulatory effort. The trade in white-tailed deer skins fell after the war to approximately 18,000 skins annually or one third the prewar levels from 1715 to 1720. See Brown, *"The Indian Trade,"* 122.

65.   Crane, *The Southern Frontier,* 193-194. The new system used five Indian commissioners; some of the first men to serve in this capacity were Colonel George Logan, Ralph Izard, Major John Fenwick, George Chicken, Jonathan Drake and Francis Yonge. Individual salaries were £150 per year.

66. Board of Commissioners Meeting, 24 July 1716, Indian Book 1: 85-86.

67. Rothrock, "Carolina Traders," 11-12.

68. Board of Commissioners Meeting, 24 July 1716, Indian Book 1: 85-87.

69. Board of Commissioners Meeting, 10 July 1716, ibid., 74.

70. Board of Commissioners Meeting, 24 July 1716, ibid., 83.

71. Board of Commissioners Meeting, 31 July 1716, ibid., 94.

72. Board of Commissioners Meeting, 14 July 1716, ibid., 79.

73. Board of Commissioners Meeting, 24 July 1716, ibid., 88.

74. Williams, *Early Travels,* 123, ftn. 5.

75. Ibid., 123, ftn.6. For modern counterparts to historic Cherokee towns, see Gary C. Goodwin, *Cherokees In Transition: A Study of Changing Culture and Environment Prior to 1775* (Chicago: The University of Chicago, Department of Geography Research Paper No. 181, 1977), 155.

76. Rothrock, "Carolina Traders," 6. The Cherokees called Wiggan "Old Rabbit."

77. Board of Commissioners Meeting, 24 July 1716, Indian Book 1: 88-89.

78. Board of Commissioners Meeting, 1 October 1716, ibid., 114.

79. Board of Commissioners Meeting, 30 January 1716/1717, ibid., 155.

80. Board of Commissioners Meeting, 24 July 1716, ibid., 89.

81. Board of Commissioners Meeting, 1 November 1716, ibid., 120.

82. Board of Commissioners Meeting, 7 November 1716, ibid., 123.

83. Board of Commissioners Meeting, 29 November 1716, ibid., 134.

84. Board of Commissioners Meeting, 1 May 1717, ibid., 176.

85. Board of Commissioners Meeting, 9 May 1717, ibid., 177-178.

86. Board of Commissioners Meeting, 20 September 1717, ibid., 211-212.

87. Board of Commissioners Meeting, 23 April 1718, ibid., 269.

88. Board of Commissioners Meeting, 8 May 1718, ibid., 272.

89. Thompson, *William Weatherford,* 9.

90. Board of Commissioners Meeting, 9 May 1718, Indian Book 1: 273.

91. Board of Commissioners Meeting, 14 June 1718, ibid., 291.

92. George Galphin to William Pinckney, 18 October 1749, Indian Book 2: 4-5.

93. Fritz Hamer, J. Walter Joseph and James D. Scurry, *Initial Archeological Investigations At Silver Bluff Plantation Aiken County, South Carolina,* Research Manuscript Series 168 (Columbia: Institute of Archeology and Anthropology, University of South Carolina, 1980), 15. Galphin married Catherine Saunderson in 1736, prior to coming to Britain's North American colonies.

94. Kathryn Holland, "The Path Between the Wars: Creek Relations with the British Colonies, 1763-1774" (M.A. Thesis, Auburn University, 1980), 4. Galphin was not the first Euroamerican to cohabit with an Indian mate. Such occurrences were common whether the trader was married within his own culture or not.

95. Ibid., 16.

96. Cashin, *Lachlan McGillivray,* 34.

97. Ibid., 48.

98. E.R.R. Green, "Queensborough Townships: Scotch-Irish Emigration and the Expansion of Georgia, 1763-1776," *William and Mary Quarterly,* 17 (1960): 183.

99. Ibid., 184-185.

100. Ibid., 186.

101. Ibid., 190.

102. Ibid., 197-198.

103. Affidavit of David Dowey, 25 May 1771, Indian Book 2: 57-58.

104. Crane, *The Southern Frontier,* 198-199. The South Carolina Indian management system continued to change. In 1723, the authority of the Indian commissioners was transferred to the governor and three members of his council. In 1724, another legislative change remanded the trade over to both houses of the South Carolina legislature with only one Indian commissioner serving. In general, this version of the Carolina Public Indian

trade functioned until the British government imposed supracolonial control over Anglo-Indian relations in 1756. See Crane, *The Southern Frontier*, 200-201.

105. Governor Glen to the Board of Trade, 23 December 1749, CO5/372: 168.

106. Affidavit of James Maxwell, 12 June 1751, Indian Book 2: 68-69.

107. Cornelius Doughtery to Governor Glen, 31 July 1751, ibid., 115.

108. Memorial of Robert Bunning and Others, 22 November 1751, ibid., 148-150.

109. Alden, "The Albany Congress," 193-195.

110. Ibid., 196-200.

111. Ibid.

112. Rough Sketch of a Plan for the Management of Indians and the Conducting of the Necessary Commerce with Them, n.d., CO5/377: 273.

113. Ibid.

114. Alden, "The Albany Congress," 200-201.

115. Ibid., 208. See John Richard Alden's *John Stuart and the Southern Colonial Frontier* (Ann Arbor: University of Michigan Press, 1944) for the complete story of the famous Indian superintendent.

116. Clarence E. Carter, "Observations of Superintendent John Stuart and Governor James Grant of East Florida on the Proposed Plan of 1761 for the Future Management of Indian Affairs," *American Historical Review* 20 (October 1914-July 1915): 815-816.

117. Ibid., 817-818.

118. Ibid., 820.

119. Ibid., 820-821.

120. Governor Boone to Board of Trade, 7 April 1764, CO5/377: 334. Boone's use of the term *insinuate* in the original letter implies that his agents were willing to intermarry with Indian women to gain the confidence of the various tribes.

121. Ibid.

122. Ibid.

123. Crane, *The Southern Frontier*, 203.

124. Alden, *John Stuart*, 181-183.

125. Robert L. Gold, *Borderland Empires in Transition: The Triple Nation Transfer of Florida* (Carbondale: Southern Illinois University Press, 1969), 173.

126. Petition of Lantagnac to Kerlerec, 1 October 1755, *Mississippi Provincial Archives: French Dominion, 1749-1763,* Vol.V,, Patricia Galloway, Dunbar Rowland, and A.G. Sanders, eds. and trans. (Baton Rouge: Louisiana State University Press, 1984), 161-165.

127. Lieutenant Governor Bull to Board of Trade, 18 November 1760, CO5/7: 264.

128. John Stuart to John Pownall, 24 January 1764, CO5/66: 342.

129. William L. Anderson, "Traders and Invaders, Assimilators and Destroyers: The Scots and Irish Among the Cherokee," Robert J. Holden, ed. (Vincennes, Indiana: *Selected Papers from the Seventh and Eighth George Rogers Clark Trans-Appalachian Frontier History Conferences,* 1991): 6.

130. Ibid., 6-7.

131. Alexander Cameron to John Stuart, 1 June 1766, CO5/66: 406.

132. Ibid.

133. Alexander Cameron to the Secretary of State of Indian Affairs, 27 August 1766, CO5/67: 218.

134. Ensign George Price to Secretary of State of Indian Affairs, 7 May 1766, CO5/66: 410. The Cherokees called the Shawnee "Norward Indians."

135. John Stuart to the Earl of Shelburne, 28 July 1767, CO5/68: 136.

136. South Carolina Traders to John Stuart, 21 May 1767, CO5/68: 140.

137. Alexander Cameron to John Stuart, 20 May 1768, CO5/69: 266.

138. John Stuart to the Earl of Hillsborough, 15 September 1768, CO5/69: 258.

139. Holland, "The Path Between The Wars," 113.

140. Stuart to Hillsborough, 15 September 1768, CO5/69: 298.

141. Stuart to Hillsborough, 1 August 1768, CO5/69: n.f.

142. Stuart to Hillsborough, 2 December 1770, CO5/72: 81.

143. Robert R. Rea, "Redcoats and Redskins on the Lower Mississippi, 1763-1776: The Career of Lt. John Thomas," *Louisiana History* 11 (Winter 1970): 11-12.

144. Ibid., 14.

145. Ibid., 21-22.

146. Ibid., 23-24.

147. Ibid., 23-25.

148. Hillsborough to Stuart, 3 July 1771, CO5/72: 240.

149. Stuart to Hillsborough, 3 January 1769, CO5/70: n.f.

150. Hillsborough to Stuart, 24 March 1769, CO5/70: 177.

151. Hillsborough to Stuart, 11 January 1772, CO5/73: 1.

152. Stuart to Hillsborough, 9 February 1772, CO5/73: 95.

153. Ibid.

154. Minutes of Congress at Hard Labour Creek, 15 October 1768, CO5/74: 39.

155. Ibid.

156. Ibid.

157. John Stuart to the Earl of Dartmouth, 8 January 1773, CO5/74: 35. The Cherokees planned to cede Cameron, Pearis and Hite some 600,000-700,000 acres.

158. Stuart to Dartmouth, 12 December 1773, CO5/75: 6.

159. Stuart to Cameron, 11 December 1770, CO5/73: 107.

160. Minutes of Congress at Hard Labour Creek, 15 October 1768, CO5/74: 39.

161. George Galphin, Robert McKay, James Jackson and Andrew McLean to Stuart, 13 November 1771, CO5/73: 99.

162. John Jamieson, George Baillie and Thomas Netherclift to Stuart, 30 October 1772, CO5/73: 97.

163. Stuart to Hillsborough, 13 June 1772, CO5/73: 156.

164. Ibid.

165. Dartmouth to Stuart, 9 December 1772, CO5/73: 454.

166. Cameron to Stuart, 11 October 1773, CO5/75: 9.

167. Alden, *John Stuart*, 314-31.5

168. Clyde R. Ferguson, "Functions of the Partisan-Militia in the South During the American Revolution," *The Revolutionary War in the South: Power, Conflict, and Leadership*, W. Robert Higgins, ed. (Durham, North Carolina: Duke University Press, 1979), 247.

169. Stuart to Dartmouth, 17 December 1775, CO5/77:22.

170. Thomas Gage to Stuart, 12 September 1775, CO5/76:187.

171. Stuart to Cameron, 16 December 1775, CO5/77:22.

172. Stuart to Dartmouth, 17 September 1775, CO5/76:172.

173. David Taitt to the Cowetas, Tallapoosas, Abechkas and Alibamous, 17 August 1775, CO5/76: n.f.

174. Helen Hornbeck Tanner, "Pipesmoke and Muskets: Florida Indian Intrigues of the Revolutionary Era." *Eighteenth Century Florida and Its Borderlands*, Samuel Proctor, ed. (Gainesville: The University Presses of Florida, 1975), 20.

175. Henry Laurens to Edward Wilkinson, 29 October 1775, CO5/77:79.

176. Stuart to Major General Henry Clinton, 15 March 1776, CO5/77: 105.

177. Ibid.

178. Stuart to George Germain, 24 January 1777, CO5/78: 83.

179. Talk from General Lachlan McIntosh to the Creeks, 23 December 1776, CO5/78:109.

180. Ibid.

181. Stuart to Germain, 22 August 1777, CO5/78: 186.

182. Alexander McGillivray to Stuart, 21 September 1777, CO5/79: 33.

183. Germain to Cameron and Thomas Brown, 25 June 1779, CO5/80: 123.

184. Cameron to George Germain, 20 September 1780, CO5/82: 88.

185. Brown to Henry Clinton, 28 December 1781, CO5/82: 283.

186. Michael D. Green, "The Creek Confederacy in the American Revolution: Cautious Participants," *Anglo-Spanish Confrontation on the Gulf-Coast During the American Revolution*, William S. Coker and Robert Rea, eds. (Pensacola: Gulf Coast History and Humanities Conference, 1982): 70.

187. Brown to Thomas Townshend, 1 June 1783, CO5/82: 367.

6

The Price of Wonder:
The High Cost of Trade

Several effects of the Indian trade on the Indians of the southern, colonial backcountry are undeniable. The trade and its attendant merchants forever changed the cycles and rhythms of traditional Indian life. Survival huntng became commercial hunting, whose profits went towards the ever-increasing debt owed the Indian trader. Native skills languished, superseded by the wrought marvels of western technology. Native peoples became culturally dependent appendages to what had once been only minority groups on their coastlines. Worse yet, they often became chemically dependent upon the liquor that was imported into their homelands despite attempts to limit it by both sides. While these facts are unchallengeable, the Indian trade was not an obedient servant to Euroamerican society : trade was a two-way street. The threat of its removal was one of the most powerful weapons Euroamerican society had to control native peoples. If the British colonials had been the sole participants in the subjugation of North America and ever had true control over their Indian trade, it would have proved an ultimate weapon indeed. Yet, rival traders, colonies and colonizing powers created competition for Indian loyalties, often allowing the Indians the leverage they needed to dictate their own trade terms. Great Britain and its North American colonies often acceded to Indian demands because of the fear they might realign with the Spanish or the French. Though the Indians were addicted to the trade, the British government was forced to supply it; the struggle for North America made the Indian trade a commodity too costly to keep and too dangerous to let go.

Native American peoples in North America had no history of mass efforts to oppose a common foe. That is one reason that no unified Indian confederation ever stopped the European advance across North America. Yet, native peoples were highly aware of their neighbors and quick to discover favoritism when practiced by Euroamericans. In 1716, the South Carolina Board of Indian Commissioners notified the colony governor that a present of 150 guns was being made to the Lower Cherokee peoples. The Upper Cherokees had been promised the same amount and the board requested that the governor honor the pledge lest the Upper Cherokees feel slighted.[1] In 1717, Charlesworth Glover, the South Carolina public trader to the Savano Indians, notified the South Carolina Board of Commissioners that the Savanos were complaining about the cost of their trade items. He noted that their prices varied, even though slightly, from those charged other tribes. The board authorized Glover to initiate price rollbacks to keep the Savanos aligned with the colony.[2] Part of the conciliatory nature of colonial government stemmed from the need to pacify a potential enemy whose forces outnumbered colonials confined to the coast. The other need was to maintain the wealth the Indian trade was generating for the individual British colonies. In the 1700s intercolonial rivalry made that job more difficult.

In May 1717, the board notified Meredith Hughes, public trader to the Wineaus, to expect a new problem in the Indian trade. They noted the arrival of Virginia traders into the backcountry and warned Hughes these rivals would stop at nothing to alienate the Indians from the Carolinians.[3] A 1717 letter from the board to Eleazar Wiggan, a public trader among the Catawbas, confirmed the intentions of the Virginians. Wiggan had written to the board of the reaction of the Catawbas to efforts by the Virginia traders to sway them from the Carolina traders. Wiggan had told the board that it seemed that the Virginians were determined to undersell the Carolinians, and the board requested a description of their goods and the prices obtained for them. Facing a potential price war and diminished profits for the traders and the colony, the board ordered Wiggan to use all means at his disposal to maintain contact and trade with the Catawbas, even if it meant lowering prices considerably.[4]

The next month, Wiggan reported a curious fact in the relationship with the Catawbas. In the past, Indian men had been used to carry trade goods into the backcountry and skins out of it. In October 1717, Wiggan reported that the Catawbas refused to act as burdeners anymore.[5] In May 1718, he explained that the Catawbas felt the Carolina traders did not supply them with enough trade items; Carolinians also expected the Indians to carry the merchandise into native homelands. Conversely, the Catawbas praised the Virginians for the great quantity of merchandise they brought, using packhorses to transport their goods, not people.[6] Not surprisingly, the Indians were using the Virginians to ameliorate a trade condition with the Carolinians they they did not like. As noted previously, the board responded by authorizing Wiggan to make a present to the Catawba king and his sister. The board also hired a packhorseman to eliminate the need for Indian labor.[7]

The Virginians moved quickly into the backcountry of Carolina. A letter from the board to William Hatton, public trader to the Cherokees, noted that they were expected soon among the Cherokees in November 1717.[8] By April 1718, they were among the Cherraws as well.[9] South Carolina hoped its assembly would pass measures preventing the encroachment of the Virginia traders. In July 1718, the board lowered the prices at William Hatton's factory among the Cherokees because they had deserted the Carolina trader for the Virginians who supplied them more cheaply. Thus, South Carolina was forced to forgo a part of its profit in the struggle to compete with the prices offered the Indians by another colony.[10] Intercolonial competition had created a price war among the traders in the Cherokee homelands, resulting in lower prices for members of that tribe at the cost of Carolina's profit. Virginia traders had their own trade goals, as expressed by a familiar representative.

In November 1728, William Byrd II noted that groups like the Catawbas warmly welcomed caravans of Virginia traders into their villages. Byrd felt his colony's traders received this treatment because they offered the Indians higher quality goods at lower prices. He noted that a group of Carolina traders lived among the Catawbas and claimed to have trade jurisdiction over them, though in his opinion, the Carolina traders greatly mistreated their Indians. "Nor has their behavior been at all better to the rest of the Indian nations among whom they reside," Byrd noted, "by abusing their women and evil entreating their men."[11] Byrd believed such practices led to the Yamassee conflict South Carolina endured in 1715. He noted "the Indians opened the war by knocking most of those little tyrants on the head that dwelt amongst them under pretense of regulating their commerce."[12] Indians, when angered, turned upon all those Euroamericans residing among them, not just a select few. Thus, the inherent danger involved in the profession becomes quite apparent.

Virginia's traffic with the southern Indians was not easy. Virginia traders had to travel great distances to extend their trade into the Cherokee lands, sometimes failing to reach their goal for want of food and fresh horses. Byrd believed that some shortcut into that region existed which, if discovered, would facilitate Virginia's profitable trade with the Cherokees.[13] Once found, Byrd believed the passage would allow his colony's traders "to undersell those sent from the other colonies so much that the Indians must have reason to deal with them preferably to all others."[14] Byrd's statement confirmed the intent of Virginia traders to undercut the business of South Carolina traders. The competition only worsened through the coming century.

Normally when Euroamericans wished to coerce Native Americans into compliance during peacetime, they threatened to withdraw trade from the Indian country. In the 1750s, when a group of Cherokees went on a rampage and killed the traders Daniel Murphy and Bernard Hughs, Governor James Glen of South Carolina reproached the Cherokee headmen. He told them to consult their old people for reminders of life before the trade with the British colonials.

Instead of the admirable fire arms that you are now plentifully supplied with, your best arms were bad bows, and wretched arrows head [sic] with bills of birds, bones of fishes, or at best with sharp stones. Instead of being decently or comfortably dressed in British cloaths [sic], you were forced to cover yourselves with the skins of wild beasts. Your knives were split canes, and your hatchets were of stone, so that you spent more days in felling a tree, than you now do in minutes.[15]

Glen's reproach carried an implicit warning using the language of trade. In chastising the Cherokees, Glen strongly reminded them what their lives would return to if he withdrew their traders. Glen further warned them that it would do them little good to turn to Virginia traders, should he withdraw the Carolina traders. He reminded the headmen that he knew their people were engaging in trade with the Virginians but that the colonials were all one people--the king would not allow one group to sell arms to the Indians for them to attack another group of colonials.[16]

The Cherokees quickly responded. In May of 1751, the Lower Cherokees sent to Glen pledging their unfailing allegiance to the British. They explained the raid and their attempts to stop it, promising that the incident would not be repeated. The headmen asked Glen not to stop the trade, since the Lower Cherokees desperately needed ammunition to fight their enemies.[17] The Upper Cherokees responded as well, using the language of trade as Glen had. Like the Lower Cherokees, they acknowledged the long-standing relationship they had with the British, emphasizing their hope that it would continue in the future. They considered the enemies of the British to be their own opponents. Thus, the Cherokees considered the French-aligned Indians as their adversaries, just as the British considered the French their rivals. As such they wrote to Glen that many of their headmen were then at war with the French Indians, though they had lost their share of people, as had the British against the French. The Upper Cherokees believed that the French purposely encouraged their Indians to kill Cherokee people. As a result, the Upper Cherokee headmen told Glen they never intended to make peace with these French forces "while we have any ammunition to go to war with, which we are at present very short of."[18] The implication of this statement is clear. Between the protestations of loyalty and affection was a blunt warning. The Cherokees would fight the French only so long as they were properly supplied with trade. The Upper Cherokees had learned to manipulate Euroamericans through such means, and their leverage rested on a possible consequence. If the British failed to respond, the French and the Cherokees might return to peaceful relations with an ensuing resumption of trade. British profits from the Indian trade would suffer, and, since Indian loyalty followed plentiful provisions, France might obtain a decisive advantage in the competition for North America.

The struggle among Spain, France and Britain improved the leverage of Indian tribes in dealing with the Europeans. Though addicted to the trade which had forever changed traditional life, they could, by threatening to realign themselves among the three European competitors, affect Euroamerican behavior as well. As in the British struggle to survive on North America's east coast, French settlers and soldiers in Louisiana survived because of their lucrative trade with the Indians.

In 1716, the *commissaire ordonnateur* Marc-Antoine Hubert observed that many French settlers in Louisiana refused to farm because it was more profitable to trade with the Indians.[19] French plans at colonization were inextricably linked with trade. At the beginning of the eighteenth century, early versions called for a chain of trading posts and tanneries guarded by armed Indian allies. Later plans envisioned extending French control of trade throughout the Mississippi Valley. In reality, since French enclaves often consisted of small numbers of troops separated by great distances, British acitivity often determined when and where scarce resources would be deployed. While traders in the upper part of the Mississippi Valley concentrated on beaver pelts, those in the lower part concentrated on deer skins. In 1714, the French built a storehouse at Natchez to extend their trade into the tribes of the backcountry and to offset British penetration into that same region.[20] British fears concerning the threat of French encroachment among the Indian tribes adjacent to their colonies were well founded. During the Yamassee War, the Alibamas, Tallapoosas and Abechkas ejected their British traders and then turned to the French in Mobile as trade partners for their deer skins. This realignment prompted the French to construct Fort Toulouse in 1717 at the confluence of the Coosa and Tallapoosa rivers. In 1716, they had built Fort Rosalie in the Natchez lands and would erect Fort St. Pierre on the Yazoo River in 1719.[21]

For the British, the French clearly were a threat. Though fierce rivals, the French and British practiced similar trade habits with respect to the southern Indians. Both colonizers had inherited trade traditions from the Spanish that included the often onerous custom of giving gifts. The French in Louisiana dealt most frequently with the Choctaws, who traveled annually to Mobile to receive presents. By 1750, these gifts were costing the French government 50,000 livres per year. The trip to Mobile was replete with custom; prior to entering Mobile, the Choctaws stopped at an Indian village at its outskirts, where they requested brandy and bread. They also changed into ceremonial clothes preparatory to greeting Mobile's commandant; then they smoked together and exchanged speeches. Once formalities had concluded, the Choctaws withdrew to await the arrival of their gifts. During the lull, native firearms were also serviced. Once repairs had been made and gifts given, the group departed, only to be followed by another. Such revolving Indian visits continued for up to six weeks.[22]

After all the groups had returned to their home range, French traders spread out through the Choctaw lands. Upon entering a specific village, the trader went to the chief's home where they smoked a pipe. Finally, the chief formally acknowledged the arrival of the trader who then proceeded to describe his wares. The next day, the chief announced the trader's arrival and described his wares. Individuals were free then to deal with the trader directly. French traders spent up to three months on these backcountry missions though profits of up to 200 percent were possible. In fact, during the French colonial occupation of Louisiana, Indian tribes supplied fifteen thousand pelts per year. By the 1730s, the French and British had become serious rivals for the southern backcountry.[23]

The relationships among Britain, France and Spain in America were affected, of course, by their continental politics. Britain's founding of Georgia in 1733 was taken as an aggressive step into Spanish domain. Further, at the conclusion of the War of Spanish Succession in 1713, Britain had received the *asiento*, allowing it to send one vessel into the Caribbean each year to trade. British traders exceeded the limit and smugglers abounded. Spanish officials caught Captain Robert Jenkins smuggling in 1731 and cut off his ear. British merchants used the incident to transform a commercial issue into an emotional, patriotic one. In March 1737, rumors of a Spanish invasion fleet reached Georgia. According to the Earl of Egmont, a trustee of colonial Georgia, an armada of seven ships and seven thousand men was amassing to attack that colony.[24] Georgia's founder, James Edward Oglethorpe, responded by building forts in southern Georgia to act as a buffer between that colony and Spanish Florida. By 1739, relationships between the two powers had deteriorated beyond repair and the War of Jenkins's Ear erupted. The distance between Britain and Georgia limited the number of troops on whom Oglethorpe could depend; this was the source of his dependency on Mary Musgrove of the Creeks.

During the War of Jenkins' Ear, the relationship between the Creeks and the British was in its honeymoon stage. Though Mary later would use her actions as a basis for monetary claims against the British government, the relationship was amiable enough at the time. In July 1742, Oglethorpe wrote to Mary that his forces had beaten the Spanish in two encounters and asked that she send as many Creek warriors as she could.[25] When Oglethorpe left the colony, his successor, William Horton, also asked Mary for Creek assistance. In July 1743, he requested the use of Creek warriors for a reconnaisance mission against the Spanish.[26] In the summer of 1744, Horton wrote to Mary again, requesting that she send as many Creeks as she could to help him against the Spanish.[27] In payment for these services, the Creeks expected gifts. In September 1744, Horton wrote to Mary, describing just how costly their services turned out to be. "I have given the Indians that came from warr [sic] very extraordinary presents but nothing will satisfye [*sic*] them tho' [*sic*] they have amongst other things eight horses."[28]

Just as that conflict began to subside, Britain became embroiled in yet another war of international scope. In 1744 the War of Austrian Succession brought Britain's slow, simmering rivalry with France in North America to the boil. Now, the question of Indian alliances in North America became critical, involving much more than mere profit margins. Indian warriors allowed a colonial power to enhance either thinly spread colonial troops or to increase the effective range of full complements. Plentiful trade goods purchased those Indian warriors, and, though costly, both sides were unwilling to risk losing their Indian allies by neglecting the trade. Such a gamble might result in a successful deployment of warriors by the enemy at a critical juncture, thus deciding the contest for North America. The Indians could not, however, be counted upon to think, react or fight according to European standards of war. British colonial officials did not gamble; they became preoccupied with containing the spread of French influence among the tribes of the backcountry.

The French used groups like the Choctaws to harass Indians aligned with the British. In so doing, they could effectively drain British resources as they struggled to minimize British influence in the backcountry. The potential effects of the escalating competition for Indian alliances were sobering. If British settlements lost an ally to the French they would lose profits from trade with that ally as well. The loss of too many former allies could have potentially ignited the tribes of the backcountry in a war against the British. In that case, the fur traders and Indian agents would have become hostages with which the tribes could have bargained with the British. As the various tribes of the backcountry gained experience with Europeans, they learned to use the language of trade to manipulate these fears to their own advantage.

In October 1744, a Cherokee headman wrote to the newly installed governor of South Carolina, James Glen. Normally, Indian groups made ceremonial trips to greet new British officials and there was little that could prevent them from doing so when they could expect gifts and lavish treatment. Having learned that the British were at war with both the Spanish and French, the headman chose to avoid a trip till the following spring, believing that Glen and his "beloved men and warriours [sic] would be very busy about ordering and preparing for the warr [sic] and that we might be troublesome at such a time."[29] The headman also told Glen that since his people owed great debts to the traders they needed to hunt that fall in order to pay those debts.[30]

One of the first tasks undertaken by Governor Glen in his new position was to thwart French efforts in the backcountry. When Cherokee headmen paid him a visit in the fall of 1746, they pledged their loyalty to the British. Despite such apparently firm feelings, the Cherokees were, in fact, divided in their loyalty. Cherokee leaders told Glen that those members of their tribe living near the Mississippi River were visited frequently by the French and French-aligned Indians. Their proximity to French forces left them somewhat vulnerable and these Cherokees cooperated with the French out of fear. Glen told the board that, at that juncture, he proposed building a fort in their homelands to counteract French influence. As Glen noted in his own style, a fort would "bar the door against the French, & be such a bridle in the mouths of the Indians themselves, & that would forever keep them ours."[31] The building, garrisoning and supplying of such a fort would be expensive. Perhaps mindful of that cost, Glen reminded the board why he thought such an outlay necessary. The Indian trade had made Carolina prosperous because it involved the exchange of low cost items produced by British manufacturers for deer skins. At that time, he noted that Charles Town was exporting six hundred to seven hundred hogsheads of skins annually with one hogshead bringing 50 guineas in Charles Town.[32]

Some tribes of the southern backcountry resisted the notion of Euroamericans building forts in their home lands. Yet, others quickly realized that such forts had many advantages. First, they provided ready shelter for the Indians should their own enemies attack. Second, such fortifications would serve as a deterrent to enemies of the tribe on whose land it was built. Third, forts often served as repositories for larger amounts of trade goods than traders could carry. In April 1747, Glen wrote to the board with an update on South Carolina's status with its Indian neighbors. He noted that while the French still tried to alienate the Cherokees from the British, the Cherokees had petitioned him for the construction of just such a fort. In fact, they had promised to cede land as its site, provide labor for its construction and help provision it for the first two years.[33] The implied French threat to the Cherokees was forcing Britain to consider building forts among its aligned Indian tribes, thus increasing costs in Indian management. If the British chose to refuse the request, they risked alienating the Cherokees and sending them into the arms of the French. Thus, the actual cost of maintaining Indian alliances and the Indian trade rose during the tension between the two intruding European powers.

In July 1748, Governor Glen regretfully informed the board that French Indians had attacked British settlements and carried off people as slaves. The threat was so great that the Indian traders were afraid to leave Cherokee lands without armed escort. He used the opportunity to press his idea about fort building, which he had expanded in light of continuing trouble in the backcountry. In addition to recommending the fort among the Cherokees, he called for building one in the Choctaw lands. He believed too that the British should construct one between the Catawbas and the Cherokees and still another between the Chickasaws and the Creeks.[34]

British forts spread among the southern backcountry could dissuade the French physically but could not defeat them. In a preliterate society built upon oral tradition, propaganda was also a deadly weapon. In 1749, Governor Glen attempted to mediate a peace settlement between the Creeks and the Cherokees. In July that year, a backcountry resident, Thomas Devall, warned Glen that the French were making inroads with some tribes among the Creeks. He also warned that the French knew about Glen's plans for peace and would prevent it if possible.[35] In December 1749, Glen wrote to the board that when he invited Creek and Cherokee headmen to Charles Town for peace talks, the French in Mobile and the Alabama Fort started rumors that the Indians had been called there to be put to death.[36] The Cherokees and the Creeks preferred to have the meeting at Fort Moore, some 150 miles from Charles Town, but Glen refused to meet that far inland and continued to pressure both groups to meet at Charles Town. Ironically, when they arrived they fell prey to disease and died in great numbers, especially the Cherokees. Cherokee survivors started back home only to learn that French Indians had attacked several of their Overhill towns.[37] Thus disease and French actions had made the rumors appear to be true.

The explosive political relationship between Britain and France often overshadowed their competition for the Indian trade, but it never replaced it. Amid their continuing political struggle, the governor of New Orleans wrote to James Glen to withdraw British traders from the Choctaws. The French official claimed the Choctaws for France, warning that one British trader among them had been killed already. The French governor further warned that he expected the death of three more British traders at any time.[38]   While trade rivalries determined who would use the southern Indians to the best advantage, the rivalry for financial gain remained a very important subtext amid the international struggle to dominate North America.

As if international competition for the Indians and their trade were not enough, internal domestic competition still plagued colonial authorities. Conflict with Virginia traders first irritated South Carolina officials, but before long, a new rival appeared to challenge South Carolina's hegemony in the backcountry. The colony of Georgia, established in 1733, quickly became a thorn in South Carolina's side with respect to the Indian trade. In 1737, the Board of Trade notified the Lords of Committee of Council that South Carolina had lodged a formal complaint against Georgia Indian traders who had interfered with South Carolina's trade. Concurrently, Georgia made a complaint against the lieutenant governor of South Carolina for interfering with a Georgia ordinance to maintain peace with the Indians. Specifically, Georgia officials complained that South Carolina had licensed Thomas Wright, a former convict, and sent him into Georgia to harass the Indians there. South Carolina officials retorted that Carolina traders operating near the Savannah River, but within the colony's border, had been driven off by Georgians, who seized their goods.[39]

The Board of Trade attempted to settle the problem by having the governor and council of South Carolina and the Trustees of Georgia issue licenses to persons of the other province if they qualified for a license in their own colony.[40] Such measures failed to solve the problems between the two colonies. Ludovic Grant, a thirty year veteran of the Indian trade, wrote to Governor Glen in May 1752 to complain of continuing problems. Grant believed that the Georgia traders, subject to fewer trade restrictions than their neighbors, would ruin the trade for the Carolinians. Both Carolina and Georgia claimed certain Indian towns as trade preserves, and their respective traders were now competing for these towns. Georgia also allowed its traders to conduct business with residents of towns claimed by South Carolina, if the Indian residents took their business to the trader. Grant characterized the Georgia traders as "a monstrous sett [sic] of rogues for the major part of whom the gallows groans."[41] While the growing competition could be viewed as merely a healthy market, it had serious repercussions for colonial Indian management.

First, the influx of traders from Virginia, Georgia and South Carolina resulted in price wars to gain Indian customers. A group of veteran Indian traders from South Carolina, Robert Bunning, Cornelius Dougherty, James Beamer and Ludovic Grant, complained of its results. The glut in the number of traders had lowered prices so much that it was impossible to make a living without resorting to dishonesty and violence, to the detriment of the Indians. Trader abuse of the Indians could prompt them to launch a surprise attack on all Euroamericans in their lands. Honest traders could not make enough to buy new merchandise to sell, much less to pay their old debts.[42] One sure way to risk losing Indian allies was to allow the supply of Euroamerican goods upon which they were dependent to falter. Ultimately, this led the Carolina Indian traders to suggest an already familiar but costly remedy. They felt the surest way to stabilize the backcountry was to build forts. "The Indians would know," the traders wrote, "that the British took care of them, . . . and the trader must be obliged to act regularly and justly."[43]

The traders did not always act properly. In September 1751, Glen authorized one of his officials in the backcountry to intercept a group of Virginia traders bound for Cherokee lands with goods and ammunition. Glen felt that since a rogue group among that tribe had murdered two traders that summer, the arrival of those supplying ammunition at such a time might provoke a backcountry war. The Virginia traders were being aided by a licensed Carolina trader, acting as a guide to help them reach their destination.[44] Competition naturally led to a race to supply the most popular Indian goods. Sadly enough, unscrupulous traders began to import more liquor than ever into the backcountry. In February 1753, Ludovic Grant wrote to Governor Glen that Georgia traders were bringing rum into the Cherokee lands, much to the displeasure of Indians in the towns of Ioreee and Cauwee. The Indians planned to seize this contraband substance, believing the Georgia traders to be no better than rogues.[45] As intercolonial competition worsened, so did international rivalry.

By the 1750s, intelligence reports about French activity dominated British communication from and to the southern colonial backcountry. In May 1751, John Pearson notified his superiors that representatives from five Indian groups were entering the Cherokee homelands, for what purpose he could not determine.[46] French influence had not stopped with the Cherokees. Although the Creeks were loyal to the British, Pat Graham noted in June 1751 that the French constantly tried to stir up trouble between them and their British neighbors. Graham's warning focused on a particular French attempt to mediate a peace among the Choctaws, French allies and Creeks. The Creeks, so far, had refused the offer unless it included their British allies, a proviso the French rejected. Graham concluded that British influence could be even greater if the government prevented "some loose, idle fellows from going to trade amongst those Indians whose bad principles and ill morals, the Indians can scarcely equal."[47]

Ultimately, smoldering embers from unsettled conflict in Europe among Spain, France and Britain erupted once more by mid century. Though the Treaty of Aix-la-Chapelle technically had ended Britain's conflict with France over the Austrian succession, the French government's determination to join the halves of its colonial empire in North America provoked British military action. When French forces pushed into western Pennsylvania and the Ohio Valley in an attempt to take over the fur trade, the governor of Virginia sent colonial forces into the region to challenge the forces building a fort at the site of modern Pittsburgh. In the spring of 1754, British troops under twenty-one year old George Washington engaged French soldiers in Pennsylvania. Washington and his troops initially defeated their French adversaries, but were forced to retreat before greater numbers. Fearful of the prohibitive cost of such a war, the government of George II hesitated to escalate the conflict deliberately. Yet, it dispatched General Edward Braddock to America in 1755 to counter a bold French move at territorial aggrandizement. Supplied with regular troops, Braddock was authorized to enlist volunteers, and so

George Washington chose to make his second foray into the Pennsylvania backcountry. In July 1755, Braddock and his forces were ambushed by French and Indian forces just eight miles short of the French fort. Though smaller in number than their victims, the French forces humiliatingly wounded or killed two thirds of the British forces. Financial considerations delayed a British response, but Britain formally declared war on France in May 1756. Now, both colonial powers would use every means at their disposal to win the contest for North America. The necessity of retaining Indian allies and countering enemy influence in the backcountry took on added meaning and required added expenditures. This European war, transplanted to North America, would be the first of two great wars in which the struggle to retain Indian allies was a critical issue.

In this great conflict, one of the easiest ways for the British and French to battle each other was through their respective Indian allies; each sought to alienate the other's closest Indian neighbors and turn them against former allies. To accomplish this task, both European powers used lies, threats, bribery and the promise of trade. In the ensuing struggle, certain groups of Indians often found themselves the beneficiaries of price wars started to lure them away from former trade partners. The Indians also found ways to manipulate both groups of Europeans by playing on their fears about losing Indian allies to each other. In this contest within a contest, the Native Americans of the Southeast were often the winners.

While the older name of "French and Indian War" is an inaccurate one to describe the conflict among Britain, France and Spain at mid century, it does identify those forces which preoccupied British colonials in North America. Since the British settlements in the Southeast bordered the Creek and Cherokee homelands, it is not surprising that those tribes were the focus of colonial attention. In December of 1754, Governor Glen of South Carolina wrote to three Cherokee headmen, Tacite of Hiawassie, Colane of Eurphorsee and the King of the Valley. He told them of his desire to hold a conference with both their people and the Creeks. Glen wanted this conference to confirm the peace between the two peoples, a peace which he warned that the French wanted to destroy. He also warned the Cherokees that the French were attempting to enlist the Tawasaws and other northern Indians against the Cherokees while bringing in the Choctaws and Creeks against them from the south.[48]

The ulterior motive of such a warning should be considered carefully. The French were seeking to attract as many Indian allies as possible, just as the British hoped to do. To that end, both sides needed to be on their best behavior among the tribes they hoped to entice. Yet, as Ludovic Grant noted, the British effort was being jeopardized by an enemy within--the traders. He wrote to warn Glen in March 1755 of trader irregularities which he believed would hurt Britain's attempt to maintain good relations with the Indians at this critical time. He noted that the Carolina traders extended too much credit to the Cherokees, more than they could ever hope to repay. Offering his own psychological opinion of the effect, Grant believed that the Indians developed a dislike of the traders because they owed them so much money. The close presence of the traders among the Indians only exacerbated their disdain for their creditors. Thus, Grant believed the Cherokees were tempted by distant traders, probably alluding to the French. He believed the problem of excessive credit was a critical one, given the French threat; if it were not corrected, Grant believed the Indians might take drastic steps to extinguish their debts--by extinguishing the traders.[49]

The French were trying very hard to alienate the Cherokees from the British. Of the two major aligned tribes, the Cherokees were the weak link. However, the French did not focus all their attention on them. In May 1755, Lachlan McGillivray wrote to Glen that a French captain met both Upper and Lower Creeks in April. Bearing gifts, the captain wanted to mediate a peace between the Creeks and France's Choctaw allies. In order to tempt the Creeks, McGillivray noted that they also showed them an impressive array of trade goods with prices matching those offered by the British. Further, they told the Cherokees they would continue to undercut British prices on trade items. The French felt they could afford to do this, since they shipped their goods by water, instead of by land.[50] The French had clearly thrown down the gauntlet. The resulting competition to obtain Indian loyalty would create a price war, lowering profits for everyone involved from British merchant to backcountry trader. The southeastern Indians enjoyed a buyer's market.

Governors of other southern colonies also began entreating their Indian neighbors to remain loyal. In December 1755, Governor Robert Dinwiddie of Virginia warned the Catawbas about the intrigues of the French. He told them that the Iroquois League had mobilized against the French and urged them to do likewise, since the French had murdered Catawba people during a recent raid on Virginia, and urged the Catawba king to join forces with the Cherokees and the Virginians to defeat the French. Many Indians chose sides in such a conflict simply on the basis of their estimation of the probable winner. Knowing this, Dinwiddie told the Catawba king that his coalition of Euroamerican and Native American forces had inflicted such defeats on the French and their allies that he believed the French would be banished to Canada the following year.[51]

Despite the gallant efforts being made to bind the Creeks and Cherokees to the British cause, veteran Indian traders continued to report trader abuse of the Indians. Such unregulated activity was fast undermining any efforts Britain was making, according to James Beamer, a trader among the Cherokees, who wrote to Governor Glen in February of 1756 warning him, as Ludovic Grant had, of the abusive behavior of some traders. Beamer reminded Glen that both Georgia and South Carolina were dependent for their safety on peace with the Creeks and Cherokees. Yet, some traders flagrantly violated trade laws and disrupted the harmony of the backcountry. Beamer noted a trader named Williams who imported great quantities of rum into the Cherokee lands. Williams sold the rum at high prices and sometimes shorted the Indians on quantity. Such cheating, Beamer noted caused " disturbances, quarrels and even murders between the white people and Indians and is the . . . cause of the Indians threatning [sic] and even beating, some traders."[52]   Perhaps even more dangerous than importing rum and cheating customers, Williams blatantly told the Indians that he did not have to obey the governor of South Carolina. He told them he could trade as he pleased, and, if he chose, take rum to any Cherokee town. Beamer wisely noted that government officials should not be surprised when the Indians flouted the rules of colonial government, having had such a teacher as Williams. Worse yet, Williams told the Cherokees that they "had done a fine piece of work to their country, that they had made themselves and their children slaves by giving up their lands and themselves to the King over the Great Water."[53] Despite an element of truth to the criticism, such statements were highly destructive to the goal of strengthening ties with the Indian tribes. Beamer warned Glen that such unbridled talk was doubly destructive when the Indians failed to see the guilty parties punished.[54]

Members of the southern Indians learned to take advantage of the conflict raging between the Europeans in North America. Headmen of the Chickasaws asked the governor of South Carolina to consider their pitiful condition. They were ill-supplied with the goods to which they had grown accustomed because they had been prevented from hunting for three years. During that time, they had been preoccupied with fighting the French, whom they knew to be enemies of the British. They noted that their traders would not advance them credit for ammunition and gunpowder because they had no skins to trade. The Catawbas also begged for help. They thanked the Carolinians for prior supplies,which had enabled them to hold out against the French to that point. In a carefully crafted sentence, they told the Carolinians that friends of the British were their friends; British enemies were Catawba enemies as well. "We hope you will stil [sic] take pity on us," the Catawbas wrote, "and give us a supply of powder and bullets and guns &c. to enable us to outlive our enemies."[55] The implication of the Catawba appeal is quite plain. If the British expected them to continue fighting the French, who the British had said were the Catawbas' enemies, then the British must supply guns, ammunition and other trade items despite the Indians' inability to pay. British profits would have to be sacrificed if British war policy were to prevail.

Other factors in the colonial Indian trade cut into British profits. By 1754, the president of the Board of Trade, Lord Halifax, authorized the construction of forts in the southern backcountry out of fear of French encroachment. Former South Carolina Governor Glen's old dream was now coming true, albeit with French help. Captain Raymond Demeré, the former commander of Fort Frederica in Georgia, was dispatched to the Cherokee homelands to begin construction on the new Fort Loudoun, located in east Tennessee at the junction of the Little Tennessee and Tellico rivers near Maryville.[56] Initially stationed at nearby Fort Prince George, near modern Pickens, South Carolina, Demeré wrote to South Carolina's new governor, William Lyttelton, in July 1756 with a report on Indian relations. An Indian leader, Little Carpenter, informed Demeré of an increasingly critical situation in the Cherokee homelands. The traders had been unable to supply the Upper Cherokee towns of western North Carolina, eastern Tennessee and northern Georgia with enough ammunition. Little Carpenter told Demeré that the traders should be well supplied with goods; if not, they would be asked to leave Cherokee lands. He also stated that the commander of the new fort always must have a supply of trade goods.[57] Obviously the Cherokees were using the European war as a vehicle through which to increase the previously lagging trade in their lands.

The Cherokees continued to be a weak link in the British buffer zone. Major Andrew Lewis wrote to Demeré in September 1756 with alarming facts. During a visit to the Cherokee town of Chota, Lewis learned that a group of French-aligned Indians, the Savannos, as well as the French themselves had made inroads into the Cherokee town of Tellico. At the heart of the intrigue was a man called French John who had lived among the Cherokees for many years. French John was aided by a Cherokee mate who spoke that tongue and that of the Savanno Indians. Little Carpenter, Old Hop and other Cherokee headmen had reportedly sent French John and his Cherokee mate to the French Alabama Fort to tell its occupants that they expected the construction of a French fort in the Upper Cherokee towns. Lewis also reported that the British traders and translators no longer felt safe among the Upper Cherokees.[58] Most likely, the Cherokees had no united plan to force the British and French to compete for them. Yet, the actions of the Tellico people were producing just that effect.

Delegates from the Creeks confirmed a growing French threat. When some Creeks were killed by Euroamericans on the Ogeechee River in Georgia, Creek headmen met to discuss the affair. At that juncture, a Lieutenant White Outerbridge told Governor Lyttelton that though the headmen dismissed the matter as accidental, French representatives were on hand to paint a disturbing portrait of the British to the Creeks, reciting the now-familiar story of how they looked on the Creeks as brothers. As such, they prepared to retaliate against the British in Georgia for their misdeed to the Creeks on the Ogeechee River. The French used the isolated incident cleverly, warning the Creeks to stay away from British settlers because they were dangerous.[59] Perhaps the most unsettling note of the report concerned intelligence information given by a trader, George Johnston. The Creek merchant noted that during a recent stay among the Creeks, he witnessed the passing of a Cherokee delegation bound for the French fort intending to repatriate two Frenchmen and to establish a relationship between the Cherokees and the French.[60]

To the benefit of the British, all of the Cherokees were not open to an association with the French. During a recent visit to Great Tellico, modern Monroe County, Tennessee, Demeré was quickly asked by the Cherokee emperor what he thought of the disaffection of one town to French influence. When Demeré replied that such a move saddened him, the emperor asked Demeré did French people not live among the British at Charles Town? Demeré tried to explain that those Frenchmen were Huguenots, coreligionists and loyal British subjects.[61] The French used half-truths and lies to weaken the British link to the Cherokees even further. In October 1756, Demeré addressed Old Hop and Little Carpenter at Tomatley in response to questions they had about the building material being sent there for construction of the fort. The French had told them that metal was being sent to clap their women and children in irons, after all the men were killed. He reassured them that the metal was for the fort they had requested, which would hold some 180 men. Demeré fully expounded on the usefulness of the fort, stating it would provide the Cherokee people protection from their enemies, yet he chastised them for allowing some of their people to request a French fort in Cherokee lands. Using trade as a threat, Demeré told them that no other nation could supply them as well as the British and no Indians were poorer than those who aligned themselves with the French. If the French could not adequately take care of their closest Indian neighbors, then the more distant Cherokees could expect even less from them.[62] Finally, Demeré resorted to an old trick, albeit with a new twist. He told the Cherokees that should they allow a French fort in their lands, such close proximity between the two European powers would result in severed supply lines for both, ending all trade. Demeré blamed the war on French ambition to dominate North America, as though the British did not aspire to the same goal. Knowing that the Indians liked to side with the winner, he told them that the French had already lost thousands of men in the conflict, though in fact Britain was losing the war in 1756.[63] While he clarified the purpose of the building materials sent to Tomatley, Demeré cleverly threatened the cessation of trade as a means to induce the Cherokees to reject the overtures of the French.

The Cherokees' response to Demeré's talk likewise hinged on trade and was, in its own way, just as clever. Old Hop told Demeré that in addition to the forts at Chota and Tomatley he wanted yet another built within such a distance that a gun fired at one would be heard by the other two. Old Hop observed that while the British had come to give them a talk, they had done so empty-handed and at a time when the Cherokee warriors were out fighting enemies or hunting. The Cherokee headman warned that his towns were dangerously low on gunpowder and bullets, strongly hinting that the British should resupply them. In an example of how Euroamerican values had changed Indian perceptions, Old Hop told Demeré that while the British men had fine red uniforms, he was naked and could not sit with Demeré without "disgracing" him. The headman expressed the wish that when the British fort was completed, it would be well stocked so his warriors and headmen might obtain clothes, so "that they might look like men, and not be ashamed to show themselves, for an empty house looks but poorly."[64] Obviously, the Cherokees had assimilated European values about nakedness and now equated clothes with prosperity. Again, the main message to the British was clear. The Cherokees expected them to supply guns and ammunition if the British wished them to continue opposing the French. At the same time, any British fort erected in their homelands would be expected to provide a plentiful supply of desired goods.

The French continued to make inroads among the Cherokee people. The Old Warrior of Tomatley wrote to Raymond Demeré in November 1756 with more news about Cherokee disaffection. He reported that not only were the Tellico people firmly under French influence but the people of Chatuga had joined them. Both towns were planning to relocate to Hiwassie Old Town. In addition, Old Warrior noted that when the Tellico people went to the Alabama Fort for presents, they had been beaten there by a group of Creeks, who took all the presents. The commanding officer of the fort received the Cherokees from Tellico warmly and told them to expect his visit in their homelands both to study the British trade and to observe abusive British Indian traders. He promised to supply the Cherokees with everything they needed and to wage a price war with the British as he was determined to undercut them. Finally, the French official told them to expect soon a great quantity of gifts for their wives and children as a prelude to their new relationship.[65]

Just as the Europeans learned that the Indians aligned themselves with the strongest military power, they also learned that the Indians aligned themselves with the best provider. Price wars and an upsurge in gifts were the natural outcome of such European competition from which the Indians benefited. In November 1756, a very concerned Raymond Demeré wrote to Governor Lyttelton that if the British lost the Tellico people, they ultimately would lose all of the Cherokee people. He believed that the fates of both South Carolina and Georgia were inexorably tied to the fates of the Creek and Cherokee tribes. If Britain lost either tribe, the other would surely soon follow. Should the Creeks and Cherokees join forces with the French-aligned Choctaws, Demeré believed the resulting coalition eventually would absorb every other Indian group of consequence in North America. The British captain noted that attracting the Cherokees was of such import that the French would spare no cost: "Indians are a comodity [sic] that are to be bought and sold and the French will bid very high for them. And on this particular occasion if we don't bid as high we shall [absolutely] lose them."[66]

From all available indicators, the British were well on their way to losing the Cherokees in the mid-1750s. Intelligence reports from an Indian named Judd's Friend[67] in December 1756 confirmed a meeting between the French at the Alabama Fort (Toulouse) and the Cherokee Mankiller[68] of Tellico. The French official told the Mankiller figuratively that the "French house" had been darkened for a long time because of the Cherokees' ties to the British. Every time the French had reached out to the Cherokees, the British called them to Charles Town. Once there, the British wined and dined them and gave them a "fine red coat." Perhaps alluding to the recent ill fated visit of the Cherokees to Charles Town to see the former governor James Glen, the French official noted that British gifts, like clothes, were tainted with death. He told the Mankiller that " the Carolina people had conjourors [sic] . . . that could send up bundles of sickness to their Nation . . . from which proceeds the decrease of their people."[69] The Frenchman accused the British of beating Cherokee warriors and molesting Cherokee women. He also brought up the issue of materials being shipped to Tomatley and stated they were to make shackles to enslave the Cherokee people. The French official ended his meeting with the Mankiller by stating that the Tellico people should go to New Orleans and guide a boatload of free goods back to the Cherokee homelands.[70]

Once more, the French were playing on Indian insecurities. North American Indians had long viewed Europeans as conjurors since they mildly experienced European illnesses which often proved fatal to the Native Americans. Indians often refused to go into heavy population centers, like Charles Town, until after the summer's heat, for fear of illness. Some British traders did cheat and misuse the Cherokees. Thus, the French over emphasized the unscrupulous behavior of some traders to represent the actions of all of them. They continued to misrepresent the purpose of British building materials shipped into the backcountry to the detriment of British interests. Other intelligence reports in

December 1756 noted that the Mankiller of Tellico expected French John to give him thirty horse loads of ammunition. Meanwhile, the Tellico people were reported to be in the process of building houses in anticipation of the arrival of the French.[71]

Subsequent intelligence from Cherokee territory revealed that the only reason for the Mankiller's visit to the construction site of Fort Loudoun had been to reconnoiter its progress. He had been instructed by the French to scalp some of the colonials there and return with their scalps as tokens of Cherokee fidelity. Then the French would attack and kill the British in their homelands.[72] To cement this new alliance, the French offered that one item more tantalizing than all others-- commerce. They increased the quantity of free gifts promised to the Cherokees to unbelievable proportions. Their subsequent offer promised a caravan of one hundred horses sent to them four times. After this massive bounty of gifts, the French planned to send one hundred horse loads of trade items for sale. As if this were not enough, the French stated they would accept as payment all manner of skins, not just deer skins.[73]

The British traders among the Cherokees in January 1756 noted the continued defection of the Tellico people. British merchants Thomas Leaper and James Kelley abandoned their trading house in Tellico fearfully and transferred their wares to the nearby town of Chatuga. They reported that a group of Indians under the direction of the Mankiller had staked out the route into Tellico from Chota and now patrolled it in search of the British scalps needed to cement their deal with the French at the Alabama Fort.[74] Demeré quickly sent out warnings to travelers to avoid the usual route into Tellico.[75]

While this group of Cherokees continued to drift into the French orbit, other members of that tribe sought to strengthen their British ties. Demeré wrote to Governor Lyttelton that Old Hop had summoned him to a meeting at Chota where the elderly Cherokee strove to convince the British captain of the loyalty of seven towns among the Overhills Cherokee. Upon returning to his fort, Demeré found the Mankiller of Tellico waiting for him. In the meeting, Demeré learned that the source of much of the disaffection of the Tellico people was trade. The Mankiller wanted better trade for his town, specifically a permanent, resident trader. Further, he wanted a steady supply of goods at cheaper prices than previously supplied. Upon investigating the matter, Demeré had found that a trader, Robert Gowdy, had been licensed to operate in Chatuga and Tellico. Yet, he had not been there to run his trade; instead, be became a middleman, selling his goods at Ninety-Six, South Carolina, to men described by Demeré as disreputable. These merchants had paid higher prices for their goods from Gowdy and so took fewer with them to Tellico and Chatuga. Once there, they charged the Indians even higher prices and would advance little or no credit.[76] Thus, one reason that the Tellico and Chatuga Indians were leaning toward the French was the lure of better trade promised by the French. Since the trade items had been incorporated thoroughly into tribal life, poor supplies and high prices were creating the frustration associated with the British alliance. That there was little or no regulation of British Indian traders by colonial government had much to do with the apparent disaffection of these two Cherokee towns. Captain Demeré dispatched Lieutenant Robert Wall to Tellico in January 1757 to address the issue of trade in connection with recent Indian behavior. The Mankiller met with Wall, telling the British lieutenant that the Tellico Cherokees had considered themselves "children of King George," but had wondered lately whether he looked upon them as his children. The reason for their doubt rested upon the issue of trade. The Tellico people felt slighted because they never received free gifts as surrounding towns did and they believed they had been abandoned by the British.[77]

Other trade irregularities began to surface in connection with the disaffection of some of the Cherokees. Old Hop summoned Demeré for a meeting, at which the elderly Cherokee leader produced a price schedule with the signature of the former South Carolina governor, James Glen. Hop stated that the traders stationed among the Cherokees had no regard for the price schedule; they charged what they wanted despite government guidelines. Glen also had promised Hop that another trader would be sent to Chota, but the government had not made good on this promise. As a result, Hop told Demeré his people looked on the schedule as "nothing but lies as they did on all the rest of the papers that came from Carolina, and that Charles Town was a place where nothing but lies came from."[78] Questioning the local trader, John Elliott, Demeré found his prices for trade goods exorbitant, especially on the most commonly requested items such as clothing.[79] Demeré, like others before such as Ludovic Grant, warned Governor Lyttelton that if colonial government continued to ignore such irregularities there always would be factionalism in the Indian country. Demeré stated "the traders are for the most part a sett [sic] of villains who studdy [sic] nothing but their own narrow views . . . without having the least regard to justice."[80] Old Hop produced a sample of red paint used by them in body adornment, long a traditional practice. Sold by the trader John Elliott, it was found to contain lead.[81]   The Indians considered the traders   representatives of Euroamerican government.   Their behavior toward members of their host tribe was taken by the Indians as a barometer of the British government's interest in them as a people. When men of low character operated among them in such a manner, they all but negated any diplomatic effort made by colonial government. Despite the intent of colonial policy formulated in Savannah and Charles Town, it was the day-to-day behavior of the traders which influenced relations between the two cultures.

During Demeré's meeting, Old Hop told him that his people had expected a supply of guns, powder and bullets for a long time and that shipment had never arrived. Using the leverage of trade, he told Demeré that the French sent their Indians to war fully supplied with all war necessities and rewarded them hand-somely for scalps once the Indians returned.[82] Thus, southeastern Indians learned to play competing European powers off each other to correct trade irregularities imposed either intentionally or unintentionally. The meaning of the message was clear: disaffection among the Cherokees was due, at least in part, to a failure of the British to live up to mutually agreed upon trade guidelines. If the British wished to maintain their loyalty, they would have to perform as well as the French. Obviously, playing off one power against the other could be done too often and for frivolous reasons. Until each side reached its financial limit, however, both would experience an upsurge in Indian expenditures with Native Americans often gaining from the contest.

As the year 1757 wore on, more evidence appeared linking British problems with the Tellico Cherokees to trader irregularities. In April, Demeré wrote to Lyttelton with a new tale of trader intrigue: the Great Warrior of Chota had told him that John Elliott, the trader who had ill used the Tellico people, had incurred a debt to him and his people for horses and supplies. Elliott had promised them rum as payment, stating that he had a supply at Keowee, and the Great Warrior had ordered eight kegs as payment. In truth, there was rum at Keowee. Lyttelton had ordered that it be confiscated there and not shipped into Cherokee lands. The treaty of Saludy which the Cherokees had signed with the former governor Glen had prohibited the shipment of rum into the backcountry. Though Demeré labored to explain this and the illegality of Elliott's behavior, the Great Warrior could not understand Demeré's failure to repay them. The Cherokee told Demeré that if the British refused to pay their debts, his people would do likewise. Demeré's refusal to comply seemed to lend credence to French talk of British duplicity in their dealings with Indians. Further, the Great Warrior intended to seize goods passing through Cherokee lands from Charles Town to recoup their losses.[83]

Demeré continued to receive intelligence reports linking problems with the southern Indians to trader activity. In April 1757, he also learned that some of the traders among the Creeks were selling trade items to French officers, who then supplied their Indian allies with the goods.[84] The French continued their recruiting activities among the Cherokees. During a meeting between the governor of New Orleans and a delegation of Cherokees and Shawnees, the governor told them again to initiate a war against the British, starting with one of their forts. He advised them to kill five hundred or six hundred British and clear them out of the backcountry so that the French might enter the Indian towns and properly supply them.[85]

By the summer of 1757, more disturbing intelligence reports seemed to confirm that the Cherokees intended to comply with French requests. Daniel Pepper wrote to Demeré stating that two headmen from the Lower Creeks had warned him that the Cherokees intended to attack the newly built Fort Loudoun; the Cherokees had requested the aid of the Creeks in the plan.[86] Events elsewhere in the colonies exacerbated deteriorating relationships. In April 1758, a delegation of Cherokees bound for Charles Town was intercepted by William Byrd II, assistant to the newly-appointed Superintendent of Indian Affairs for the Southern District, Edmund Atkin. Byrd wanted the delegation, led by Little Carpenter, to go to Virginia and join in efforts to engage the French at Fort Duquesne. Earlier groups of Cherokees had gone and been dissatisfied with the presents given as payment by the Virginians. Once this latest group arrived, they too asked for presents--more presents than the British commander, Colonel George Washington, could give. Unfortunately, Native American styles of combat differed greatly from European ones. The Cherokees grew impatient as they waited for the British to build posts and supply houses along the route to attack the French fort. Ultimately, the Cherokees abandoned the effort and started home through Virginia, taking horses and other goods in recompense.[87]   Little Carpenter eventually reached an understanding with the colony of Virginia in time to participate in the raid on Fort Duquesne. Two days before the final assault, the Cherokees were told by the Savannos that the French were abandoning their fort and so they too abandoned the fray once more. The move angered colonial officials and Little Carpenter was taken before the expedition commander, Brigadier General John Forbes, Governor Francis Fauquier of Virginia, and Governor William Lyttelton of South Carolina. Relations with the Cherokees were so shaky that colonial officials decided not to press the matter.[88]

Once Little Carpenter was back in the Cherokee homelands, his people decided to recoup their perceived losses for services rendered by attacking the Carolina backcountry. This situation, combined with the rumors about an attack on Fort Loudoun, prompted Lyttelton to dispatch reinforcements to Loudoun and to order replacements for dwindling food supplies. The colonial governor also initiated an embargo on trade goods, including arms and ammunition, against the Cherokee people. The cessation of trade was so drastic that the Cherokees sent a small delegation, led by Occonostotah, to reason with Lyttelton. Unmoved, he detained the Cherokee emissaries for a time, before sending them home with an armed escort. En route he dispatched a messenger with the trader John Elliott to reassure the Cherokees such measures were for the party's safety in the unsettled backcountry. Unfortunately, the messenger, at Occonostotah's suggestion, told the Cherokees en route that the delegation were indeed slaves and their colonial escorts planned to destroy their homes and enslave their women and children.[89]

Ultimately, Lyttelton's party reached Fort Prince George in December 1759 without incident. They concluded a peace treaty with the Cherokees in which the latter promised to surrender twenty-four of their people responsible for the murder of Euroamericans in the backcountry. While awaiting the guilty, twenty-two Cherokees would be held hostage at Fort Prince George, released as the murderers surrendered. The one provision directly benefiting the Cherokees called for the return of the traders. The Cherokees further agreed to kill any French agents who came among them and to detain anyone guilty of fomenting trouble between the Cherokees and the British. Led by Attakullakulla, others including Kittagusta, Occonostotah, Oconeca and Killianca signed the treaty.[90]

Though Attakullakulla had secured the release of some Cherokees, he had effectively condemned others in a treaty despised by many of his people. The British had come to the bargaining table armed with the trade goods desperately needed by the Cherokees but would not release those items until the murderers surrendered. Incensed over the treaty and taking of hostages, many Cherokees turned against the most readily available Euroamericans in their midst--the traders. Shortly after the treaty was signed, two groups of Cherokees killed and dismembered the trader John Kelly.[91]

In January 1760, a group of Cherokees bearing concealed weapons requested permission to enter Fort Prince George to exchange murderers for hostages. Their leader tried unsuccessfully to secure the hostages' release; failing, he departed without bloodshed. Concurrently, another group of Cherokees turned on John Elliott's trading house at New Keowee. Elliott, guilty of over charging the Cherokees, was killed along with nine other Euroamerican men.[92] On 16 February 1760, the Cherokees moved against Fort Prince George. Luring its commander, Lieutenant Richard Coytmore, outside on the pretext of a desire to make a trip to Charles Town, they murdered the British officer. In retaliation, soldiers inside the fort murdered the Indian hostages.[93]

Coytmore's death signaled a general war between the two cultures now occupying the southern backcountry. The trader Thomas Beamer carried the news to Charles Town, and Carolina officials hurried to organize a colony ill prepared for war. Governor Lyttelton summoned troops from North Carolina and Virginia while Governor Henry Ellis tried to marshal the Creeks to fight on the side of the colonists against their traditional enemies. Of major concern were the two forts isolated in a now hostile environment. Military officials organized a relief expedition for Fort Prince George, though Fort Loudoun was completely surrounded. Colonel Archibald Montgomery led the relief expedition bound for Fort Prince George, which was ambushed by Cherokees. Montgomery failed in his attempt to crush the Cherokees, leaving Fort Loudoun at the mercy of its enemies. The Cherokees starved the besieged fort into submission but released its British occupants in exchange for the fort's remaining ammunition and guns. Marching out of the backountry, the garrison was attacked. Attakullakulla took Loudoun's sole surviving officer, John Stuart, to Virginia where he ransomed the British officer.[94]

The British war effort elsewhere was generally more successful after William Pitt became the new chief minister in December 1756. He allowed Britain's Prussian allies to do most of the fighting in the European theater while he deployed British troops in North America to cut off New France. Utilizing the talents of innovative younger officers like James Wolfe and Jeffrey Amherst, Britain secured victory with the fall of Quebec in 1759. With respect to the war for Indian loyalties, the French were losing well before 1759. At the outset, British naval blockades were unable to keep out French ships bearing Indian goods. By the war's end, however, the blockades were effectively limiting the French trade. By 1757, the Choctaws, encouraged by the Chickasaws, threatened to abandon their French allies for the British. The scarcity of goods prompted unscrupulous French traders to cheat the Choctaws further exacerbating the situation between France and its Indian allies.[95]

In November 1760, Lieutenant Governor William Bull notified the Board of Trade of a recent meeting with the Choctaws, who told Bull that the bulk of their people had few remaining ties with the French and wished to open diplomatic relations and trade with the British.[96] Nonetheless, French agents, such as Lantagnac, still worked to alienate the Cherokees from the British. As noted earlier, Lantagnac originally was a soldier stationed at Mobile who became lost in the forest on a hunting expedition. Turned over to the British by their Indian allies, he remained in Charles Town for a time until he became a trader among the Cherokees. He acquired a Cherokee mate during his stay among them, though he traded among the Creeks as well. Aided by his Cherokee wife, he continued his efforts to align the Cherokees with France.[97]

Perhaps the major French defeats after 1756 and trade problems prompted the Choctaws to consider aligning with the British. In any event, more colonial officials began to report a correspondence with them. In October 1760, Georgia Governor Henry Ellis reported to the board that the French had persuaded a small group of Choctaws to murder a British packhorseman. Another group of Choctaws joined by some Creeks pursued the original assailants until driven off by the gunfire from a nearby French fort. Ellis promised the Choctaws liberal trade and used the new relationship to discipline an old one. Ellis told the Creeks that traders bound for Choctaw lands would have to pass through their own. He warned the Creeks that if they molested these traders, they would have new enemies--the Choctaws.[98]

Though the physical battles of the Great War for Empire had ended, two facts became apparent to colonial officials. First, many problems with the Indian tribes aligned with Britain had been caused or exacerbated by insufficient trade goods and ungovernable traders. Second, these weaknesses had allowed the French to use the Indians to harass British settlements quite effectively. South Carolina Lieutenant Governor Bull wrote to William Pitt in February 1761 with information concerning French activities. He noted that the often lucrative nature of the Indian trade tempted many sorts of men to engage in it. Further, French supplies from Mobile bound for the Cherokees had weakened Britain's hold on that tribe. In fact, French efforts had almost disrupted British relations with the Creeks as well. As a result, Bull informed Pitt that South Carolina had enacted a series of laws placing stringent controls on material bound for the Indian country.[99]

South Carolina did take steps to regulate the trade with the Cherokees better, much as it had planned to regulate the trade with other tribes after the Yamassee War in 1715. A new governor, Thomas Boone, planned to make the Cherokee trade a public monopoly with a board of five directors to govern the trade and a resident factor to implement policy. A rough draft of this plan illustrated that the colonials well knew the source of many of their old problems. It also indicated they would no longer tolerate many traditional native practices which were becoming increasingly expensive. In a very bold opening statement, the draft noted that "neither the Indian traders nor Indians can be at all depended on; the first are the refuse of the Earth, [and] stick at nothing to obtain a temporary advantage."[100] The plan called for uniform policies in dealing with one group of Indians when two or more colonies were involved. Trade would take place at outposts located only so deep in the backcountry as could be readily defended in case of attack. The factors employed in the public trade were to be men of good character and even temper. Trade goods would consist of the usual items, and ammunition and rum were included on the list. The authors of the plan deemed credit extension to the Indians as the source of many past disputes and strictly forbad its use. The plan called for factors to be authorized to seize persons trafficking in goods illegally in the Cherokee lands and to hold their wares as a guarantee that such persons would appear at the proper time to answer charges. Punishments for Indian offenses were quite harsh. If a Cherokee killed a Euroamerican, then the government would be empowered to kill two members of his tribe. In order to prevent the Indians from engaging in retributive justice, all trade with the tribe would cease until the Indians accepted the judgment and punishment. Not surprisingly, the plan called for an end to Indian conferences, which it termed disgraceful. It asked that such practices "be forever laid aside, those ignominious tributes be utterly abolished, & that immense expense of provisions be saved."[101] Colonial Indian expenditures had risen steadily during the critical contest to gain the loyalty of the various tribes of the backcountry. Now officials were attempting to pare down those expenditures, a move bound to conflict with tribal values and with the custom of giving presents, established by the Spanish, and practiced by the British with the southern Indians for 150 years.

The South Carolina act for regulating the Cherokee trade was quite similar to its draft. The purposes of the act were to maintain the peace recently reestablished with the Cherokees and to encourage their withdrawal from French interests through a steady supply of needed goods. Honest, trustworthy men were to operate the trade out of a storehouse at Fort Prince George, located at Keowee. The trade was to be governed by a board of directors. Thomas Lamboll, Thomas Shubrick, Gabriel Manigault, John Savage and Thomas Smith were chosen as those directors. They planned to hire a resident factor for Fort Prince George at an annual salary of £300. That factor would take an oath and enter a bond pledging to enforce the trade regulations under penalty of a £1,000 fine.[102]

His duties included enforcing uniform prices for trade goods sold and skins received. Interestingly, the factor was to prevent the Indians from entering Euoamerican settlements for any reason whatsoever.   No members of the governor's council or the assembly could be members of the board of directors.[103] In July 1762, the board chose Edward Wilkinson as factor and gave him instructions which covered weaknesses recognized by the colonials as detrimental to their relationship with the Cherokees. Neither Wilkinson nor any of his assistants was allowed to issue credit. Nor was Wilkinson allowed to leave his post, except in extreme emergency. He and his associates had to maintain friendly relations with the Indians though they were to avoid making them any promises. The factor had to record various aspects of the trade and notable events in Cherokee life.[104]

Unfortunately for both Native American and Euoamerican cultures, the policy had virtually no time to correct old ills. In 1763, King George III issued a royal proclamation opening the trade to all subjects. Thus, South Carolina's monopoly was illegal and was dissolved by an ordinance on 6 October 1764. Supervision of the trade in the South reverted to the office of Superintendent of Indian Affairs John Stuart. Stuart's ascendancy over the colonial governors, albeit incomplete and brief, ushered in a new age in Britain's relationship with the southern tribes.

NOTES

1. Board of Commissioners Meeting, 11 July 1716, Indian Book 1: 75.

2. Board of Commissioners Meeting, 10 September 1717, ibid., 205. Public factors were government-sponsored traders used to control the trade by keeping free traders out of the backcountry.

3. Board of Commissioners to Meredith Hughes, 1 May 1717, ibid., 176.

4. Board of Commissioners to Eleazar Wiggan, 20 September 1717, ibid., 211-212.

5. Board of Commissioners Meeting, 24 October 1717, ibid., 221.

6. Board of Commissioners Meeting, 8 May 1718, ibid., 272.

7. Board of Commissioners Meeting, 9 May 1718., ibid., 273.

8. Board to Captain William Hatton, 2 November 1717, ibid., 223.

9. Board to Meredith Hughes, 11 April 1718, ibid., 265.

10. Board of Commissioners Meeting, 19 July 1718, ibid., 306.

11. Byrd, *The Prose Works,* 311.

12. Ibid. The Yamassees wreaked havoc on South Carolina when their source of income, hunting and slave procurement, failed and their creditors kept pushing them to pay their trade debts.

13. Ibid., 274.

14. Ibid., 275.

15. Governor Glen's Talk to the Cherokees, n.d., Indian Book 2: 45.

16. Ibid.

17. The Headmen and Warriors of the Lower Cherokees to Governor Glen, 10 May 1751, ibid., 62-63. The Cherokees traditionally warred with the Creeks but were subject to attack from the Shawnees, often called the Norward Indians.

18. Talk of the Overhill Cherokees at Great Tellico to Governor James Glen and the South Carolina Assembly, 9 April 1751, ibid., 64.

19. Daniel H. Usner, "The Deerskin Trade in French Louisiana," *Proceedings of the Tenth Meeting of the French Colonial Historical Society,* Philip P. Boucher, ed. (New York: University Press of America, 1985), 76.

20. Ibid., 76-77.

21. Ibid., 77.

22. Ibid., 78-79.

23. Ibid., 79.

24. Robert G. McPherson, ed., *The Journal of the Earl of Egmont: Abstract of the Trustees Proceedings for Establishing the Colony of Georgia 1732-1738* (Athens: University of Georgia Press, 1962), 246.

25. Oglethorpe to Mary Matthews, 13 July 1742, *Colonial Records of Georgia,* 27, 3.

26. Major William Horton to Mary Matthews, 23 July 1743, ibid., 5.

27. Horton to Mary Bosomworth, 13 June 1744, ibid., 6.

28. Horton to Mary Bosomworth, 21 September 1744, ibid., 8.

29. Emperor of the Cherokees to Governor Glen, 10 October 1744, CO5/371: 6.

30. Ibid.

31. Glen to the Board of Trade, 29 September 1746, CO5/371: 104.

32. Ibid. A guinea, last issued in 1813, was worth 21 shillings. One hogshead by the mid eighteenth century was equivalent to 52.5 imperial gallons. An imperial gallon was 20 percent more than a standard U.S. gallon. Thus, 1 hogshead contained the equivalent

volume of 63 gallons.

33. Glen to Board of Trade, 28 April 1747, CO5/371: 133.

34. Glen to Board of Trade, 26 July 1748, CO5/372: 67.

35. Thomas Devall to Governor Glen, 20 July 1749, CO5/459: 26.

36. Glen to Board of Trade, 23 December 1749, CO5/372: 168.

37. Glen to Board of Trade, 23 December 1749, CO5/372: 168.

38. Governor Glen to Board of Trade, 23 December 1749, CO5/372: 168.

39. Board of Trade to the Lords of Committee of Council, 14 September 1737, CO5/401: 224.

40. Board of Trade to the King, 21 June 1738, CO5/401: 269.

41. Ludovic Grant to Governor Glen, 3 May 1752, Indian Book 2: 263.

42. Memorial of Robert Bunning and Others to Governor Glen and Council, 22 November 1751, ibid., 150.

43. Ibid.

44. Governor Glen to Captains Gibson, Fairchild and Minnick, 12 September 1751, Indian Book 2: 123-124.

45. Ludovic Grant to Governor Glen, 8 February 1753, Indian Book 2: 367. Colonial traders before the advent of the superintendency were not enjoined from selling liquor to the Indians.

46. John Pearson to George Hunter, 26 May 1751, ibid., 77.

47. Pat Graham to Governor Glen, 15 June 1751, ibid., 81.

48. Glen to Tacite of Hiawassie, Colane of Eurphorsee and King of the Valley, *Colonial Records of South Carolina: Documents Relating to Indian Affairs 1754-1765*, William L. McDowell, Jr., ed. (Columbia: South Carolina Department of Archives and History, 1970), 26. Hereafter referred to as Indian Book 3.

49. Ludovic Grant to Glen, 27 March 1755, ibid., 42-45.

50. Lachlan McGillivray to Glen, 13 May 1755, ibid., 72-73.

51. Lieutenant Governor Dinwiddie to the Catawba Nation, its King, Sachems, and Warriors, December 1755, ibid., 102.

52. James Beamer to Governor Glen, 21 February 1756, ibid., 105

53. Ibid., 106.

54. Ibid.

55. Headmen and Warriors of the Chickasaw Nation to the King of Carolina and His Beloved Men, 5 April 1756, ibid., 109-110.

56. McDowell, Jr., Indian Book 3: xxiii.

57. Raymond Demeré to Governor Lyttelton, 19 July 1756, Indian Book 3: 144. Attakullakulla was called Little Carpenter by the British. Both names are used in the text as records refer to him by both.

58. Major Andrew Lewis to Demeré, 11 September 1756, ibid., 202-204. Lewis was the British commander in charge of the group of Cherokees sent to help the Virginia colony deal with attacking Shawnees in February 1756. See John P. Brown, *Old Frontiers: The Story of the Cherokee Indians from Earliest Times to the Date of their Removal to the West, 1838* (Kingsport, Tennessee: Southern Publishers, 1938), 57.

59. Lieutenant White Outerbridge to Governor Lyttelton, 22 October 1756, ibid., 210-211.

60. Ibid., 211.

61. Demeré to Lyttelton, 13 October 1756, ibid., 214. Ammonscossittee, a younger leader of the Overhill Cherokees resided at Tellico, though Connecorte, known to the British as Old Hop, considered himself the more fitting leader of the nation and his town of Chota,

the more proper seat of power. Politically and economically, a rivalry of sorts existed between the towns of Tellico and Chota. See E. Raymond Evans, "Notable Persons in Cherokee History: Ostenaco," *Journal of Cherokee Studies,* Volume I, No. 1 (Summer 1976): 42.

62. Demeré to Old Hop and the Little Carpenter, 3 October 1756, ibid., 222. Like Attakullakulla, Old Hop had an Englsih name and his own Cherokee name, Connecorte. Colonials called him Old Hop because of his lameness.

63. Ibid., 222-223.

64. Old Hop's Reply to Captain Demeré, 3 October 1756, ibid., 223-224.

65. Old Warrior to Demeré, 9 November 1756, ibid., 244-245. Chatuga was located on the Tellico River, near Tellico, in modern Monroe County, Tennessee. Hiwassee was located on the Hiwassee River at Savannah Ford in modern Polk County, Tennessee. See Goodwin, *Cherokees in Transition,* 153-156.

66. Demeré to Lyttelton, 18 November 1756, ibid., 249.

67. Judd's Friend, known otherwise as Ostenaco, was a Cherokee leader noted for both diplomatic and military accomplishments. He most likely was born in the town of Hiwassee. In addition to his given name, he earned the right to be called "Mankiller" for his military prowess. He was called Judd's Friend because of his close association with a Euroamerican named Judd. Often based at Chota, Ostenaco used his diplomatic skills for many years to maintain amicable relations between the Overhill Cherokees and the government of colonial South Carolina. See Evans, "Notable Persons," 41-53.

68. Possibly more than other Cherokees, the Mankiller of Tellico was firmly identified by the English translation of the great war title "Outacite," at least in colonial records. Born in the town of Tellico, this Cherokee leader did try to establish an alliance between the French at Fort Toulouse (Alabama Fort) and the Tellico Cherokees. Though close scrutiny indicates this alliance was possible because British traders so badly mismanaged the trade with Tellico, South Carolina government came to view the Mankiller as an unreliable mercenary. See Fred Gearing, "Priests and Warriors: Social Structure for Cherokee Politics in the 18th Century," *American Anthropologist,* Volume 64, No. 5, Part 2 (October 1962): 64.

69. Intelligence from Judd's Friend to Captain Raymond Demeré, 10 December 1756, ibid., 265. In *Empire of Fortune: Crowns, Colonies, and Tribes in the Seven Years War in America,* Francis Jennings noted that British soldiers at Fort Pitt deliberately infected enemy Indians with smallpox in 1763, see 200.

70. Ibid., 265-266.

71. Intelligence from Indian Nancy to Captain Raymond Demeré, 12 December 1756, ibid., 269.

72. Intelligence from Nancy Butler to Captain Raymond Demeré, 20 December 1756, ibid., 276.

73. Talk of the Blind Slave Catcher of Chatuga, 2 January 1757, ibid., 305-306.

74. Known alternately as the Alabama Fort and Fort Toulouse, the French enclave was located just north of the modern Alabama capital of Montgomery.

75. Demeré to Governor Lyttelton, 4 January 1757, ibid., 306-307. Thomas Leaper and James Kelly were two packhorse traders who worked out of Tellico. See David C. Corkran, *The Cherokee Frontier: Conflict and Survival: 1740-1762* (Norman: University of Oklahoma Press, 1962), 104.

76. Demeré to Governor Lyttelton, 15 January 1757, ibid., 315. Unfortunately for researchers, some of the Indian traders of the late colonial period are mentioned briefly or indirectly and little other information is available on them.

77. Report of Lieutenant Robert Wall to Captain Raymond Demeré, 13 January 1757, ibid., 321-322.

78. Demeré to Governor Lyttelton, 5 February 1757, ibid., 333-334.

79. Ibid. Elliot's other questionable trade practices included the use of a shortened yardstick for measuring and a rigged scale that consistently measured two pounds less than actual weight.

80. Ibid., 334.

81. Ibid. Lead poisoning occurs when the substance is ingested or absorbed through the skin, resulting in anemia, constipation, colic, paralysis or muscular cramps.

82. Ibid., 335.

83. Demeré to Lyttelton, 2 April 1757, ibid., 360. Keowee was located on the Keowee River, adjacent to Fort Prince George in modern Pickens County, South Carolina. See Goodwin, *Cherokees in Transition,* 154.

84. Demeré to Lyttelton, 11 April 1757, ibid., 366.

85. Abstract of a Talk Between the Governor of New Orleans and the Cherokee and Shawnee Indians, n.d., ibid., 369.

86. Daniel Pepper to Demeré, 27 June 1757, ibid., 390. Pepper is again one of those figures whose name surfaces in connection with the Indian trade but who is hard to identify further against the backdrop of Anglo-Indian conflicts in the 1750s.

87. Ibid., xxix-xxx.

88. Ibid., xxx-xxxi.

89. Ibid., xxxii-xxxiii.

90. *The South Carolina Gazette,* 1325, 5 January-8 January 1760, 1.

91. David H. Corkran, *The Cherokee Frontier: Conflict and Survival, 1740-62* (Norman: University of Oklahoma Press, 1962), 189-191.

92. Corkran, *The Cherokee Frontier,* 191-192.

93. David H. Corkan, *The Carolina Indian Frontier* (Columbia: University of South Carolina Press, 1970), 58.

94. McDowell, Jr., Indian Book 3: xxxiv-xxxv.

95. Patricia Dillon Woods, *French-Indian Relations on the Southern Frontier 1699-1762* (Ann Arbor: University of Michigan Research Press, 1980), 164-166.

96. Lieutenant Governor William Bull to Board of Trade, 18 November 1760, CO5/7: 264.

97. Ibid.

98. Henry Ellis to Board of Trade, 20 October 1760, CO5/7: 270.

99. Lieutenant Governor William Bull to Secretary of State, William Pitt, 18 February 1761, CO5/20: 95.

100. Rough Sketch of Plan for Management of Indians and the Conducting of the Necessary Commerce with Them, n.d., CO5/377: 273.

101. Ibid.

102. Documents Accompanying the Journal of the Directors of the Cherokee Trade 1762-1765, Indian Book 3: 557-560.

103. Ibid., 560-562.

104. Instructions to Edward Wilkinson, 19 July 1762, ibid., 570-573.

7

Stuart's America: Relations with the Southern Indians During the Superintendency of John Stuart

Had John Stuart not survived the attack of Fort Loudoun nor Edmund Atkin died, Stuart would never have attained the unique position of Indian superintendent. As Britain's political representative, Stuart was responsible for diplomatic relations with native peoples stretched out over an immense territory (Figure 7). Though Spanish and French threats receded into the background, trade issues continued to dictate the relationship between the two cultures.

Stuart's initial task after the war centered on a series of conferences in the Southeast to familiarize the Indians with the Proclamation of 1763 and its intent to halt westward expansion. As noted previously, Stuart met with the Upper and Lower Creeks and Choctaws in November 1763, telling them the French had been banished west of the Mississippi for their deceitful ways. Secretary of State for the Southern Department Lord Egremont authorized £4,000-£5,000 worth of gifts to support British policy.[1]

Though off to a lavish start, British officials were actually bent on minimizing costs for Indian affairs. From the government perspective, Indian expenses had grown enormously during the war years, especially since Britain's

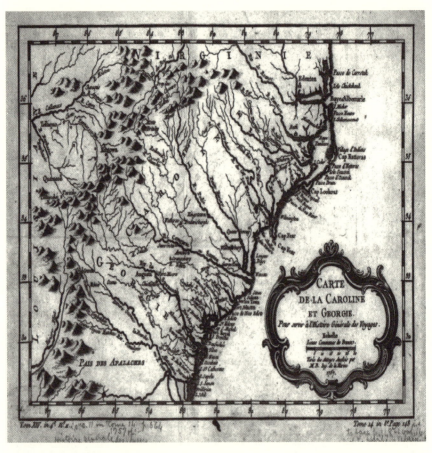

Map of Carolina Backcountry. Courtesy of Hargrett Rare Book and Manuscript Library/ University of Georgia Libraries.

Indian allies had not performed as well as hoped. Stuart, in a May 1763 letter to General Jeffrey Amherst, promised to avoid unnecessary expenditures for Indian presents while acknowledging his responsibility to police the Indian trade for fraud. Stuart noted half-heartedly that without the coercive power to make traders obey, he stood little chance of success.[2] He believed true military rank would have helped him deal with the traders and governors.

Some problems had not changed. Though the French and Spanish had been banished past the Mississippi River, they still managed to harass British settlements using their Indian allies. Indian traders and land-hungry colonials irritated some Indian groups already unhappy with the British. In February 1763, when the commander of Fort Detroit, Major Henry Gladwin, announced the end of the Great War for Empire to the tribes of the Old Northwest, they rallied together under Pontiac, an Ottawa chief, to attack the British. For three years, Indians from the Ottawa, Chippewa, Potawatomi, Huron, Shawnee and Delaware tribes laid siege to the fort and laid waste to the surrounding countryside. Eventually, the attackers' patience waned when the fort, steadily supplied by Fort Niagara, did not capitulate. Gradually the Indians also realized that France had ceded Canada to the British. In 1766, Pontiac surrendered to Northern Superintendent William Johnson.[3]

In January 1764, Stuart wrote to Board of Trade Secretary John Pownall that a group of New Orleans merchants had been supplying the Indian incendiaries of the Illinois country, including Pontiac himself. Stuart dispatched a group of Cherokees and Chickasaws to that area to seize any French traders they encountered. He also mentioned that General Thomas Gage had suggested a plan to aid Stuart in his continuing job of making allies out of former enemies. Gage proposed that Stuart try to hire a former French Indian expert, Monsieur Monberaut, a former commander of Fort Toulouse in the Creek lands. As noted earlier, Monberaut had previously worked to alienate the Creeks from the British, but Stuart now felt he could put those persuasive talents to use, especially since Monberaut felt ill used by his own government. He accepted the offer and Stuart hired him as a deputy to help strengthen ties with the Creeks.[4]

In 1765, Stuart again met with groups such as the Creeks and the Choctaws. Concurrently, colonial governors continued sending their own representatives among the southern tribes, though George III had urged them to exercise caution in picking agents. At an Indian conference in West Florida, Stuart issued regulations jointly with West Florida's governor George Johnstone. Stuart's aides were expected to cooperate with colonial officials like Johnstone. At the conference, Stuart issued a list of nineteen guidelines for those engaged in the Indian trade: liquor, rifles and ammunition were not to be sold by traders. Stuart established limits on the amounts of undressed skins that could be purchased by the traders and also limited credit available to Native Americans to thirty pounds of deer skins. Stuart imposed a uniform set of weights and measures and a list of fixed prices for goods sold to the Indians. The superintendent placed a tariff on goods sold in the trade and confined it to Indian towns. The traders were not to strike or misuse the Indians nor hold meetings with them without Stuart's permission.[5]

Unfortunately, Stuart's ability to enforce such regulations was hampered by old problems. Neither he nor his assistants could be everywhere at once. Nor could they make sure that only decent, honest Euroamericans became Indian traders or colonial agents. As noted earlier, Alexander Cameron wrote to Stuart in June 1766, appalled at the fraudulent business tactics practiced by the traders in Cherokee lands.[6] "It is no wonder," Cameron wrote, "that the Cherokees should withdraw their affections from us when we allow such villains to trade or reside amongst them."[7]

With the end of the Great War for Empire, intercolonial rivalry again took center stage after the peace of 1763. As previously described, Virginia subsidized its traders and the Cherokees in the Carolinas were almost at the point of war in their resentment of what they thought were unfair trade prices.[8]

Despite such setbacks, Stuart tried to fulfill the duties of his office. One of his responsibilities was to secure land cessions from the southern Indians for various colonies, such as Florida. Specifically, West Florida needed large cessions from the Chickasaws, Choctaws and Creeks, and many of Stuart's meetings from March to June 1765 dealt with that subject. Stuart met with the Upper and Lower Creeks at Pensacola and with the Chickasaws and Choctaws at Mobile.[9] The language of trade played a large part in those negotiations. The Creeks were present at Pensacola from 27 May 1765 until 4 June 1765. They were anxious to stabilize trade ties in order to receive more regularly the items upon which they had become dependent. Stuart told the Creeks that their "Great King" could not take care of them properly if they did not cede the land requested by colonial officials.[10] The Creek land cession proved to be a hard bargain, for, despite Stuart's requests for more, they ceded only fifteen miles. Further, Stuart anticipated future problems in dealing with the Upper Creeks and Choctaws because the French traditionally had given them large presents; he believed that weaning these tribes from such practices would be difficult.[11]

The Mobile Conference had ended the month prior to the beginning of the Pensacola meeting but had perhaps netted more significant results for the British. Here, Stuart was able to draw upon the expertise of his new employee, the Chevalier de Monberaut. The conference began on 26 March 1765 though smallpox delayed one group of Choctaws. Governor Johnstone opened the meeting by introducing Stuart as the Indians' protector and Monberaut as his assistant. Johnstone told the delegates of the British desire for peace in the Indian lands and proposed regulation of the prices of trade staples. Johnstone also planned to station agents at Fort Tombecbe. Of course, colonial officials wanted a land cession from these Indians as well. Monberaut underscored the finality of the new diplomatic order by telling the Indians that the French had departed, never to return. The British could supply them well, he reassured them, adding that his concern for their well-being had prompted him to stay instead of returning to France. The only obstacle in these negotiations came when the Choctaws delayed by illness arrived. They stubbornly refused to exchange their French medals for British ones until Monberaut hinted that Stuart would choose his own recipients, replacing the recalcitrant leaders with new ones.[12] Though Stuart received the land cessions, he had taken important steps in supplanting French influence among the Choctaws and Chickasaws.[13]

Despite some successes with new allies, problems festered among old ones. Alexander Cameron in 1766 noted that the Indian traders among the Cherokees were beginning to appoint their own Indian assistants. Cameron found that, to impress their Indian employees, the traders would tell all manner of lies, and they continued to eliminate all competitors in the trade, no matter the cost.[14] Since Stuart had no direct coercive power to deal with renegade traders, he sought to stem their source. In April 1767 he appealed to Lord Charles Montagu of South Carolina and Joseph Wright of Georgia, asking the two governors to recall all licenses issued to trade generally in the backcountry. Stuart wanted licenses granted to responsible people who would trade in specific towns.[15] Stuart went further, asking the governors to issue licenses only to traders who could produce persons of high character willing to take out bonds with the traders as proof of their good behavior. Once licensed, traders would be required to follow directions from colonial governors or the superintendent under penalty of a £300 fine. Traders also would have to accept responsibility for their assistants, providing their names and addresses with their original bond.[16]

Though Stuart moved to minimize trader competition, trader grievances continued to grow. As discussed earlier, in May 1767, South Carolina traders complained to Stuart about a Cherokee demand either to lower prices on their trade goods or to allow them access to traders from Georgia who could offer lower prices. These backcountry merchants blamed their problems on the excessive number of people engaged in the trade, contributing to the decline in profits. Also, the Cherokees had been so preoccupied with enemy attacks they were unable to hunt and process as many skins as formerly. As a result they charged more for the few they had. Competition to sell European goods had produced so much price cutting that the Indians had come to expect it. The Carolina merchants stated that the Cherokees wanted to deal exclusively with Carolina traders, as the Indians liked their quality of goods and traders better. They blamed part of their economic problem on a Carolina ordinance which forbade Indian traders to receive their clients in Euroamerican settlements. The Georgia merchants, however, could trade in Indian or Euroamerican towns, giving them a decided advantage over the Carolinians in a competitive, glutted market.[17]

In that same petition, the Carolina traders noted some aspects of trade that the colonials had learned in the late war. They blamed some of the irregularities in the trade on the practice of giftgiving, noting that those who gave the greatest gifts had the most influence over the Indians. The merchants also disapproved of the limitations that South Carolina imposed over the importation of rum into the Cherokee lands. Though they respectfully complied with the law, they believed the Indians simply would travel to settlements where they could purchase it. Since the Cherokees were going to purchase rum anyway, the Carolina traders were being deprived of yet another way to compete with other traders. These backcountry merchants wanted to be free of cumbersome trade regulations, despite the disastrous results for the Indian tribes. Ironically, they acknowledged the difficulty caused by other traders while disclaiming any blame themselves: "your memorialists are sorry to hear that the name of Indian trader has been in some degree a reproach; they are not sensible that any of their substitutes have so atrociously offended as to reflect upon their employers."[18]

As trade problems increased once more, Stuart found himself juggling diplomatic problems as well. In early 1768, the Cherokees complained of Euroamerican encroachment on their lands. This was particularly irritating for Stuart as the tribe recently had ceded large chunks of their land to stop further encroachment.[19] The governments of both the Carolinas permitted these movements. In fact, the North Carolina governor, William Tryon, opened land in the Great Smoky Mountains, an area deep within the heart of Cherokee lands, for settlement. When the Cherokees petitioned Stuart, the superintendent forwarded a copy of the Proclamation of 1763 to Tryon. With trade problems once more on the increase and with colonial governors deliberately ignoring royal edicts, Stuart needed all the resources at his disposal to carry out the duties of his office.

What he received in 1768, instead, was a serious blow. In that year, George III officially returned control of the Indian trade to the colonies. Both Stuart and William Johnson continued in their posts and Stuart was permitted to retain two deputies along with an annual budget of £3,000 per annum for Indian gifts, though his expenses were not to exceed that budget for any reason.[20] Though the outcome of the Great War for Empire had been favorable to Great Britain, it left the nation with a tremendous postwar debt. The transfer of power was designed to alleviate extra expenses; to that end, Britain planned to withdraw all posts in the interiors of its colonies. Stuart worried about the psychological effects of such a move on Britain's Indian allies. If an insufficient quantity of trade goods were perceived by the Cherokees as lack of attachment, withdrawal might well be perceived as hostility. Stuart instructed Alexander Cameron to tell the ever-fragile Cherokees that the sole reason for the pullout was British faith in the Cherokees to regulate their own affairs.[21]

Though dealt a disastrous blow in the running of his office, Stuart rechanneled his energy into achieving old goals through new avenues. He wrote to Hillsborough in the fall of 1768 requesting that colonial governors require the Indian traders to obey him when he summoned them for meetings. Stuart also queried Hillsborough where he might refer Indian complaints, now that the trade had reverted to individual colonies.[22] Such a question was justified since Indian complaints were on the rise once more.

One of Stuart's larger problems, which concerned the Cherokees and the Virginia governor, Francis Fauquier, illustrates the problems caused the superintendent by colonial governors. In the fall of 1766, Virginia and the Cherokees were renegotiating their boundaries. The colony appeared to be dragging its heels in the matter and Stuart queried Fauquier about the delay. Fauquier wrote back explaining the delay as his failure to receive a copy of the Proclamation of 1763 and an explanation of its new policy toward settlement.[23] Such actions as this only worsened deteriorating relationships. The Cherokees were eager to end the matter, having already coined the term "Virginian" to describe any land-hungry settler.[24] The Cherokees and Virginians were also trying to settle a murder. Colonists murdered a group of Cherokees and the Virginia governor agreed to compensate the tribe with a quantity of presents. Stuart relayed the terms of the settlement to the Cherokees, but then Fauquier was remiss in honoring his end of the deal. Stuart noted that such actions impeded the cause of Indian management because they made him appear untrustworthy.[25] Fauquier died before fulfilling his agreement with the Cherokees, and so Stuart tried to reason with Fauquier's successor, John Blair. Stuart told Blair that the Cherokees simply did not understand the delay; they interpreted it as an outright breach of promise.[26] One lesson which few Euroamericans, except Indian officials like Stuart, learned was that Native Americans did not fully perceive the differences among Euoramericans. When Virginians murdered Cherokees, the slighted parties viewed all Euroamericans as guilty. They neither understood the importance of boundary lines separating Virginians from North Carolinians nor differentiated good Indian traders from bad ones. They viewed each Euroamerican as a representative of George III. One thoughtless official could undo half a century's diplomatic work.

In May 1768, Alexander Cameron wrote to Stuart about just such a person. Cameron noted that a trader named Waters had opened an outpost near Fort Charlotte and begun selling large quantities of liquor. Euroamerican settlers began complaining of abusive treatment by the Cherokees soon after the liquor sales started. Such liquor sales violated Stuart's instructions to Cameron and the last treaty concluded between the Cherokees and the British.[27]

Though the marginal coercive power of Stuart's office effectively had been transferred to the colonial governors, he still held certain responsibilities. He needed to include more linguists in his budget in order to deal with both peripheral tribes and longstanding allies. Stuart hired an interpreter for the Chickasaws and Choctaws, one for the Creeks and a third to accompany him or his two deputies on special occasions. As a result of this growing bureaucracy, Stuart's budget for Indian gifts was reduced from £3,000 to £1,500.[28]

The year 1770 began poorly for John Stuart. The Virginia House of Burgesses asked him for even larger cessions of Cherokee lands that would place Euroamerican settlements within sixty miles of the Cherokee villages, virtually destroying their hunting grounds. The Creeks were beginning to complain of Euoramerican encroachments along the Mississippi River.[29]

By year's end, Stuart wrote to Hillsborough that every Indian group in his district had implored him to send agents to deal with the traders. Stuart had hoped the colonies would voluntarily formulate a uniform comprehensive Indian management system. Since they had not, he began to reassert his own policy. The Chickasaws had been friendly to the British since 1702 mainly because of trade enticements; Stuart wanted to station a resident deputy among them to relay intelligence reports from that more distant region. He also felt it vital to post an agent among the smaller tribes of the Mississippi. Stuart found men to accept both assignments but noted that his budget would not cover the agent dispatched to Natchez to handle the smaller tribes.[30]

In the spring of 1771 he wrote to Hillsborough that the deregulation of the Indian traders was, once again, the cause of growing unrest among the southern Indians. Specifically, Stuart noted that traders among the Cherokees were allowing their hosts to contract credits far beyond their ability to pay.[31] Hillsborough responded that Stuart's complaint was indeed justifiable. Trader irregularities, Hillsborough feared, ultimately would lead to disastrous consequences. Yet, the secretary noted that the individual colony governors had prevailed over Stuart in the contest for Indian affairs; they had convinced the king that they were the best arbiters of the trade.[32] One of the most dangerous consequences of credit over extension was a resulting demand for land cession. Indians beset by heavy debt occasionally ceded tracts to land-hungry Euroamericans. Dishonest traders knew that and sometimes extended credit to facilitate land acquisition.

In 1771, traders allowed the Cherokees to over extend themselves and then requested land as an alternative to payment with deer skins. Hillsborough instructed Stuart to intervene in this negotiation process to prevent further disastrous results. At the same time, he ordered Governor James Wright of Georgia to discontinue such practices.[33] Stuart likewise told Deputy Cameron to warn all traders with such claims to relinquish them. This problem had the potential to ignite the backcountry as the Creeks claimed part of the land proposed for cession by the Cherokees.[34] Trade threatened to exacerbate the unsteady relationship between two traditionally antagonistic tribes. If the conflicting claims resulted in an Indian war, it would only be a matter of time before the colonials were drawn into the conflict. Unsupervised trade endangered Britain's diplomatic ties with its Indian clients in the interwar years.

The Earl of Hillsborough's tenure as Secretary of State for the American colonies ended in 1772. His replacement, the Earl of Dartmouth, wrote to Stuart, to complain of the cost of Indian conferences and to prohibit him from calling them unless absolutely necessary.[35] Such moves were risky since Indians interpreted any reduction in attention, especially where trade was concerned, as a sign of waning attachment.

As if Dartmouth's cost cutting measures were not binding enough, Stuart found himself harried by individual Indian traders pushing for the land cession. The traders who, as mentioned before, asked Stuart to allow a Cherokee land cession were well aware of its diplomatic dimensions. Unless the cession were allowed, traders would abandon their calling and, if so, the Cherokees would lack the goods upon which they had come to depend. Without them they might resort to combat. Alliance with European enemies of Britain was no longer a possibility, but a hostile Indian confederacy certainly was.[36]

As stated previously, in October 1772, a group composed of John Jamieson, George Baillie and Thomas Netherclift petitioned Stuart to use his influence in the proposed land deal. The traders wanted him to persuade the Creeks to give up their claim over the land the Cherokees wanted to cede. They bluntly told Stuart they had large sums of money invested in the venture and offered lavish presents if he thought that might settle the conflicting claim.[37] Since trade and diplomatic issues were inseparable, trader greed had transformed a business issue into a political one. Unsupervised trade practices produced results more incendiary than calculated attempts to manipulate the tribes through trade.

In the face of the frustrated land deal, traders who previously had been fierce rivals found a new unity. As noted earlier, David Taitt, Stuart's deputy to the Creeks, reported the Creek traders were hard at work trying to induce the Indians to renounce their claim to the Cherokee cession. Perhaps even more dangerous was the fact that these same traders insulted Taitt in front of the Upper Creeks. Since they showed Taitt no deference, he felt the insult cost him the respect of the Creek headmen, thus diminishing his effectiveness.[38] To compound matters, the new Secretary for the American colonies, Dartmouth, notified Stuart in December 1772 that he planned to support the land cession plan to King George III.[39] Stuart responded by warning that continued land aggrandizement was forcing the southern Indians into a political realignment with the fiercer northern tribes.[40]

Until 1775, the role of the Superintendent of Indian Affairs had been to secure land and trade from the southeastern Indians, to maintain peace between them and their Euroamerican neighbors and to minimize Indian expenses. In 1775, Stuart was confronted with emissaries of a new foreign power in the backcountry. Like his own agents, these spoke English and several Indian languages. They also knew how powerfully trade issues affected diplomatic ones. They were the American traders who had Patriot leanings in the smoldering conflict between Great Britain and her American colonies. Perhaps more dangerous than even French traders, these agents had exactly the same background and experiences as the Loyalist traders with whom they now competed. Indians who had encountered difficulty in distinguishing among Georgians, Carolinians and Virginians would have even more difficulty in distinguishing between Patriot and Loyalist traders. More importantly, the sudden competition between the Euroamericans for Indian loyalty would once again create conditions where the southern tribes could dictate trade terms more to their liking. Traders who had shown them kindness and honesty in the past would be the ones to whom they returned to deal, regardless of the traders' political allegiance. Loyalist officials would come to fear Patriot traders and Indian agents as much in the Revolution as they feared French officials in the Great War for Empire.

In July 1775, Governor James Wright of Georgia notified Stuart of the activities of these new rivals. As previously discussed, Wright told Stuart that the Patriots were sending agents into the backcountry to compete for the allegiance of the southern Indians. This rivalry intensified when the Patriots intercepted a shipment of ammunition bound for East Florida and Georgia. Since part of the shipment was meant for the Indians, the interruption in supply would make Loyalist officials appear unable to deliver goods, an undesirable condition which might cost them Indian loyalty.[41]

Stuart informed the Earl of Dartmouth in December 1775 of the full extent of the Patriot threat. As previously noted, not only would Patriot leaders be vying for control of the trade which shaped Indian behavior, the Continental Congress had appointed three former traders as rival Patriot Indian superintendents. Stuart noted that George Galphin, Edward Wilkinson and John Rea had gone to meet with a group of northern superintendents, also appointed by the Congress.[42] The choices for the Patriot superintendents exemplified the threat posed by the newest rival Indian officials. In years past, George Galphin had supplied Indian Commissioner William Pinckney of South Carolina with intelligence reports about French activities among the Creeks in the late 1740s and early 1750s. Edward Wilkinson was the short-lived public factor to the Cherokees in South Carolina's attempt to establish a monopoly in the trade with that tribe. Rea was guilty of illegally pumping rum into Cherokee lands in the 1750s. Thus these men, either in accordance with the law or acting outside it had extensive experience in dealing with the southern Indians.

John Stuart was based, originally, in Charles Town, South Carolina. Patriot forces there, however, suspected him of marshaling Indian troops against them and forced him out of the colonial port. Taking refuge in St. Augustine, Florida, Stuart soon was confronted with the handiwork of the rebel Indian agents, as Patriot officials began using trade threats to manipulate the Indians, as the French had twenty years earlier. In September 1775, he wrote to Dartmouth of George Galphin's dealings with the Creeks, telling them the Patriots were fighting to stop the Loyalists from withdrawing trade from the southern Indians.[43] Patriot forces readily employed trade and the threat of its cessation to manipulate the natives of the backcountry. The Georgia Council of Safety presented a talk to the Lower Creeks explaining the cause of the current hostilities between the Euroamericans. They told the Creeks that violence had erupted when the Great King had demanded more money from the Patriots than they could pay and had sent soldiers to collect that money forcibly.[44] The Patriots obviously hoped to tap into the frustration the Indians had experienced in trying to pay their own debts to traders over the years.

Stuart was forced to resort to his own brand of propaganda in trying to counter the effects of the Patriot superintendents. Through his agent, David Taitt, he informed the Creeks that there was a dispute among the Euroamericans though it did not concern the Indians. Knowing what mattered most to them, Taitt pledged to keep the trade flowing. In return, Loyalist officials expected them to remain attached to the king and to ignore the talks given by the Patriots.[45] A few months later, in December, Patriot forces learned that during a conference with the Cherokees, Alexander Cameron had warned them that without the king's intervention they would have lost all their land to voracious colonials.[46] Loyalist forces knew how to tap Indian fears as well.

As discussed earlier, Patriot suspicion about Stuart's use of his office drove him from Charles Town. To his credit, not until December 1775 did Stuart notify his assistants of instructions from General Thomas Gage to employ the southern Indians to harass Patriot forces. Stuart was quick to point out to his deputies that he did not interpret this as permission to launch indiscriminate attacks on the frontier, but only to engage those subjects involved in armed rebellion. Assistants, such as Alexander Cameron, were to persuade Indian warriors to organize and join Loyalist forces. Not surprisingly, Stuart authorized Cameron to inform the various chiefs that they would be properly supplied with arms and ammunition for the venture. Also unsurprising is the order to apprehend the rebel Indian agents if at all possible.[47] Stuart's job before the war had been to maintain peaceful relations with British colonials, sometimes by encouraging intertribal warfare. Now his job required peaceful intertribal relations so that Indian warriors would be free to harass Patriot forces. Such a swift transition would require much diplomatic skill and an increase in expenditures for arms and presents for the Indian tribes.

In March of 1776, Stuart wrote to Major General Clinton about the stiff opposition he encountered with the rebel Indian agents. Schooled by years of experience with the Indians in the backcountry, these rebel agents appeared to be well funded, so that the competition with them to control the southern Indians would be great. Stuart used the opportunity to lay blame for his current dilemma on years of overlapping jurisdiction in Indian affairs. Stuart observed that all of the southern Patriot officials had been employed by colonial governors in Georgia and South Carolina, the same governors whose independent actions often had made Stuart's job more difficult. In closing, Stuart warned Clinton to expect an upsurge in Indian expenses.[48]

Such warnings were well founded. The southern Indians once again realized the power they had to affect the trade, given the situation among warring Euroamericans. Emistisiguo, a headman among the Creeks, sent word to Stuart in November 1776 reaffirming their loyalty to the Great King. Further, they would provide the warriors requested by Stuart, but only if he had provisions for them. Emistisiguo had refrained from choosing sides in the conflict, but encroachment on his land by the Virginians had convinced him to side with Stuart's forces.[49]

After Lord George Germain replaced the Earl of Dartmouth as Secretary for the American colonies, Stuart asked him for budget increases to subsidize the Indian tribes fighting in their behalf, reminding Germain that keeping the Indians ready to act in the war effort was not an easy task though it was an expensive one.[50] In fact, given Stuart's limited budget of £3,000, it was an exorbitant expenditure. In January 1777, Stuart submitted a summary of his expenses covering the period from 1 January 1775 until 31 December 1776 amounting to £25,021 12s 11d. sterling. He also predicted a steep increase in the future of Indian expenses. Hunting among the Creeks and Cherokees had come to a halt because of the war; without means of purchasing goods and engrossed in fighting, both tribes had become entirely dependent on British supplies. Thus Stuart was required to increase both the supplies of ammunition and the gifts sent to the Indians of the backcountry. He deemed this turn of events the source of the great upsurge in expenditures during the last two years.[51] Where government policy sought to minimize expenses, the war actually accelerated the cultural dependency of the southern Indians on the British.

Expenses were not confined to these two allies. One of Stuart's tasks in the postwar years had been to court peripheral groups like the Chickasaws and the Choctaws. Now, they too had to be supplied to maintain their allegiance. In August 1777, he wrote to Germain that a general meeting of the Choctaws had worsened an already growing expense. A supply ship carrying the presents expected at any such congress had failed to arrive on time. Thus, Stuart was forced to buy presents from local merchants. He also felt bound to send extra gifts to those groups already fighting on the British behalf since such activity disrupted hunting schedules and their own productivity.[52]

Stuart's same letter chronicled the effectiveness of Patriot Indian officials. George Galphin organized a group of Creeks to attack the Georgia frontier. Descending upon a fort, they drove away its supply of horses, though a surprise maneuver by the Loyalists led to a Patriot defeat.[53] Not all Patriot plots were so easily countered. As discussed previously, in September 1777, Alexander McGillivray notified Stuart that he had discovered a Patriot-sponsored Indian plot to kill the Loyalist Indian officials David Taitt, Alexander Cameron and William Moniac, a translator. Upon meeting with Creek headmen, McGillivray found they had been hired to kill for trade goods. Though McGillivray convinced the majority to abandon their scheme, his efforts were not entirely successful--a group of Tallapoosa Indians did attack the stores of Taitt and Cameron at Hickory Ground, though both men survived.[54]

As in the last war, other colonial powers sought to exert their influence over the southern Indians as a part of the larger struggle, rather than out of concern for the American colonials or the American Indians. Stuart had been notified that the Spanish governor of New Orleans, Don Bernardo Galvez, had been courting all the Indians around the Mississippi, including the Choctaws. The British both claimed and supplied this tribe and deemed a recent gift exchange between the Spanish and the Choctaws a threat. Stuart ordered his deputies in that area to pay special attention to Spanish interaction with the Indians.[55]

Attempts by the Loyalists to strike at the Patriots necessarily involved trade. In March 1778, Germain praised Stuart for his recall of Loyalist traders from the backcountry. In conjunction with a British effort to prevent supply ships from reaching Patriot forces, Stuart hoped to withhold his own trade while eliminating Patriot Indian supplies. The combined effort was gauged to convince the southern Indians to abandon their dalliance with Patriot traders; instead they were to remain ready to add their manpower to British forces fighting the Patriots. Few weapons were as powerful as the threat of trade cessation. Germain was convinced that the Spanish government at New Orleans was attempting to use trade to manipulate the southern Indians against the British war effort and urged Stuart to continue gathering intelligence reports from that quarter.[56]

As in the Great War for Empire at midcentury, both Patriot and Loyalist forces were frustrated in trying to use the southern Indians. Both groups expended increasingly larger amounts of money to secure Indian loyalty but often found as their reward a bungled military operation. Unfortunately, not even the highest bidder for Indian warriors could make them fight European style. In 1778, the British relearned that hard lesson. Early in that year, British officials began hearing rumors of an impending attack on West Florida. Specifically, the colonials, under James Willing, were expected to bring an attack force of forty-two boats down the

Ohio and Mississippi rivers to strike the isolated province. In response, John Stuart ordered his deputies among the Choctaws to organize a group of them to be stationed on the Mississippi to intercept the Patriots. To that end, he assigned a group of Choctaws to a place called Walnut Hills.

Willing embarked on his mission on 11 January 1778 aboard the U.S.S. *Rattletrap*. Unfortunately for the British, the Indian style of fighting did not include long low, activity periods like watches. The first group of Choctaws tired of their duty and departed for home before a second group arrived. In the ensuing gap, the Willing party landed at Walnut Hills on 18 February 1778. Undeterred by Native American forces, the Willing party continued on to Fort Panmure at modern day Natchez, Mississippi. Taking that fort, the Patriot flotilla continued as far south as New Orleans, recruiting men and collecting materiel all along the way.[57]

Similarly, when rebel forces were expected to attack East Florida also in 1778, Governor Peter Tonyn wrote to Stuart desperately requesting Indian forces to protect the province.[58] Patriot forces numbering three thousand engaged Loyalists on the St. Marys River, but this time, a contingent of five hundred Seminoles was present to fight the Patriots. Their presence did not, however, prevent the Patriots from winning the day.[59] Thus, even when Patriots or Loyalists purchased Indian fighters, they were neither the equivalent of European solders nor guarantors of victory. While the efficacy of Indian troops was often questionable, there was no doubt that their expense continued to climb.

Originally limited to a budget of £3,000 for Indian expenses in the years after the Great War for Empire, Stuart soon incurred increases as he struggled to maintain some semblance of order after the Indian trade was deregulated in 1763. His task to reaffirm old allies, such as the Creeks and Cherokees, while gaining new allies, such as the Chickasaws and Choctaws, added to that increase. In fact, the upsurge in expenditures was so great that Germain wrote to Stuart in March 1779 that the matter had become a subject of concern in Parliament.[60] Stuart to that point had spent £77,306 8s 2.5d.[61] The extraordinary jump in expenses, plus the unreliability of Indian troops once secured, prompted Germain to notify Stuart that he could no longer support Stuart's requests for funds from the Public Treasury.[62] Stuart died on 21 March 1779 before Germain's letter arrived. In the summer of 1779, Germain appointed Alexander Cameron and an Augusta Loyalist, Thomas Brown, as dual superintendents for West and East Florida, respectively.[63]

Cameron was well aware of the power of trade over the southern Indians; it took Brown precious little time to learn. As noted earlier, in September 1780, Cameron wrote to Germain that his influence among the Indians was in direct proportion to the goods he could give them. Cameron acknowledged the great financial burden that his department had become. Be that as it may, he warned Germain that it would be impossible to bind the Indians to British plans unless they were provided with sufficient gifts, ammunition and arms. As noted, Cameron observed that the southern Indians had grown accustomed to a steady supply of gifts whether their services were required or not.[64] He reminded Germain of the ultimate economic equation involving the Indians by warning that a reduction in gifts and arms might push the southern Indians, especially the Choctaws, toward better trade partners, like the Spaniards.[65]

As the British tried to hold onto their Indian allies, they became more deeply committed to supplying them, despite their intentions to hold down cost. In December 1781, Thomas Brown wrote to Henry Clinton that Cherokee society had been so disrupted by the war that hunting had virtually stopped. As a result, he was having to send them basic necessities including clothing and ammunition. Likewise, he reported that the Creeks were completely dependent on the government for similar reasons.[66] Thus, the goal to utilize the Indians as auxiliary forces was incompatible with economizing on Indian expenses. In fact, the war accelerated the transition away from traditional life for the Indians and made them even more dependent on British trade.

Ultimately the war ran its course. The final disposition of Britain and Native Americans of the southern backcountry ended, as it had begun, with issues of trade. At war's end, Thomas Brown wrote to Thomas Townshend, acknowledging his order to withdraw Brown's men from the backcountry. As noted earlier, Brown feared for the safety of his men should groups like the Creeks learn that the British were withdrawing from the area. Once more, backcountry traders could be used as hostages if the Indians were provoked.[67]

Groups of Indians began to make visits to St. Augustine pledging their loyalty to the British. In June 1784, Brown wrote to Lord North that a group of five hundred to six hundred Indians with their families planned to visit. Britain had lost the war but was not yet free of the burden of the Indian trade. Though Brown's Indian stores had been exhausted, he felt bound to request the gifts necessary for an impending diplomatic courtesy call even after the war.[68]

The Indian trade superficially appears to be a case of the total dependency of a technologically inferior civilization to a technologically superior one. Yet, the relationship was much more complex, involving a mutual dependency of sorts. In the early 1700s, various southern colonies competed for the Indian trade, creating conditions that allowed the Indians to dictate their own terms. During the Great War for Empire and the American Revolution, international rivalry intensified this bargaining power. Euroamericans knew that, although Indian allies did not assure victory, they might be effective at a critical juncture. Retaining such allies entailed expenditures for talks, congresses, gifts, feasts and a steady flow of trade. Indian alliances were an expensive gamble, yet one that the British, Spanish, French and Americans felt compelled to take, almost as though they had become addicted to the trade as well.

NOTES

1. Alden, *John Stuart,* 17. This conference, which met at Augusta, Georgia, ran November 5-10, 1763.

2. John Stuart to General Jeffrey Amherst, 31 May 1763, CO5/63: 145.

3. Francis Jennings, *Empire of Fortune: Crowns, Colonies, and Tribes in the Seven Years War in America* (New York: W.W. Norton and Company, 1988), 443-445. See also Francis Parkman, *The Conspiracy of Pontiac and the Indian War After the Conquest of Canada* (Boston: Little Brown and Co., 1909).

4. John Stuart to John Pownall, 24 January 1764, CO5/66: 342.

5. Gold, *Borderland Empires,* 173.

6. Alexander Cameron to Stuart, 1 June 1766, CO5/66: 406.

7. Ibid.

8. Ensign George Price to the Secretary of State for Indian Affairs, 24 January 1764, CO5/66: 342.

9. Gold, *Borderland Empires,* 173-174.

10. Ibid., 175.

11. Ibid., 177-178.

12. Milo B. Howard, Jr., and Robert Rea, trans., *The Memoire Justicatif of the Chevalier Montault de Monberaut: Indian Diplomacy in British West Florida, 1763-1765* (University: University of Alabama Press, 1965), 30-34.

13. Ibid., 175.

14. Cameron to Secretary of State, Indian Affairs, 27 August 1766, CO5/67: 218.

15. Stuart to Secretary of State, Indian Affairs, 11 April 1767, CO5/68: 119.

16. Stuart to the Earl of Shelburne, 28 July 1767, CO5/68: 136.

17. South Carolina Traders to Stuart, 21 May 1767, CO5/68: 140.

18. Ibid.

19. Stuart to Shelburne, 7 May 1768, CO5/69: n.f.

20. Stuart to the Early of Hillsborough, 15 September 1768, CO5/69: 258.

21. Stuart to Shelburne, 1 August 1768, CO5/69: n.f.

22. Stuart to Hillsborough, 15 September 1768, CO5/69: n.f.

23. Stuart to Francis Fauquier, 21 July 1767, CO5/70: n.f.

24. James H. O'Donnell III, "The South on the Eve of the Revolution: The Native Americans," *The Revolutionary War in the South: Power, Conflict, and Leadership,* W. Robert Higgins, ed. (Durham, North Carolina: Duke University Press, 1979), 66.

25. Stuart to Hillsborough, 17 October 1768, CO5/70: n.f.

26. Stuart to John Blair, 19 August 1768, CO5/70: n.f.

27. Cameron to Secretary of State, Indian Affairs, 20 May 1768, CO5/69: 266.

28. Stuart to Hillsborough, 14 April 1769, CO5/70: n.f.

29. Stuart to Hillsborough, 14 April 1769, CO5/70: n.f.

30. Stuart to Hillsborough, 2 December 1770, CO5/72: 82.

31. Stuart to Hillsborough, 27 April 1771, CO5/72: n.f.

32. Hillsborough to Stuart, 3 July 1771, CO5/70: n.f.

33. Hillsborough to Stuart, 11 January 1772, CO5/73: 1.

34. Stuart to Hillsborough, 9 February 1772, CO5/73: 95.

35. Earl of Dartmouth to Stuart, 23 September 1772, CO5/73: n.f.

36. George Galphin, Robert McKay, James Jackson, and Andrew McLean to Stuart, 13 November 1771, CO5/73: 99.

37. John Jamieson, George Baillie, and Thomas Netherclift to Stuart, 30 October 1772, CO5/73: 97.

38. Stuart to Hillsborough, 13 June 1772, CO5/73: 156.

39. Dartmouth to Stuart, 9 December 1772, CO5/73: n.f.

40. Stuart to Dartmouth, 4 January 1773, CO5/74: 45.

41. Stuart to Dartmouth, 21 July 1775, CO5/76: n.f.

42. Stuart to Dartmouth, 17 December 1775,CO5/77: 22.

43. Stuart to Dartmouth, 17 September 1775, CO5/76: n.f.

44. Helen Hornbeck Tanner, "Pipesmoke and Muskets: Florida Indian Intrigues of the Revolutionary Era," *Eighteenth Century Florida and Its Borderlands,* Samuel Proctor, ed. (Gainesville: The University Presses of Florida, 1975), 20.

45. David Taitt to the Cowetas, Tallapoosas, Abechkas and Alibamous, 17 August 1775, CO5/76: n.f.

46. Henry Laurens to Edward Wilkinson, 29 October 1775, CO5/77: 79.

47. Stuart to Cameron, 16 December 1775, CO5/77: 28.

48. Stuart to Major General Clinton, 15 March 1776, CO5/77: 107.

49. Emistisiguo to Stuart, 19 November 1776, CO5/78: 81.

50. Stuart to Lord George Germain, 23 August 1776, CO5/77: n.f.

51. Stuart to Germain, 24 January 1777, CO5/78: 83.

52. Stuart to Germain, 22 August 1777, CO5/78: 186.

53. Ibid.

54. Alexander McGillivray to Stuart, 21 September 1777, CO5/79: 33.

55. Stuart to Germain, 22 August 1777, CO5/78: 186.

56. Germain to Stuart, 10 March 1778, CO5/79: 54.

57. J. Barton Starr, *Tories, Dons, and Rebels: The American Revolution in British West Florida* (Gainesville: The University Presses of Florida, 1976), 85-92. Early in 1777, Sir William Howe, Commander-in-Chief of British Forces in America, authorized Stuart to enlist Loyalist civilians and Indians in a support group known as the Loyalist Refugees.

58. Patrick Tonyn to Stuart, 16 May 1778, CO5/79: n.f.

59. J. Leitch Wright, *Florida in the American Revolution* (Gainesville: The University Presses of Florida, 1975), 55-57.

60. Germain to Stuart, 31 March 1779, CO5/79: n.f.

61. James H. O'Donnell III, *Southern Indians in the American Revolution* (Knoxville: The University of Tennessee Press, 1973), 90.

62. Germain to Stuart, 2 June 1779, CO5/79: n.f.

63. Germain to Alexander Cameron and Thomas Brown, 25 June 1779, CO5/79: n.f.

64. Cameron to Germain, 20 September 1780, CO5/82: 88.

65. Ibid.

66. Colonel Thomas Brown to Henry Clinton, 28 December 1781, CO5/82: 283.

67. Brown to Thomas Townshend, 1 June 1753, CO5/82: 367.

68. Brown to Lord North, 8 June 1784, CO5/82: 432.

Bibliography

PRIMARY SOURCES

Adair, James. *Adair's History of the American Indians*. Edited by Samuel Cole Williams. Johnson City, Tennessee: The Watauga Press, 1930.

Bartram, William. *Travels Through North and South Carolina, Georgia, East and West Florida*. Savannah, Georgia: The Beehive Press, 1973.

Bossu, Jean Bernard. *Travels in the Interior of North America 1751-1762*. Translated by Seymour Feiler. Norman: University of Oklahoma Press, 1962.

Byrd, William. *The Prose Works of William Byrd of Westover: Narratives of a Colonial Virginian*. Edited by Louis B. Wright. Cambridge: Belknap Press, 1966.

_____.*The London Diary (1717-1721) and Other Writings*. Edited by Louis B. Wright and Marion Tinling. New York: Oxford University Press, 1958.

Coleman, Kenneth, ed. *The Colonial Records of the State of Georgia: Original Papers of Governor John Reynolds 1754-1756*. Vol. 27. Athens: University of Georgia Press, 1977.

Galloway, Patricia, Dunbar Rowland and A.G. Sanders, eds. *Mississippi Provincial Archives: French Dominion, 1749-1763*. Vol V. Baton Rouge: Louisiana State University Press, 1984.

Grant, Ludovic. "Historical Relation of Facts etc." *South Carolina Historical and Genealogical Magazine*. (10): 54-68.

Great Britain. Public Records Office, Kew. *Colonial Office, Series Five Material*. (Volumes 7-459, but primarily volumes 67-79).

Howard, Jr., Milo B. and Robert Rea, trans. *The Memoire Justicatif of the Chevalier Montault De Monberaut: Indian Diplomacy in British West Florida, 1763-1765.* Tuscaloosa: University of Alabama Press, 1763-1765.

Imlay, Gilbert. *A Topographical Description of the Western Territory of North America.* New York: Augustus M. Kelley, Publishers, 1964.

Lawson, John. *A New Voyage to Carolina.* Edited by Hugh Talmadge Lefler. Chapel Hill: The University of North Carolina Press, 1967.

Lloyd's Evening Post. (London, 12 April 1773).

McDowell, William L., ed. *The Colonial Records of South Carolina: Journals of the Commissioners of the Indian Trade, September 20, 1710-August 29, 1718.* Columbia: South Carolina Archives Department, 1955.

_____. *The Colonial Records of South Carolina: Documents Relating to Indian Affairs: May 21, 1750-August 7, 1754.* Columbia: South Carolina Archives Department, 1958.

McDowell, Jr., William L., ed. *The Colonial Records of South Carolina: Documents Relating to Indian Affairs 1754-1765.* Columbia: South Carolina Department of Archives and History, 1970.

McPherson, Robert G., ed. *The Journal of the Earl of Egmont: Abstract of the Trustees Proceedings for Establishing the Colony of Georgia 1732-1738.* Athens: University of Georgia Press, 1962.

McWilliams, Richebourg Gaillard, trans. and ed. *Fleur de Lys and Calumets: Being the Penicaut Narrative of French Adventure in Louisiana.* Baton Rouge: Louisiana State University Press, 1953.

Milfort, General Louis. *Memoirs of a Quick Glance at My Various Travels and My Sojourn in the Creek Nation.* Translated and Edited by Ben C. McClary. Kennesaw, Georgia: Continental Book Company, 1959.

Moore, Alexander, ed. *Nairne's Muskhogean Journals: The 1708 Expedition to the Mississippi River.* Jackson: University Press of Mississippi, 1988.

Romans, Bernard. *A Concise Natural History of East and West Florida.* New Orleans: Pelican Publishing Company, 1961.

The South Carolina Gazette. (Columbia, 5-8 January 1760)

Stiggins, George. *George Stiggins.* Edited by Virginia Pounds Brown. Birmingham: Birmingham Public Library, 1989.

Timberlake, Henry. *Lieutenant Henry Timberlake's Memories 1756-1765.* Edited by Samuel Cole Williams. Marietta, Georgia: Continental Book Company, 1948.

SECONDARY SOURCES

Books

Alderman, Pat. *Nancy Ward: Cherokee Chieftainess.* Johnson City, Tennessee: The Overmountain Press, 1978.

Axtell, James. *After Columbus: Essays in the Ethnohistory of Colonial North America.* New York: Oxford University Press, 1988.

_____. *The Invasion Within: The Contest of Cultures in Colonial North America.* New York: Oxford University Press, 1985.

_____. *The European and the Indian: Essays in the Ethnohistory of Colonial North America.* New York: Oxford University Press, 1981.

Belshaw, Cyril. *Traditional Exchange and Modern Markets*. Edited by Wilbert E. Moore and Neel J. Smelser. Englewood Cliffs, N.J.: Prentice Hall, Inc., 1965.

Boucher, Philip P., ed. *Proceedings of the Tenth Meeting of the French Colonial Historical Society*. New York: University Press of America, 1985.

Bridenthal, Renate, Claudia Koonz and Susan Stouard, eds. *Becoming Visible: Women in European History*. Boston: Houghton Mifflin Company, 1987.

Cashin, Edward J. *Lachlan McGillivray, Indian Trader: The Shaping of the Southern Colonial Frontier*. Athens: The University of Georgia Press, 1992.

Coker, William S. and Thomas D. Watson. *Indian Traders of the Spanish Borderlands: Panton, Leslie and Company and John Forbes and Company 1784-1847*. Pensacola: University of West Florida Press, 1986.

Coker, William S. and Robert Rea. *Anglo-Spanish Confrontation on the Gulf-Coast During the American Revolution*. Pensacola, Florida: Gulf Coast History and Humanities Conference, 1982.

Corkran, David H. *The Cherokee Frontier: Conflict and Survival, 1740-62*. Norman: University of Oklahoma Press, 1962.

_____. *The Creek Frontier 1540-1783*. Norman: University of Oklahoma Press, 1967.

_____., *The Carolina Indian Frontier*. Columbia: University of South Carolina Press, 1970.

Crane, Verner W. *The Southern Frontier: 1670-1732*. Ann Arbor: University of Michigan Press, 1964.

Gibson, Charles and Howard Peckham. *Attitudes of Colonial Powers Toward the American Indians*. Salt Lake City: University of Utah Press, 1969.

Gold, Robert L. *Borderland Empires in Transition: The Triple Nation Transfer of Florida*. Carbondale: Southern Illinois University Press, 1969.

Goodwin, Gary C. *Cherokees in Transition: A Study of Changing Culture and Environment Prior to 1775*. Chicago: The University of Chicago Press, 1977.

Gridley, Marion E. *American Indian Women*. New York: Hawthorn Books, Inc., 1974.

Hamer, Fritz, Joseph J. Walter and James D. Scurry. *Initial Archeological Investigations at Silver Bluff Plantation Aiken County, South Carolina*. Research Manuscript Series 168. Columbia: Institute of Archeology and Anthropology, University of South Carolina, 1980.

Higgins, W. Robert, ed. *The Revolutionary War in the South: Power, Conflict, and Leadership*. Durham, North Carolina: Duke University Press, 1979.

Hoffer, Charles P., ed., *Indians and Europeans: Selected Articles on Indian-White Relations in Colonial North America*. New York: Gailand Publishing, Inc., 1988.

Holden, Robert J., ed. *Selected Papers from the Seventh and Eighth George Rogers Clark Trans-Appalachian Frontier History Conferences*. Vincennes, Indiana: n.p., 1991.

Holland, Kathryn. "The Path Between the Wars: Creek Relations with the British Colonies, 1763-1774." Master's Thesis, Auburn University, 1980.

Hudson, Charles B. *The Southeastern Indians*. Knoxville: The University of Tennessee Press, 1984.

Jennings, Francis. *The Invasion of America: Indians, Colonialism, and the Cant of Conquest*. New York: W.W. Norton and Company, 1976.

_____. *Empire of Fortune: Crowns, Colonies, and Tribes in the Seven Years War in America*. New York: W.W. Norton and Company, 1988.

Jones, Jr., Charles Colcock. *Antiquities of the Southern Indians, Particularly of the Georgia Tribes*. New York: A.M.S. Press, 1973.

Martin, Calvin. *Keepers of the Game: Indian-Animal Relationships and the Fur Trade*. Berkeley: University of California Press, 1978.

Martin, Joel. *Sacred Revolt: The Muskoghee's Struggle for a New World.* Boston: Beacon Press, 1991.

Mereness, Newton G. *Travels in the American Colonies.* New York: Antiquarian Press, Ltd., 1961.

Norton, Mary Beth. *Liberty's Daughters: The Revolutionary Experience of American Women, 1750-1800.* Boston: Little, Brown and Company, 1980.

O'Donnell III, James H. *Southern Indians in the American Revolution.* Knoxville: The University of Tennessee Press, 1973.

O'Meara, Walter. *Daughters of the Country: The Women of the Fur Traders and Mountain Men.* New York: Harcourt, Brace & World, Inc., 1968.

Paper, Jordan. *Offering Smoke: The Sacred Pipe and Native American Religion.* Moscow, Idaho: The University of Idaho Press, 1988.

Perdue, Theda. *Slavery and the Evolution of Cherokee Society 1540-1866.* Knoxville: The University of Tennessee Press, 1979.

Picket, Albert James. *History of Alabama and Incidently of Georgia and Mississippi: From the Earliest Period.* Tuscaloosa, Alabama: Willo Publishing Company, 1962.

Proctor, Samuel., ed. *Eighteenth Century Florida and Its Borderlands.* Gainesville: The University Presses of Florida, 1975.

Randolph, Randolph F. *British Travelers Among the Southern Indians, 1660-1763.* Norman: University of Oklahoma Press, 1973.

Schoolcraft, Henry R. *Information Respecting the History, Condition, and Prospects of the Indian Tribes of the United States.* Vol. 5. Philadelphia: J.B. Lippincott and Co., 1855.

Silver, Timothy. *A New Face on the Countryside: Indians, Colonists, and Slaves in South Atlantic Forests, 1500-1800.* Cambridge: Cambridge University Press, 1990.

Starr, Emmet. *History of the Cherokee Indians and their Legends and Folklore.* New York: Kraus Reprint Company, 1969.

Starr, J. Barton. *Tories, Dons, and Rebels: The American Revolution in British West Florida.* Gainesville: The University Presses of Florida, 1976.

Swanton, John Reed. *The Indians of the Southeastern United States.* Grosse Pointe, Michigan: Scholarly Press, 1969.

_____. *Social Organization and Social Usages of the Indians of the Creek Confederacy.* New York: Johnson Reprint Corporation, 1977.

Terrell, John Upton and Donna M. Terrell. *Indian Women of the Western Morning: Their Life in Early America.* New York: The Dial Press, 1974.

Thompson, Lyn Hastie. *William Weatherford: His Country and His People.* Bay Minette, Alabama: Lavender Publishing Company, 1991.

Todd, Helen. *Mary Musgrove: Georgia Indian Princess.* Chicago: Adams Press, 1981.

Washburn, Wilcomb E. *The Indian in America.* New York: Harper & Row, Publishers, 1975.

Williams, Samuel Cole, ed. *Early Travels in the Tennessee Country 1540-1800.* Johnson City, Tennessee: The Watauga Press, 1928.

Woods, Patricia Dillon. *French-Indian Relations on the Southern Frontier 1699-1762.* Ann Arbor: University of Michigan Research Press, 1980.

Woodward, Grace Steele. *The Cherokees.* Norman: University of Oklahoma Press, 1984.

Wright, J. Leitch. *Florida in the American Revolution.* Gainesville: The University Presses of Florida, 1975.

Articles

Alden, Richard. "The Albany Congress and the Creation of the Indian Superintendencies." *The Mississippi Valley Historical Review*. 27 (September 1940): 193-210.

Brown, Philip M. "Early Indian Trade in the Development of South Carolina Politics, Economics, and Social Mobility during the Proprietary Period, 1670-1719." *The South Carolina Historical Magazine*. 76 (July 1975): 118-128.

Carter, Clarence. "Observations of Superintendent John Stuart and Governor James Grant of East Florida on the Proposed Plan of 1764 for the Future Management of Indian Affairs." *American Historical Review*. 20 (October 1914-July 1915): 37-56.

Dalton, George. "Economic Theory and Primitive Society." *American Anthropologist*. 63 (1961): 1-25.

Green, E.R.R. "Queensborough Townships: Scotch-Irish Emigration and the Expansion of Georgia, 1763-1776." *William and Mary Quarterly*. 17 (1960): 183-199.

Kardulias, Nick. "Fur Production as a Specialized Activity in a World System: Indians in the North American Fur Trade." *American Indian Culture and Research Journal*. 14: 1 (1990): 25-60.

McClary, Ben Harris. "Nancy Ward: The Last Beloved Woman of the Cherokees." *Tennessee Historical Quarterly*. 21 (December 1962): 352-364.

Moore, Jr., W.O. "The Largest Exporters of Deerskins from Charles Town, 1735-1775." *The South Carolina Historical Magazine*. 74 (July 1973): 144-150.

Rea, Robert R. "Redcoats and Redskins on the Lower Mississippi, 1763-1776: The Career of Lt. John Thomas." *Louisiana History*. 11 (Winter 1970): 5-35.

Rothrock, Mary U. "Carolina Traders Among the Overhills Cherokees, 1690-1760." *East Tennessee Historical Society's Publications*. 1 (1929): 3-18.

Wolf, Peter H. "Vasomotor Sensitivity to Alcohol in Diverse Mongoloid Populations." *American Journal of Human Genetics*. 25 (1973): 193-199.

Index

About the Author

MICHAEL MORRIS is an Adjunct Instructor of History at the University of South Carolina–Aiken. His previous publications include articles on Native Americans and Trade in the American Southeast.